"Brett McCracken is one of this generation's leading thinkers on the intersection of faith and culture. In *Gray Matters*, he explores Christianity's natural extremes with his feet firmly planted in Scripture. He charges headfirst into controversial questions and leaves no stone unturned. The result is a truly spectacular book that carves a path between an oppressive, rules-based religion and a powerless, free-for-all 'faith.' If you start reading it, beware—you won't be able to put it down."

—**Jonathan Merritt**, faith and culture writer; author, *A Faith of Our Own: Following Jesus Beyond the Culture Wars*

"This book is not only clear and engaging but also careful and wise. *Gray Matters* is a helpful, critical, reflective exploration of how we should consume culture as Christians, one that is neither reactionary nor defensive, triumphalist nor despairing. Few younger Christians have navigated these turbulent waters with as much even-handed clarity as this book does, which makes it an important read."

—**Matthew Lee Anderson**, MereOrthodoxy.com; author of *Earthen Vessels: Why Our Bodies Matter for Our Faith*

"Idealism is all the rage among bright young evangelicals today, but Brett McCracken brings something all too rare to the table: he holds his earnest idealism in tension with lucid good sense and winsome moderation. May his tribe increase!"

—**John Wilson**, editor, *Books & Culture*

"Martin Luther said the world was like a drunken man, first falling off one side of the horse and then the other. With a fresh and thoughtful look at challenges such as food, music, film, and alcohol, Brett McCracken has offered a new generation a way to stay on the horse."

—**Roberta Green Ahmanson**, writer and speaker

"In *Gray Matters*, Brett McCracken does something quite refreshing—he serves as a wise and discerning guide to the consuming of culture. Many books condemn 'secular' culture, just as many books advocate (consciously or unconsciously) accommodating ourselves to culture. Brett has written something much different: a biblically informed and culturally savvy approach to consuming culture in a God-honoring, community-building, and mission-advancing way. Not everyone will agree with Brett's method or his conclusions, but that is part of his point. Central to modern discipleship to Jesus is wrestling through 'gray matters'—those areas where there is room to think, pray, study, and consume—in the ways we eat, drink, listen, and watch. Brett seeks to redeem our consumption in surprising and helpful ways."

—**Mike Erre,** pastor; author, *The Jesus of Suburbia: Have We Tamed the Son of God to Fit Our Lifestyle?*

"Brett McCracken has long been my favorite reviewer of both music and movies, so it's no surprise to me that he has written this needed book on consuming culture. A number of wonderful books have been written encouraging readers to create culture, but Brett takes the reader into the everyday world of consuming culture. Brett is an incredibly capable writer, thinker, and connoisseur, and all of this shines through in his work—bringing back into focus that how we engage the world around us matters deeply."

—**Tyler Braun,** worship pastor; writer; author, *Why Holiness Matters: We've Lost Our Way—But We Can Find It Again*

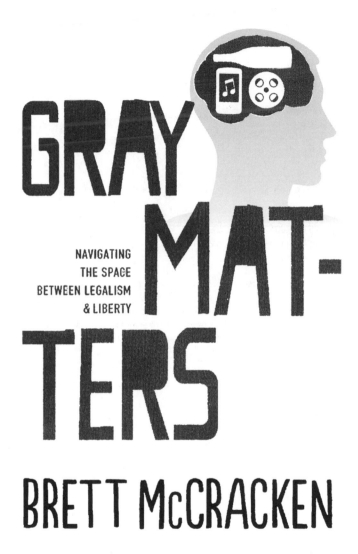

GRAY MAT-TERS

NAVIGATING THE SPACE BETWEEN LEGALISM & LIBERTY

BRETT McCRACKEN

BakerBooks

a division of Baker Publishing Group
Grand Rapids, Michigan

Published by Baker Books
a division of Baker Publishing Group
P.O. Box 6287, Grand Rapids, MI 49516-6287
www.bakerbooks.com

Printed in the United States of America

Library of Congress Cataloging-in-Publication Data is on file at the Library of Congress, Washington, DC.

ISBN 978-0-8010-1474-1

Published in association with the literary agency of Wolgemuth & Associates, Inc.

13   14   15   16   17   18   19   7   6   5   4   3   2   1

Contents

Introduction

Into the Gray

Let me tell you about two friends of mine—both twenty-something Christians who grew up in the evangelical sub-culture and graduated from Christian colleges several years ago. The first—we'll call him Lee—is a deeply pious, Bible-toting conservative who believes there's pretty much no value in secular music, movies, and television. He's something of a wet blanket at parties, always giving disapproving grimaces when he sees fellow Christians (gasp!) watch R-rated movies or (horror!) sip a fermented beverage. He's well intentioned and a nice guy if you get to know him, but his indifference to art and culture (unless it can be purchased in a Christian bookstore) is bothersome, and his legalistic stance on media consumption can be downright noxious.

My other friend—let's call him Lance—grew up in a household that espoused many of Lee's legalistic views. However, in college, everything changed for Lance. He was introduced to secular music and foreign films, and he hung out mostly with art and sociology majors. He came to view his old fears of secular culture as ludicrous. He threw away his "Christian"

CDs and threw his arms wide open to any and every bit of envelope-pushing secular culture he could find. He started smoking—first cloves, then cigarettes, then pot—and especially relished lighting up when he was around more conservative fellow graduates of his evangelical college. He got drunk at any party where liquor was on hand. He learned to cuss with the best of them. No outside observer would have ever guessed that Lance—painfully desperate to distance himself from his legalistic youth—was a follower of Jesus Christ.

Between Legalism and License

Among the many things the divergent paths of Lee the Legalist and Lance the Libertine demonstrate is this unfortunate fact: Christians have a hard time with nuance. Gray areas are not our strong suit. It's way easier to just say yes or no to things, rather than "well, maybe, depending. . . ." But simple responses to complicated questions are exactly what lead to extremists like Lee and Lance.

Certainly there are *plenty* of places where a clear yes or no is absolutely appropriate, even necessary. But there are also many areas where it's not that black and white. God gives us minds with the capacity for critical thinking so that we might navigate the complexity of these less-straightforward areas of existence.

Culture, including what we consume or abstain from within culture, is one such gray area. The Bible doesn't give us easy answers about whether this or that HBO show is okay to watch, or whether it's appropriate for Christians to enjoy the music of Outkast. Scripture contains no comprehensive list of acceptable films, books, or websites. Contrary to what some Christians maintain, the Bible neither endorses nor forbids all sorts of things it could have been clearer about.

But scriptural silence about the particularities of twenty-first-century media habits is no reason to just throw up one's hands and indulge in an "anything goes" free-for-all. Rather, it's an invitation to think about the gray areas more deeply, to wrestle with them based on what Scripture *does* say and what we've come to know about the calling of Christians in this world. The gray areas matter.

Christians have a tendency to approach secular culture from one of two opposite extremes. On one extreme you have Christians (like Lee) who separate from it completely, opting instead to hide away in an alternative "Christian culture." They fear the corrupting influences of the secular realm and, out of fear (some of it well-founded), try to regulate it through legalism or else avoid it completely.

The other extreme (the Lance type of Christian) emphasizes "arms wide open" Christian liberty and exercises little discernment in what, if anything, is unsuitable for Christian consumption. This approach—pretty widespread among my generation of millennial Christians—tends to overcompensate for the stifling excesses of "hands off!" legalism but in the end is just as problematic for its uncritical embrace of things that are hardly worthy or edifying for the Christian life. In the introduction to the fantastic book *Everyday Theology*, theologian Kevin Vanhoozer writes,

> We must therefore do all that we can to resist two opposing temptations, each equally dangerous inasmuch as each compromises the integrity of the church's mission. The first is an uncritical acceptance of and fascination with the newfound religiosity and spirituality of popular culture. The second is to write off popular culture as one more symptom of sinful rebellion.[1]

I would concur and add that both of these extreme positions toward culture err in that they both tend to look at culture as a monolith—either one big vice factory or one big funhouse of goodness. Both of these positions lack nuance and critical thought, and both have a tendency to turn culture into something that can be used to make a point rather than something that can truly enrich lives.

I've seen so many Lance-type Christians my age who, after having grown up in a somewhat legalistic, church-centric environment—usually where drinking and dancing and all manner of potential vice were outlawed—make a point of showing themselves to be *anything but* legalistic in their adulthood. They gamble, they smoke, they carry flasks; they tell people how much they love the (envelope-pushing) films of Todd Solondz and Pedro Almodóvar. Certainly some of them probably do find pleasure in these things and approach them with intentionality, but I suspect that a lot of their cultural consumption is driven by a concerted effort to distance themselves from the legalism of their youth. In this way, they *use* culture to shore up a part of their identity in which they have issues or vulnerability (in this case, the "Christians are legalistic" chip on their shoulder).

Likewise, I've seen plenty of Christians who *use* culture in another way. Perhaps a film is family friendly and contains some sort of moral lesson. Christians, pastors, and churches are often quick to embrace films like this through which they can make a point or evangelize. Or maybe a famous actor or musician turns out to be a Christian. Soon they show up on the covers of evangelical magazines, make the youth group speaking circuit, and become "owned" by Christians as a sort of signal to secular culture that "Christians can be just as successful in media as anyone else." In these instances, the cultural objects themselves are given little critical attention; they are merely used by Christian consumers for their own personal agendas.

In *An Experiment in Criticism*, C. S. Lewis has plenty to say about "using" versus "receiving" art and culture. Using art, says Lewis, deprives us of the true benefits we might enjoy if only we relinquished our insistence on control. "We are so busy doing things with the work," says Lewis, "that we give it too little chance to work on us. . . . 'Using' is inferior to 'reception' because art, if used rather than received, merely facilitates, brightens, relieves or palliates our life, and does not add to it."[2]

Tragically, culture is frequently relegated to the "facilitates, brightens, relieves, palliates" realm. We use alcohol to soothe our nerves or to numb our pain, food to satiate hunger, movies to titillate, fashion to make a point, and so on. But is there more in culture to appreciate beyond these surface-level satiations? What can be discovered about the world, about the beauty of creation, if we dare go deeper into the gray? It's a risk, going deeper—to plunge into the depths, the complexity, the potentially hazardous ocean of culture. But there are so many treasures to be found.

Culture Making and Culture Consuming

When I was a kid, I wanted to be an architect. I loved drawing pictures and floor plans of buildings. I spent weeks designing everything from houses to high schools to amusement parks themed around Old Testament stories (my "Plagues of the Nile" white-water rafting ride would have been awesome). As a fifth grader I read *Architectural Digest* while my mom stood in line at the supermarket. But alas, when I opted to go to a college that didn't have an architecture program, my creative ambition to be the next Frank Gehry faded.

That's when I thought I might want to be a filmmaker. Movies had been another great passion of mine, and ever since the moment in high school when I first saw Terrence Malick's *The Thin Red Line*, I dreamed about becoming a director. I started writing scripts. I took film classes and spent a semester in Los Angeles learning the ropes of "the industry." All the while, I was writing film reviews, something I'd been doing since my freshman year of college.

At some point I realized that when it came to my passion for the art of film, perhaps what I enjoyed even more than making films was the process of closely *watching* films, thinking deeply about them, and writing about them. It was a hard thing to give up on the dream of being the next Terrence Malick, but I realized that perhaps being the next Roger Ebert was just as noble a goal.

I decided to go to graduate school in cinema and media studies at UCLA, which happened to be the same program that a film theorist I admired—Paul Schrader—attended. During the two years I was there, countless people asked me what I planned to do with my master's degree. Will you be a director? Screenwriter? Producer? Some gave confused looks when I answered that no, I didn't want to make films; I just wanted to be a better consumer of them.

Perhaps this could be an activity just as God-honoring as my dreams of building skyscrapers and directing Oscar-winning films might have been. Perhaps the activity of discerning culture—sifting through it to highlight its most worthy and discard its most unredeemable—is as essential as the activity of making culture.

Thus this is not a book about *making* culture. It's a book about *consuming* culture well: discerningly, maturely, thoughtfully. It's about being so intentional, so careful, so passionate about getting the most out of the cultural goods we consume that those around us can't help but wonder: Why do we care so much?

I'm a big believer that if anyone is going to be a good *creator* of culture—whether filmmaker, musician, poet, chef, or writer—they had better first be a good *consumer* of it. Great filmmakers can discern important films from mediocre ones. Great chefs appreciate exceptional food and, over time, develop a refined palette that knows which cheese goes best stuffed in which kind of dried fruit and with which kind of garnish.

But we live in a world that beckons us to create. To be a consumer of culture is no longer good enough, it seems. And it's easier than ever to be a creator. Get out your computer and go to work on Pro Tools or Final Cut. Start a blog. Film a movie on your cell phone and upload it to YouTube. Launch an Etsy page for your handcrafted stationery. Become a Twitter journalist. A Pinterest wedding planner.

Meanwhile, social media like Facebook and Twitter reinforce our sense of self-importance, urging us to say whatever is on our minds because some audience, somewhere, really wants to know. On top of this, we've grown up being told by parents, teachers, presidents, principals, and most everyone else that we can be or do whatever we wish. The horizons are infinite. So *of course* we're not satisfied to just appreciate other people's creations or consume other people's products. We believe we too have something to contribute.

In many cases this is true. We do have things to contribute. We are all, each of us, imbued with creativity by a Creator. We have minds and abilities with immense potential for making beautiful things and for making sense of the world around us. Each of us does have something to add, but it doesn't always have to be in the form of a new created work. Sometimes what we contribute is just our thankfulness and understanding. Sometimes the most significant thing we can do for culture is simply to seek it out passionately and thoughtfully, to receive it well, and to support the further creation and appreciation of it. Sometimes the best thing we can do is to consume a piece of culture in moderation, or not at all.

Being Better Consumers

This book is for any Christian who lives in an environment where the commodities of popular culture (clothes, music, movies, food, alcohol, television, etc.) are ubiquitous and consumed on a regular basis. Which is pretty much every Christian. Ours is an ecology of cultural consumption.[3]

It has been well established that Christians can find value in exploring secular pop culture. Boatloads of books, conferences, and blog posts in evangelical circles have offered a needed corrective over the last few decades, making the case that Christians should actually care about engaging pop culture rather than separating from it or ignoring it. That's great. We've come a long way.

What I'm interested in is not so much making the case for the good of culture (because the case, I believe, has already been made—see the sidebar "15 Books on Christians and Culture"). I'm interested in making the case for a more *mature consumption* of culture. It's not enough to just affirm the value of "engaging culture." That's black-and-white thinking. We must do the work of engaging it *well*. Consuming culture is something we do every day and won't stop doing. So why not do it better?

My goal in this book is to help us think about how a healthy consumption of culture honors God, enriches the Christian's life, strengthens community, and advances the Christian mission. I intend it to be a guidebook for anyone who wishes to better integrate their Christian identity with their habits of cultural consumption.

15 Books on Christians and Culture

Dorothy L. Sayers, *The Mind of the Maker* (1941)

Richard Niebuhr, *Christ and Culture* (1951)

Francis A. Schaeffer, *Art and the Bible* (1973)

Madeleine L'Engle, *Walking on Water: Reflections on Faith and Art* (1980)

Nicholas Wolterstorff, *Art in Action: Toward a Christian Aesthetic* (1980)

Jeremy Begbie, *Beholding the Glory: Incarnation Through the Arts* (2000)

Walter Brueggemann, *The Prophetic Imagination* (2001)

Robert K. Johnson, *Reel Spirituality: Theology and Film in Dialogue* (2000)

William D. Romanowski, *Eyes Wide Open: Looking for God in Pop Culture* (2007)

Kevin J. Vanhoozer, Charles A. Anderson, and Michael J. Sleasman, eds., *Everyday Theology: How to Read Cultural Texts and Interpret Trends* (2007)

D. A. Carson, *Christ and Culture Revisited* (2008)

Andy Crouch, *Culture Making: Recovering Our Creative Calling* (2008)

James K. Smith, *Desiring the Kingdom: Worship, Worldview, and Kingdom Formation* (2009)

Makoto Fujimura, *Refractions: A Journey of Faith, Art, and Culture* (2009)

David O. Taylor, *For the Beauty of the Church: Casting a Vision for the Arts* (2010)

What Is Cultural Consumption?

Consumer is a four-letter word to many in the world today, mostly because of its association with the concept of "consumerism," the great bogeyman of capitalistic society that leaves a trail of trash, credit card debt, high-fructose corn syrup, and candy wrappers wherever it goes.

But at its most basic level, *consumer* is a neutral word. It refers to those people who buy things (i.e., everybody). It's about commerce—the exchanging of money for goods—and it doesn't have to be a bad thing. We are all consumers. Almost daily we participate in economic transactions for goods and experiences that we consume for a price.

One of this book's aims is to rehabilitate the term *consumption*, which in our world today most often connotes something indulgent, reckless, and altogether unseemly: capitalism run amok. But when done well, consumption—the receiving of a product at the other end of production—can be a healthy, wonderful activity that contributes to personal growth as well as broader human flourishing.

Part of why *consumer* enjoys such a poor reputation is because we've cheapened the process of consuming. We've been bad consumers. We've been reckless in both the scale (overindulging) and the selectivity (undiscerning) of our consumer habits. We've been too prone to fall for glossy advertising, too undisciplined to resist what we know isn't good for us, and too willing to make consumer choices based mostly on questions like "Will it make me look cool?"

But now, of all times, we should not be haphazard in how we consume. Why? Because consumerism is now irrevocably bound up with identity. Technology has made our consumption all the more conspicuous. Our consumer lives are fully on display on Facebook, Twitter, Pinterest, Amazon, Instagram, and other sites yet to come where we willingly, deliberately identify ourselves by the brands, books, bands, and products we like. On our "profiles," we are defined by our "likes," so that who we are to the world appears mostly

16

as an ingredient listing of consumer tastes and preferences. Regrettable though it may be, consumerism has become the front line of our witness, the outer layer of identity.

Therefore, in this fast-paced, consumerism-as-social-media-identity world, we as Christians must be more intentional about being present, active, and critical in our consumer choices. People are watching. We are observed, processed, known through our consumptive habits. What message are we sending?

We should also be passionate about engaging culture well because we want to know God more through his creation. We should live our consumer lives with the overarching goal of wanting to "taste and see that the LORD is good" (Ps. 34:8), understanding that God speaks to us everywhere—in food and drink, in melodies and rhythms, in the multiplex and the church sanctuary, on the beach or atop a mountain. Indeed, "The earth is the LORD's, and everything in it" (Ps. 24:1).

We should be better consumers because at the end of the day, the very activity of consuming is an extravagant gift of God. We don't deserve it. But we have it nonetheless. So let's make the most of it.

Ways We Cheapen Consumption

- By consuming solely to satiate temporary desires
- By consuming as a means of escaping our lives, fleeing problems
- By consuming too quickly
- By consuming primarily as a status-marking activity
- By consuming as a means of rebellion
- By overindulging
- By amassing "stuff" just to have more
- By discarding things when bored with them

Cultured Christians

We need more cultured Christians—not in the sense of being fashionable, well-heeled aristocrats who frequent the opera and attend gallery openings but simply in the sense that we take the consumer role seriously and approach culture with nuance, intentionality, and an open mind.

Cultured Christians are willing to explore all sorts of things in the realm of art and culture, even if they ultimately don't accept all of it. They're brave enough to try new things but wise enough to know that not everything is valuable or edifying.

Cultured Christians recognize how complex, ambiguous, and personal words like *edifying* and *discernment* are, and they accept that there is no easy formula or checklist for Christians wondering whether something is or isn't appropriate. Nevertheless, they recognize that the question is important, and they accept the challenge.

Cultured Christians don't treat culture as a mercenary, using it only to improve their own status in the world (by wearing fashionable clothes, name-dropping esoteric indie bands, etc.). They love culture for its inherent goodness, truth, or beauty. Not for what it can do for them.

Cultured Christians don't care about "the scene." They don't choose a bar or restaurant because it's a hot spot but because of its quality. They aren't ashamed to like Coldplay, college basketball, superhero movies, or any number of other consumables just because they have mass appeal. They embrace culture because they deem it valuable, regardless of what the "in crowd" says.

Cultured Christians don't rush to judgment. They don't look at something fancy on a menu and say, "No thanks. I'll go with what I know!" They don't walk out of a difficult, complex film saying, "I didn't get it. What a waste of my time." They understand that good things in culture rarely

18

lend themselves to immediate and easy understanding. It takes time, effort, the development of taste, and a patient sensibility to get the most out of culture.

Cultured Christians recognize the global impact of healthy, thoughtful consumption. They consider factors such as sustainability, fair trade, and the origins of the products they consume. Beyond trendiness, they take time to learn what "grass fed" actually means and why "locally grown" may be a good thing.

Cultured Christians don't separate the realm of culture from the realm of faith. They don't pit their Christianity in opposition to culture or understand their faith as being uninformed or uninfluenced by culture. They avoid looking at things in terms of sacred/secular dichotomies, recognizing that common grace lends dignity to all manner of cultural activity—even while they recognize that common grace isn't the same as *saving* grace.

Cultured Christians recognize that there are good things within culture that, when recklessly received or abused, can become evil, but that in moderation, these things can still be good. For cultured Christians, moderation is key—moderation not in the sense of compromise or lukewarm tepidness but in the sense of knowing that the best of things often comes in small doses.

Cultured Christians are not pendulum people. They aren't always reacting against some bad iteration of the faith by going too far in the other direction. They embrace the stasis of the middle—the pendulum at rest—because it is in that nonreactive space where a true, deep, rewarding appreciation of culture can occur.

Eating, Drinking, Hearing, and Seeing the Glory of God

Part of living as a Christ follower in the here and now is recognizing—sometimes all too painfully—that the here and now is not what we were made for, that the world as it is only offers glimpses of the world as it is meant to be (and will be again, in the new creation). But within the bittersweet, keenly felt absences of the heart lies a stirring hope—an inkling that our present and future pleasures are linked, that the experience of great-tasting food, transcendent music, or beautiful images now is but a practice for our future enjoyments.

As C. S. Lewis writes in *The Weight of Glory,*

> At present, if we are reborn in Christ, the spirit in us lives directly on God; but the mind and, still more, the body receives life from Him at a thousand removes—through our ancestors, through our food, through the elements. The faint, far-off results of those energies which God's creative rapture implanted in matter when He made the world are what we now call physical pleasures; and even thus filtered, they are too much for our present management. What would it be to taste at the fountainhead that stream of which even these lower reaches prove so intoxicating? Yet that, I believe, is what lies before us. The whole man is to drink joy from the fountain of joy.[4]

One day we will drink from the fountainhead, but that we can even now drink from the lower reaches means that consuming good things has a purpose in this life. Enjoyment of food exists. Why? A recognition of pleasant-sounding harmony exists. Why? Because God receives glory when we take pleasure in his creation. Thus, we must take that project seriously: "So whether you eat or drink or whatever you do, do it all for the glory of God" (1 Cor. 10:31). We must live for the glory of God *now*, as a foretaste of the life to come.

This book is about pursuing God and giving him glory as mature, nuanced consumers of the "gray areas" of culture. I'll be focusing on four areas of pop culture that we don't often think about as necessarily theological: food, pop music, movies, and alcohol. Indeed, some of these areas have had a historically volatile relationship with evangelical Christianity.

The book begins with food, because we all eat food. It's a daily activity of cultural consumption (whether or not we think of it as "culture"), and by considering what it means to "eat Christianity," we will set the stage for further explorations in the book. This section then gives way to a discussion of popular music—one of the most explosive and emotional areas of contested culture within Christianity, but also one of the most widely beloved. Pretty much everyone listens to music and bonds with others over it. The third area of culture we'll explore is film, often a flashpoint for debates about what is and isn't appropriate for Christians' consumption. And finally we'll tackle the ever-controversial and highly debated topic of alcohol. Younger evangelicals largely affirm alcohol; in many cases their parents do not. Is there an appropriate, moderate balance when it comes to the Christian consumption of alcohol?

Seven key themes will guide this discussion of consuming culture well. First is the recognition that partaking in culture is part of our *mission*. Kevin Vanhoozer says, "The most compelling reason I can give for learning to read culture is that the mission of the church demands it."[5] As missionaries tasked with the spreading of Christ's kingdom and the stewardship of God's creation, we simply cannot make a dent if we are lazy cultural interpreters. The world watches Christians and how they interact with culture. Do we protest it? Boycott it? Fund it? Abuse it? Learning to be healthy, thoughtful creators and consumers of culture is vital for our witness as ambassadors of Christ on earth.

A second theme is the idea that mature cultural consumption requires wise *stewardship* of resources. Consumer power is economic power, and what we choose to support with our money says a lot about the kind of consumers we are. Third is the recognition that *community* plays a vital role in our partaking of culture. Most of the time, consuming culture isn't just an isolated activity but rather takes place among other people; this is a blessing that gives consumption another layer of meaning. A fourth theme is the notion that enjoying God's good creation is an act of *worship*—that more than culture being just banal, everyday diversions or enjoyments, receiving culture is in some sense the receiving of grace, which is something for which we should praise God. Fifth is the value of cultivating *taste* in the process of consuming culture. It's the idea that we get the most out of culture when we take the time to refine our taste and expand our palates. A corollary to taste is *discernment*, the ability to critically assess the relative merits, truth, goodness, and beauty of a complicated aspect of culture, which also takes work. The final key theme is the notion that the healthiest enjoyment of culture requires *moderation*—the idea that too much of anything good can become bad, just as wholesale abstinence from something wonderful can also be a bad thing.

My hope is that each of these themes will equip us to be better navigators of cultural gray areas, resisting the polarities of legalism and absolute liberty by becoming more discerning both in *what* we consume and in *how* we consume it. My hope is that we will each come to a fuller appreciation of the finer things in life, the glories and goodness of God's common grace, and that we would worship the Creator ever more through receiving the fruits of his creation.

So often we blaze through life, moving from temporary enjoyment to temporary enjoyment, haphazardly consuming things so that none of it ever grows us in any significant way. But I know we can be better. And I know that if we take the time to really dig in and do the work of being the best consumers of culture we can be, it will not only enhance our faith and witness but also glorify God. He's the source of everything good, after all, and he makes everything good taste, sound, look, and feel all the more magnificent.

PART 1

EATING

We all eat. We eat to live. It's required for survival on this planet. In that way, this section is unique among the four parts of this book. We can survive without music, without movies, without alcohol. But we cannot live without food.

That food is necessarily a part of our day-to-day lives means that the question of how we consume it is incredibly important. If we are spending so much of our lives doing this thing—ingesting various plants, animals, sugars, and grains, multiple times a day—shouldn't we take at least some time to consider how this activity does or does not edify our lives, or whether or not it brings us closer to God and to other people? Is food simply a necessary evil, a bodily requirement that annoyingly requires lots of money, time, and (occasionally) indigestion on a weekly basis?

Are we consuming food in a manner worthy of the gospel of Jesus Christ? That may sound like a silly question, and indeed, for many of us the whole notion of food as a spiritual discipline or missional activity might be a new idea. But if we are talking about being cultured Christians—believers who receive culture well and consume things in a healthy and mature manner—we should not neglect a discussion of food.

Food is the ultimate in global pop culture. Every day, across the world, billions of people eat. Each person receives food as sustenance, but sometimes also as a meaningful pleasure. They receive it around tables, with friends, after a long day of work, as part of festivals or celebrations. They taste it and savor it, satiating not only their physical body but their emotional and spiritual being. Food brings us pleasure, sometimes even joy. How can we get the most out of food? Is there a biblical approach to food? Why does food simultaneously bring about such pleasure and such stress, and what does a healthy approach to consuming it look like? The following two chapters ask those questions, first by looking at biblical themes related to food and then by applying them to our modern world.

* * * * * * * * * * *

Interlude

Food as Worship

* * * * * * * * * * *

It may sound lofty and pretentious to describe food as worship. All I know is that when I took my first bite of chicory-rubbed filet mignon in bordelaise sauce on a Sunday afternoon in 2010, it felt like tasting a little bit of heaven. It felt like the pleasure of God.

That filet mignon was one course of a ten-course dinner prepared by my friend Jessica Kemp, who does things with food I've never seen done before. And this meal, in which each course was creatively inspired by one of Jessica's favorite songs of the year, was unsurpassed in the pantheon of great meals I've ever had.

At this dinner, which probably lasted six hours or more, seven friends and I enjoyed mind-blowing homemade delicacies: quail confit with poached kumquats, tempura basil and sage, blue cheese ice cream with Madeira poached fig and wildflower sage honey, and a strawberry rose milkshake with rose-laced cream.

How could I not experience God through food like that—sitting in good company, enjoying never-before-tasted flavor combinations, anxiously awaiting the next carefully concocted course, and never getting full? (The courses were all nearly bite-sized.)

Dinners like this can be worshipful experiences. In community, with hours and hours of conversation and exquisite cuisine, how can our thoughts not orient us toward God in thanksgiving for friends, creativity, and the fact that he gave us tongues to taste and not just stomachs to fill?

* * * * * * * * * * *

1

Food and Faith

When I think of "evangelicals and food" in the context of my upbringing, I think of a few things: church potlucks, mayo-based casseroles, church ladies cooking food for those in need, and Chick-fil-A. Let me take those in order:

Church potlucks: A staple of evangelical church culture. At the midwestern Baptist churches of my youth, church potlucks happened every so often after worship services and especially during revivals. These community-building events usually occurred in the "fellowship hall" and consisted of every wife in the church bringing some sort of dish and placing it on a series of tables from which church members would fill their plates, cafeteria-style. (For those who have never experienced such a thing, the movie *Junebug* features a particularly accurate portrayal.) Typically potluck fare fell within six genres: brownies (there were always at least four variations), desserts with some sort of Jell-O and/or crunchy topping (cornflakes or pretzels), fried chicken (sometimes straight from a KFC bucket), pasta salad, dishes incorporating cream of mushroom soup, and mayo-based casseroles.

Mayo-based casseroles: A prominent genre at church potlucks is the mayo-based casserole. (The word *casserole* goes hand in hand with *mayonnaise*, doesn't it, with its onomatopoeic connotations of squishy, coagulating, gelatinous textures?) Typically improvised dishes in which random vegetables, spices, meats, cheeses, and elbow macaroni are mixed and baked with a hearty helping of Miracle Whip, these home-cooked, heavy dishes made my stomach churn as a kid and perhaps contributed to my deathly phobia of mayonnaise today. Spoiler alert: none of these casseroles were as miraculous as the primary ingredient would have you believe.

Cooking food for those in need: In my experience, evangelical church ladies seize upon any opportunity to cook something for someone in need. Any time a member of the church community has a baby, a death in the family, a serious illness, or an economic hardship, a team of church ladies tend to get cracking on a schedule for who will make what food and bring it over on what night. Then there are the many churches with pantries for distributing food to the poor and those with an organized outreach to local soup kitchens or missions. For evangelicals, food as service and hospitality seems always to be central.

Chick-fil-A: The corporate face of evangelical food. Chick-fil-A's delicious, family-friendly food—most prominent in the Southern United States—was a favorite of my family growing up. Owned and operated by the unapologetically evangelical Cathy family, Chick-fil-A remains one of the most successful Christian-run food companies, marked not only by tasty food but also by high-quality customer service and disarmingly nice staff members.

Those four associations represent some positive aspects of evangelical approaches to food: an emphasis on community, celebration, feasting, and thanksgiving (potlucks); an emphasis on hospitality and service (baking food for others, Chick-fil-A's customer service); and—to some extent, if you like mayo—an emphasis on rich, tasty food. They also represent a dearth of other positive things: healthiness, unprocessed foods, non-fried things, gourmet cuisine, and the like.

These days, however, my experience with the Christian community and food is changing. Community, feasting, celebration, and service are all still there, but increasingly it seems as though there is a true appreciation for quality food as well as the value of healthy, local, and "just" food (see chap. 2 for further discussion of this). It seems as though more and more of my Christian peers care about things like "grass-fed" beef and "free-range" chicken, seek out restaurants that regularly change menus according to what's in season locally, and order dishes like ricotta gnocchi with brown butter and truffle honey. They care about gourmet and interesting food, even if they can't always afford to eat it.

When I look at how some of my Christian friends are so deliberately, thoughtfully consuming food, I'm encouraged. I'm encouraged by my friend Brittany, a former resort pastry chef who told me—as she was making chocolate truffles with fig balsamic reduction and 55 percent dark chocolate—that "God wants me to use the culinary arts as a form of his creation." Brittany said Psalm 34:8 ("Taste and see that the LORD is good") inspires her to try new things and experiment with the flavors God has created: melon mousse with candied cucumbers, fig Bavarian cream, feta cheesecake. "It's not my flavors," she said. "It's God's flavors."

And I'm encouraged by my friend Jessica, whose culinary experimentation I highlighted earlier. She uses syringes to create laboratory-style food (foamed hickory, blackberry whiskey sour marshmallows with candied orange olive oil) and injects a healthy bit of irony and nostalgia into her creations. She once made a series of breakfast-themed cupcakes for dessert, including a scrambled eggs and bacon cupcake (the frosting was literally a sweet scrambled egg).

People like Brittany and Jessica are good models for what it means to love food, creatively prepare it, even experience it as a form of worship. They inspire me to be more thoughtful in how I understand food and more open to the possibilities and joys that come with an open mind and refined palette. They remind me that food—the most quotidian and seemingly meaningless of all cultural items we daily consume—can be a significant experience in our lives, beyond just giving us the calories we need to keep on moving.

A Distinctly Christian Approach to Food?

Does a distinctly Christian approach to food exist? Does it even make sense to talk about how Christians consume food as opposed to how anyone else consumes it? Aren't good principles for eating applicable to everyone?

Yes and no. Much of this chapter, and indeed this book, will explore principles that anyone—believer or unbeliever—can learn from and grow from in their pursuit of a healthier, more meaningful experience of culture. But it will also be driven by a commitment to Christian values and an overarching concern for what the Bible has to say about these questions. Ultimately, I hope, the Christian ethic of consumption set forth in this book will be an ethic with helpful things to say to everybody, no matter what you believe about God. Belief in God, after all, isn't a prerequisite for enjoyment of his creation. But a deeper, more meaningful enjoyment of creation can, I believe, give birth to belief or enhance one's faith. And that's one of the things this book is about.

What's a Foodie?

Urban Dictionary defines a *foodie* as "a person that spends a keen amount of attention and energy on knowing the ingredients of food [and] the proper preparation of food, and finds great enjoyment in top-notch ingredients and exemplary preparation." I confess: I'm a foodie, and many of my friends are too. We love gourmet burgers with blue cheese and port-caramelized onions; we head to food festivals where we taste bruschetta with pistachio butter and red wine figs; we chase gourmet food trucks specializing in Korean-Mexican fusion; we gather for birthdays at the exotic grilled sausage tavern downtown, where Belgian truffle-oil fries are the perfect addition to alligator, pork, and smoked andouille sausage. We love food and spend a good chunk of our disposable income on it. Can it get out of hand? Certainly. But in moderation, as delighting in the goodness of God's creation, it can also be a wonderful thing.

Food in the Beginning

In the beginning, God created all things and pronounced them "good" (see Gen. 1). Among those good things: eating. God said to mankind, "I give you every seed-bearing plant on the face of the whole earth and every tree that has fruit with seed in it. They will be yours for food" (Gen. 1:29). From that moment on, eating food became an essential motif of human existence, and indeed a biblical motif.

Interestingly, though food was created "good," it also proved to be the enticement that led to the fall of man and the beginning of sin. God told Adam and Eve they could eat fruit from any tree in the garden save one: the tree of the knowledge of good and evil (see Gen. 2:16–17). Sadly, they opted to eat the forbidden fruit in spite of this command, and thus came the fall of humanity. What this illustrates with regard to food (or any form of cultural consumption) is the fact that though something may be "good," it can lead us astray when we approach it in the wrong way. Adam and Eve could have eaten fruit from every other tree and been perfectly happy, honoring God by enjoying his goodness in creation. Instead, they consumed the outlawed fruit not because they wanted to honor God but because they wanted to be like him. For them, consumption became a selfish rather than worshipful act, and that's where it always goes wrong.

The next major food-related command from God comes in the Noah story when, after the flood, God tells Noah, "Everything that lives and moves about will be food for you. Just as I gave you the green plants, I now give you everything" (Gen. 9:3). Here, God grants humans permission to be carnivorous, with one stipulation: don't eat the blood, because in blood is the sacred life, which belongs to God (see Gen. 9:4). This first "dietary law" establishes a principle of eating and drinking that we should remember even today: eat and drink out of reverence to God, acknowledging that all life is from him and not to be abused.

Eventually God's directives on food—what and how to eat it—become a lot more specific and important as part of his covenant with Israel. As outlined in Leviticus 11 and Deuteronomy 14, the "dietary laws" for the people of Israel are extensive and detailed, offering guidelines for eating "clean" and avoiding "unclean" animals as a way to honor the covenant, approach holiness, and demonstrate reverence for God. These dietary distinctions between clean and unclean also served to reinforce the separation of Jews (pure) from Gentiles (impure), defining Israel as culturally and spiritually set apart as the people of God. Though eventually these dietary laws were nullified when the new covenant rendered the Jew-Gentile distinction obsolete as a factor in defining the people of God (see Acts 10), we can still garner from them some valuable lessons about food and faith. Just as eating food for the Israelites was a way to honor God, so it is for us today. We aren't bound by specific "do-and-don't eat" regulations, but we should still retain the spirit of eating food in humility and out of reverence for the Creator who ultimately provides it all.

Food as Thanksgiving

A major biblical theme of food is *thanksgiving for God's provision*. One of the most interesting food-related stories in Scripture is the miraculous appearance of manna each morning for the Israelites as they wandered in the wilderness (see Exod. 16). That they gathered only enough for one day on each morning demonstrated the extent to which they had to trust and depend on God's faithfulness. For them, the manna was a very tangible, honey-tasting reminder of why eating food is an act of thanksgiving.

Frequently in Scripture, thanksgiving manifests itself through celebration and feasting on food. In the Old Testament, meals were often events that symbolized the ratifying of an agreement. After Isaac and Abimelek made a covenant of peace, Isaac "made a feast for them, and they ate and drank" (Gen. 26:30). Similar feasts happened after Jacob and his father-in-law made an agreement of peace (see Gen. 31:54) and when David and Abner patched things up at Hebron (see 2 Sam. 3:20).

For the Israelites, feasting together on food was the central act of public, communal thanksgiving for God's provision. In the Jewish calendar, a cycle of seven annual feasts celebrated food and the blessings of God.

"The covenant requires human response to God's initiatives of created goodness and blessing," writes L. Shannon Jung in

Food for Life. "Understanding food as created good, a blessing, and a gift from God leads to a central aspect of human response: *appreciation.* In response to Yahweh's gift, the creatures are to enjoy that gift; they are to celebrate, feast, and party."[1]

Chief among the important symbolic meals in Jewish culture was Passover, a special annual feast commemorating Yahweh's deliverance of Israel from Egyptian bondage. Importantly, the Old Testament Passover meal anticipates and takes on new meaning in the New Testament, as it is reflected heavily in the Lord's Supper, which is to be a new feast of remembrance for the people of God. The Jewish Passover commemorated not just past deliverance but the continuing covenant faithfulness of Yahweh, as Brian MacDonald-Milne writes:

> It was an annual renewal by each family and of the whole nation of their covenant relationship with God. In the case of the Eucharist, many of the ideas associated with the Jewish Passover are taken over into the Church. It is a feast or family meal celebrated by old and young as a commemoration of God's saving action in Christ and of his present rule and care, and it renews the covenant relationship established in baptism.[2]

From the Old Testament we are reminded of the importance of food as an act of appreciation, of thanking God for his faithful provision, and of celebrating his goodness by enjoying the bounty of his creation. In this way, eating food is surely an act of worship—something that should always be done in a spirit of praise and thanksgiving.

Eating with Jesus

When Jesus Christ arrives on the scene of history in the New Testament Gospels, food and eating do not become less important in the biblical narrative; arguably they become more.

The fact that Jesus ate food should not surprise us—he had a stomach, after all—but the fact that the narratives of his life so regularly highlight his eating should strike us as significant.

As Tim Chester notes in *A Meal with Jesus*, the New Testament completes the sentence "The Son of Man came . . ." in three ways: "not to be served but to serve, and to give his life as a ransom for many" (Mark 10:45 ESV); "to seek and to save the lost" (Luke 19:10); and "eating and drinking" (Luke 7:34).

"The first two are statements of purpose," writes Chester. "*Why* did Jesus come? He came to serve, to give his life as a ransom, to seek and save the lost. The third is a statement of method. *How* did Jesus come? He came eating and drinking."[3]

In the New Testament, Jesus eats and drinks a lot. In the Gospel of Luke, there are numerous mentions of Jesus fellowshiping at the tables of others: at a banquet in the house of Levi (5:27–39), at dinner in the house of Simon the Pharisee (7:36–50), breaking bread at Bethsaida (9:10–17), enjoying hospitality at the homes of Martha (10:38–42) and later Zacchaeus (19:1–10), and dining at the homes of Pharisees (11:37–54; 14:1–24), culminating in the breaking of bread at Emmaus (24:30), in which the disciples' "eyes were opened" (24:31) and "he was known to them" (24:35 ESV) in the act of the breaking of bread. This crucial event, and the subsequent final meal (24:36–53) with the disciples and Jesus—in the resurrected flesh, still hungry for fish—not only bolsters the case for the importance of mealtime fellowship in the life of Christ, but also foreshadows the new era, in which we would gather as the body of Christ, over a meal, in remembrance of him.[4]

Jesus seemed to value the sacredness of dining with others, not just for sustenance but for community and mission. "[Jesus] was a party animal," writes Chester. "His mission

Why Is Food Tastier Than It Needs to Be?

Have you ever wondered why food tastes so good? God didn't have to create a planet that produced tasty edible plants, spices, and pleasing aromas, after all. He might have just as easily created food to be bland and tasteless—merely fuel. But he *did* create such things as curry, cocoa, sugar cane, and coffee beans. What does this say about God? What does it say about eating?

The fact that food is more delicious than it needs to be and that God was generous and went over the top in creating both taste buds and tasty food means, to author Tim Chester, that "the quality of food should matter to us. We're to treat food as a gift, not merely as fuel."[5]

It should also be a reminder to us that God created all things—lettuce, raspberries, almonds, pineapples—and declared them to be good, just as he created man in his image, with the creative faculties and desires to cultivate, combine, and cook food in ways that are extravagantly tasty. As Episcopal priest and former *New York Times* food critic Robert Farrar Capon wrote in *The Supper of the Lamb,*

> The world exists, not for what it means but for what it is. The purpose of mushrooms is to be mushrooms; wine is in order to be wine: Things are precious before they are contributory. . . . To be sure, God remains the greatest good, but, for all that, the world is still good in itself. Indeed, since He does not need it, its whole reason for being must lie in its own goodness; He has no use for it; only

strategy was a long meal, stretching into the evening. He did evangelism and discipleship round a table with some grilled fish, a loaf of bread, and a pitcher of wine."[6]

What can we learn from Jesus about how to better approach food and eating? For one thing, we can learn—or simply remind ourselves—that when we eat, we are participating in an activity that our Savior himself, God incarnate, participated in daily. Jesus didn't just talk about eating. He ate. He ate bread, fish, honey, and figs, among other things we also eat. The reality of his human fleshiness, eating then delight. Just think what that means. We were not made in God's image for nothing. The child's preference for sweets over spinach, mankind's universal love of the toothsome rather than the nutritious is the mark of our greatness, the proof that we love the secular as He does—for its secularity. We have eyes which see what He sees, lips which praise what He praises, and mouths which relish things, because He first pronounced them *tov*. The world is no disposable ladder to heaven. Earth is not convenient, it is good; it is, by God's design, our lawful love.[7]

The recognition of the superfluous, over-the-top nature of food's taste, and of man's ability to make out of it a culinary work of art, should lead us to a place of worship. As L. Shannon Jung writes,

If the world is more beautiful than it is useful, we are confronted—nay, struck down—by the beauty of kiwis, apples, bananas, artichokes, broccoli, carrots, and peaches. The beauty of fields of wheat and sunflowers and pecan orchards and gigantic stalks of corn—all are more beautiful than they need to be. They manifest the beauty of God. They awaken us to the sensibility of the world; they call us to an appreciation of all that is.[8]

Indeed, as we consider the importance of gratitude and thankfulness in the activity of eating, let us not take for granted for one moment this most mind-blowing of all facts about food: it has a *taste* when it doesn't need to, and it tastes good!

as we do now, should cause us to feel the majesty and closeness of the incarnation all the more acutely.

We should also learn from the life of Jesus that food is not *merely* a necessary fact of existence; it's a gift to be grateful for, something to be celebrated. In one of the more striking food-related episodes of the Gospels, the feeding of the five thousand (see Luke 9:10–17), Jesus takes the five loaves and two fish, looks up to heaven, and gives thanks for them (v. 16) before multiplying the food miraculously for a vast and hungry crowd.

"In receiving the bread with thanksgiving," notes Chester,

"Jesus affirms the goodness of creation. And by affirming the goodness of God's creation as he promises a new world, Jesus reminds us that this world is not going to be trashed, but redeemed. Food matters because it is part of God's good creation and part of God's new creation."[9]

Another important lesson from the "eating and drinking" Jesus is the importance that food and meals play in the building of fellowship, community, trust, and love. The scandalous thing about Jesus's eating habits was not *what* he ate but *with whom* he ate. He dined with tax collectors, Pharisees, outcasts, and sinners of all sorts. For Jesus, the table was a prime opportunity to live out his generous gospel of grace—a symbolic activity that underscores the social significance of dining in community. Jesus's critics couldn't stand the inclusiveness of his table and angrily called him "a glutton and a drunkard, a friend of tax collectors and sinners" (Matt. 11:19). As Chester notes, this particular criticism goes to show how important eating and drinking were in the mission of Jesus: "They were a sign of his friendship with tax collectors and sinners. His 'excess' of food and 'excess' of grace are linked."[10]

The communal activity of dining with Jesus symbolized the open-to-all grace of his gospel. We are all invited to his table and reject the invitation at our peril—something Jesus also explores in story form in the parable of the wedding banquet (see Matt. 22:1–14). In the story of Jesus told in the Gospels, food is about thanksgiving, grace, and anticipation of a future messianic banquet. And it all comes together in the apex of biblical meals: the Last Supper.

The Meal Jesus Gave Us

The Last Supper is the most important documented meal in Jesus's life, and it shows up in each of the four Gospels (see

Matt. 26:20–30; Mark 14:17–26; Luke 22:14–23; John 13–17). It was a farewell meal between Jesus and his inner circle, the most intimate of gatherings, as death loomed. Here, Jesus famously spoke of his body being "given for you" (Luke 22:19) and of his blood "poured out for you" (22:20), which in light of the Passover background that would have been in the disciples' minds would likely have been taken to mean, "This is my *sacrificial* flesh. . . . This is my *sacrificial* blood" (i.e., "I am the new sacrificial Lamb").[11] Jesus instructs his disciples to "do this in remembrance of me" (22:19), thus establishing the Lord's Supper as an event that was to be (and has been) a crucial part of the Christian experience.

Why is the Eucharist such a big deal? Well, for one thing it is the central symbolic action of the Christian life. In this meal, as we take the bread and the cup, we remember and give thanks for the suffering and sacrifice of Jesus for us, we join in communion with our fellow believers, and we look forward to the second coming of Christ and the messianic feast to come. In many ways, it all comes together in this meal.

Peter Leithart says the Lord's Supper is "the world in miniature; it has cosmic significance." He continues,

> Within it we find clues to the meaning of all creation and all history, to the nature of God and the nature of man, to the mystery of the world, which is Christ. It is not confined to the first day, for its power fills seven. Though the table stands at the center, its effects stretch out to the four corners of the earth.[12]

In his book, *The Meal Jesus Gave Us*, N. T. Wright suggests that what is going on in the Eucharist is "the central Christian action, which links us in an unbroken line to that little church in Turkey nineteen hundred and some years ago," and "to Jesus and his friends in the Upper Room," and "to almost all Christians throughout the world today."[13]

Though today our experience of the Eucharist is typically very unlike a meal—just a shot of juice and a tiny wafer of bread—the early church's experience of it was as part of a full meal.

Pauline scholar Robert Banks notes that for the early church, the Lord's Supper always occurred in the home, and that the word *deipnon* (as in 1 Cor. 11:20), meaning "dinner," indicates that it was likely an entire meal:

> With the exception of the words that accompany it, it was in no respect different from the customary meal for guests in a Jewish home. The breaking and distribution of the bread was the normal way of commencing such a meal, just as the taking of a cup was the usual way to bring it to a conclusion; prayers of blessing accompanied both.[14]

The "meal" aspect of the Lord's Supper should not be disregarded. The idea of communion, after all, is to *commune*. The meal is about remembering Christ, yes, but it's also about embodying the revolutionary, grace-available-for-all values that Jesus's own dining habits expressed. It has an important social aspect.

In *Making a Meal of It*, Ben Witherington points out that these early Christian meals "had elements that worked against the prevailing hierarchy and stratification of society," which Witherington finds unsurprising given that Jesus himself told his followers that when they had a banquet they should not invite their relatives or rich neighbors but rather the poor, the crippled, the lame, and the blind, even if they couldn't repay anything (Luke 14:12–14). What Jesus is saying "is that he is rejecting the idea of using meals to reinforce reciprocity cycles and, instead, is suggesting that the meals of his followers should be more gracious and less self-serving."[15]

Thomas Schreiner, in his Pauline theology *Paul: Apostle of God's Glory in Christ*, sees the divisive 1 Corinthians 11 situation as one more example suggesting that the central idea of Paul's ethic is love. When the rich Christians of Corinth are gorging on food and getting drunk while the poor lack food, Paul is outraged by their lack of the Christlike love of "putting others before oneself and living so that others will be strong in the Lord."[16]

Paul's point is that the Lord's Supper, of all meals, should do away with these inequalities and instead bring to the foreground the love and grace of Christ. It should be a meal that always reminds us that Christ's sacrifice is for *all*. And that's something worth toasting to with friends.

Around the Table

I was recently invited to attend a Friday night Shabbat dinner with a small community of twentysomething Messianic Jews in Los Angeles. Enticed by the promise of plenty of good food—fish tacos, margaritas, and cake were on the menu—and the opportunity to get to know more about the culture of Jesus-believing Jews, I happily accepted the invitation. It was a beautiful experience. As the kickoff service of the day of rest (for Jews, beginning at sunset on Friday night), the Shabbat dinner was a rich, sacred, long meal full of prayers, songs, Scripture reading, laughing, and plenty of "*L'chaim!*" toasts.

Though I was a "goy" (Gentile) guest in this intimate gathering, I didn't feel like an outsider. We were all believers, and we joined together in the breaking of bread, the drinking of wine, and the joyful consuming of fish tacos. Some of those in attendance had read my book *Hipster Christianity*, so we talked about that, and we talked about Israel and Palestine, and the Jesus people movement, even Rob Bell and the *Love Wins* controversy. The whole evening actually reminded me of a Bell quote from *Velvet Elvis* on the Christian duty to master "the art of the long meal":

> What was the ritual the first Christians observed with the most frequency? Exactly. The common meal, also called the Eucharist or the Lord's Supper. And what did this meal consist of? Hours of talking and sharing and enjoying each other's presence. Food is the basis of life, it comes from the earth, and the earth is God's. In a Jewish home in Jesus's day—and even now—the table is seen as an altar. It's holy. Time spent around the table with each other is time spent with God.[17]

The Shabbat experience was a great reminder to me of the sacredness of the dinner table and its knack for bringing together people of diverse classes, ethnicities, and cultures who together break bread in fellowship, celebration, and thanksgiving for the bounty of God's provision for us.

L. Shannon Jung argues that the biblical themes of eating coalesce around two poles: "the pole of enjoyment, providence, goodness, delighting," and "the pole of hospitality, justice, mission, *sharing.*"[18] Indeed, as we've seen in our brief survey of food in the Bible, these two broad themes come up again and again. There's a vertical component to how we should eat: as an act of gratitude to God and worship of him. There is also a horizontal component: eating in community, missionally, counterculturally. Both the vertical and horizontal were in wonderful harmony at the Shabbat dinner I attended, and it offered me a picture of how meaningful, rich, and transformative food can be in the context of faith.

Feasting in Memory and Hope

For Christians, consuming food should have aspects of the vertical (worship) and the horizontal (community), but I would argue that there is another dynamic at play here too: a "backward and forward" continuum in which memory of the past and longing for the future collide in the sacred, tasty moment of present feasting.

Some say taste and smell are the senses most tied to memory, and I believe it. There is something sacred about my memories of former feasts: the Sunday evening church potlucks full of casseroles and pies, the summer barbecues with grilled hot dogs and sweet corn on the cob, Christmas dinners at my grandma's house with fluffy dinner rolls and pecan pie, Super Bowl parties with my mom's "Mississippi mud" brownies. Or the meals with friends that I'll never forget: eating *nasi goreng* off banana leaves in Malaysia; enjoying long meals in Spain at 11:00 p.m., savoring every bite of crunchy lemon potatoes, paella, serrano ham, and Spanish omelettes; having dinner in Matsumoto, Japan, with a friend and a sweet older Japanese couple who ordered us everything on the menu.

We remember eating, and in eating, we remember. Perhaps God made smell and taste so saturated with memory because he wanted us to always be remembering and reflecting upon the gift that is food. In the moment I taste a spoonful of flourless chocolate cake with hazelnuts and sea salt caramel, I worship God for his goodness. Years later I can still remember that taste, and I thank God again. Memory plays a big role in our enjoyment of eating, and it's one of the reasons why a meal—the Lord's Supper—is one of our most important rituals of reflection and thanksgiving.

But in the Lord's Supper, remembrance is only part of the meaningfulness of eating. It's also a foreshadowing of eating in the future—a foretaste of the magnificent feasts to come in God's kingdom. Similarly, when we eat our everyday meals, we should be reminded that there is a future to this activity.

We will be eating in the world to come, thanks be to God! There is food, eating, feasting after death and resurrection. We see in the Bible that the resurrected Christ eats (see Luke 24). As Chester notes, the resurrection of Jesus

> is the promise and beginning of the renewal of all things, and the future is a physical future on a renewed earth. It's a future with broiled fish. We will enjoy not just food, but cooking and fermenting and brewing. "On this mountain the Lord of hosts will make for all people a feast of rich food, a feast of well-aged wine, of rich food full of marrow, of aged wine well refined" (Isa. 25:6).[19]

What does it mean, though, that we will be eating in our resurrected bodies? Will hunger exist too? Will we *need* to eat?

In his theology of the body, *Earthen Vessels*, Matthew Lee Anderson suggests that our human dependence on things like food, clothing, and shelter will be ended in the new creation, pointing to 1 Corinthians 6:13: "'Food is meant for the stomach and the stomach for food'—and God will destroy both" (ESV). And yet Scripture seems to indicate that we will be eating. One of the major eschatological images in the final chapters of the Bible is that of the great wedding feast of the Lamb (see Rev. 19:9). We can only conclude that eating in the new creation must be for some other purpose than sustenance or survival. "In the resurrection," writes Anderson, "our bodies will no longer be dependent upon resources for their ongoing existence, suggesting that when we consume, it will be for the purposes of pleasure."[20]

Eating in the Now-and-Not-Yet

In the resurrection, the apparent sole purpose of food is for pleasure. In the here and now, food is pleasurable but also necessary—something we need to survive. That now-and-not-yet tension should guide our ethic of eating today.

Because it's about survival and sustenance now, we must approach food thoughtfully and graciously, aware that food is correlated with our health. We should consume food with a humility before God, who alone sustains us and provides us with nourishment.

But by God's grace, food is more than that. It's tasty and transcendent when it doesn't need to be. It's a foretaste of God's coming world—something we can delight in, something through which we can taste the goodness of God. "Food is revelatory of the goodness and joy of the earth," writes Jung.

> It is also how we come to taste the language of grace and love; it is how we come to know community. Food opens up in us the visceral channels of knowledge. It enables us to experience love before we have a name for it. God comes to feed us, to fill us, to love us. We know grace first through our bodies.[21]

We must never forget that food is a sacred gift, an invitation to joy and grace. It may be easy to take food for granted, to cheapen it or scarf it down because we need to fill our stomachs, but as we've seen in our brief biblical survey, to eat food is to partake in something significant. How we eat, what we eat, why it matters—these questions should inform our culinary habits as, with every bite, we seek to honor God.

****

Interlude

A Timeline of Food Memories

****

Eating is about remembrance. That God created us to have such capacity for food memories seems to indicate that there's something important—even sacred—about eating: what we eat, who we eat with, and where we are in life. It's about thanksgiving.

As an exercise in remembering and giving thanks to God for how he's provided for me my entire life, I sat down to record one food memory from every year of my life (as far back as I could recall such memories, which was twenty years). You should try it too. It's healthy, I think, to think about such things. Thanks be to God for allowing us to taste his goodness and relive it in memory.

1992: Dinner at my favorite childhood restaurant, Casa Bonita in Tulsa, Oklahoma. I loved their Mexican rice and sopapillas (with honey!). Also, the puppet show was fun but kind of scary.

1993: Fourth of July barbecue in my grandparents' backyard in Boulder, Colorado. Hamburgers, hot dogs, sweet corn on the cob, and my grandmother's blueberry pie with homemade vanilla ice cream.

1994: In San Francisco with my family, dinner at Empress of China. Best Chinese food I'd tasted up to that point. I think I recall especially loving the sweet and sour pork.

1995: Christmas in Kentucky with all the McCracken relatives. On Christmas Eve, a unique tradition that persists even today: steak sandwiches with a side of orange slices.

1996: Camping in Yellowstone with my family. Nothing can compare to eating slightly charred hot dogs and gooey s'mores roasted over the campfire while foreboding tales of bears cause the kids' eyes to widen.

1997: On vacation with my family in Lake Tahoe, I had the best meal of my life up to that point, at a restaurant called Jack Rabbit Moon in Incline Village, Nevada. Realization: "New American" is my favorite genre of food, even though I couldn't name it then.

1998: New Year's Day tradition of a packed house of neighbors, friends, and family, while an array of game-day food filled the kitchen: Cincinnati chili, pigs in a blanket, Christmas cookies, and my dad's amazing taco-seasoned Chex mix.

1999: Friday night family reunion in the Chicago suburbs, eating Chicago-style pizza (Gino's or Nancy's) before we all headed to Lake Geneva for Bible camp.

2000: For senior prom, we splurged for dinner at Café Sebastienne in Kansas City's Kemper Museum of Contemporary Art. I had rabbit, and it was amazing.

2001: My first year of college. The Wheaton College cafeteria (aka "Saga") was the best. "Student Appreciation Dinners" occasionally featured prime rib and lobster tail.

2002: Studying abroad in Malaysia, eating all sorts of things my taste buds had never encountered. Realization: it's all bananas in Malaysia—banana pancakes, fried bananas with ice cream, fried rice on banana leaf, etc.

2003: Wednesday nights at Baker's Square in Wheaton with Ryan, Aubrey, Kevin, and our regular waitress Tanya. As we were driving back to campus one night after pie, the radio reported the beginning of the Iraq war.

2004: In Paris with friends for spring break, trying to eat on the cheap. Munching on baguette slices with Nutella on the train to Versailles.

2005: On a senior year road trip through the South, four friends and I enjoyed barbecue (in Charleston and Memphis), soul food (in Savannah), fried chicken (in Tennessee and Alabama), and even a Waffle House breakfast or two.

2006: Dinner at a random Tex-Mex restaurant in Fresno with four friends, shortly after the car we were driving in nearly got hit by a truck that ran a red light. We were jumpy at that meal, happy to be alive, glad to be together.

2007: Dinner in Matsumoto, Japan, with my traveling companion, Mark, and a local couple, the Watanabes. We didn't speak Japanese and they didn't speak English (well), but we still managed to have a wonderful meal of tempura, rice, and sake.

2008: Thanksgiving dinner with my friend Will, his parents, his aunt and uncle, and a somewhat random collection of local international students in Magalia, CA.

2009: At the Trout Inn outside Oxford, a summer dinner of steak and ale with friends Donna and Tammy on the riverbanks where Lewis and Tolkien once dined.

2010: Spent a day in San Diego eating and drinking good things with good friends, starting at the Goldfish Point Café in La Jolla and ending at Red Tracton's steakhouse in Del Mar, with stops for sushi, coffee, and desserts in between.

2011: In Altea, Spain, a hot summer evening of tapas and red wine with friends, migrating from café to café until 3:00 a.m. Realization: I could get used to Spanish culture.

2012: At Studio restaurant in Laguna Beach, a seven-course dinner at sunset that I'll never forget. During the dessert course (some sort of strawberry Napoleon), I got down on one knee and proposed to Kira. The happiest moment of my life. (She said yes!)

* * * * * * * * * *

2

Where We Go Wrong (and Right) in Eating

* * * * * * * * * *

Food can be a wonderful thing. But when abused or thoughtlessly consumed, it can also be a dangerous thing. I love coffee, for example. But I've come to learn that if I drink too much of it too often, I get headaches. I also love almond croissants but know from experience that too many of them too often can leave me feeling gross, indulgent, and a little paunchy.

Any good thing can become a bad thing when consumed poorly. This is one of the core tenets of this book. But what does "consumed poorly" look like? And with respect to food, what does the flip side—consuming well, consuming *Christianly*—look like? How do we honor God in the way that we eat?

In this chapter I want to raise five cautions about how we sometimes go wrong in the way that we consume food. But with each I believe there is an opportunity to do better—not only to avoid the pitfalls but to cultivate healthier habits. From there I think we can begin to understand just what an ethic of Christian eating might look like today when built upon biblical principles and applied to our contemporary world.

Caution #1: Food as Escapism

Food can be a great escape. Those of us lucky enough to live in places where food is relatively plentiful know it is often a convenient go-to comforter in times of stress, sadness, or anxiety. There's a reason "comfort food" is a culinary genre. Eating fried chicken or pecan pie can take the edge off a hard day.

This isn't necessarily a bad thing. Escapism, as we'll discover in later chapters, has its place. Consuming food as a means of self-soothing can be fine, but it shouldn't be our primary mode of eating. For one thing, food as escapism turns eating into a self-centered act. It's about what food can do *for me*, not about what food is (a beautiful, tasty gift) or what it can be when enjoyed in community. The occasional late-night doughnut run or ice cream study break is one thing; habitually eating unhealthy food as a way to de-stress is another. It can become an addiction. The "food as escapism" mentality cheapens food by making it a habit-forming drug that goes dangerously beyond the gratuitously tasty giver of life that it is.

But food as escapism is not limited to the realm of gorging on Twinkies and potato chips after a bad breakup. It can be a bad habit of foodies as well. Sometimes our obsession with eating gourmet or "artisan" food can be equally consuming and self-focused. The *gourmands* who get weak in the knees over the Valdeón cheese samples at Whole Foods and can't go a day without some sort of Marcona almond acai granola bar are equally at risk of relying on food for narcissistic boosts of self-esteem or comfort.

The temptation to turn to food for comfort is widespread and—to an extent—understandable, but is it the best way?

Opportunity #1: Eat for Connection

Instead of using food to ameliorate our stress or emotional turmoil, perhaps we should instead think of food as a way to—paradoxically, perhaps—get outside of ourselves. Eating food should bring together rather than isolate human beings. Instead of eating food as a way to detach from the world, perhaps we might try eating as a way to reconnect. It's actually a pretty natural fit.

"Food connects," writes Tim Chester.

> It connects us with family. It turns strangers into friends. And it connects us with people around the world. Consider what you had for breakfast this morning. Tea. Coffee. Sugar. Cereal. Grapefruit. Much of it was produced in another state or country. Food enables us to be blessed by people around the world and to bless them in return.[1]

As a habit that every human has in common, eating brings us together. And as something that involves ingredients from all corners of the globe—sometimes all at once—food connects us with one another. It reminds us that we are part of a global ecology; that what we are eating originated somewhere, from someone; that the spices we take for granted have origins in specific cultures and geographical locations. It's like a World Civilizations class every time we eat.

In his book *Food and Faith: A Theology of Eating*, Duke Divinity School professor Norman Wirzba suggests that in a trinitarian theology, "all reality is communion" and that even eating should be conceived of in relational terms of membership, belonging, responsibility, and gratitude. Eating "joins people together, to other creatures and the world, and to God through forms of 'natural communion' too complex to fathom," writes Wirzba. "It establishes a membership that confirms all creatures as profoundly in need of each other and upon God to provide life's nutrition and vitality."[2]

Far from a solitary and self-indulgent activity, the universality of food should remind us of our interconnectedness every time we eat. As embodied, fleshly creatures, we cannot maintain an isolated posture in our habits of consumption, suggests Tom Beaudoin in *Consuming Faith*. "The body is not a closed system but an open one, utterly reliant on the world," he writes.[3] As L. Shannon Jung says, our dependence "on air, on water, on food, on each other, and on God is integral to health and bodily well-being."[4]

Indeed, the greatest of all meals for Christians—the Eucharist—rebuffs the isolationist mode of consumption. It's a sacred means of connection and solidarity. In it we identify with the suffering of Christ. We connect with our Savior and his body: our fellow believers throughout the ages. And it's thoroughly countercultural.

Movies about Food

- For the chocolate lover: *Chocolat*
- A Danish dinner party: *Babette's Feast*
- Family run restaurant: *Bella*
- Japanese home-cooking: *Still Walking*
- Class and cooking: *Ratatouille*
- A cooking class: *Julie & Julia*
- The ethics of eating: *Food, Inc.*
- Chefs in love: *Mostly Martha*

It may seem odd to think about eating in terms of connection, solidarity, humility, and suffering rather than as a matter of satiating our primal needs and emotional urges. But in the meal Christ gave us, the Eucharist, the former is exactly what eating is. It's about getting outside of ourselves and reflecting on the bigger picture.

Caution #2: Too Much Food

Eating to excess is one of the most widespread and dangerous ways that we abuse food. Especially in America, we eat *a lot* of food, and coupled with poor dietary choices and a sedentary lifestyle, our overeating has led to an epidemic of obesity.

Statistics tell the story. Over the past three decades, childhood obesity rates in America have tripled, and today, nearly one in three children in America are overweight or obese.[5] About one-third of United States adults (33.8 percent) are obese, and the number of states with an obesity prevalence of 30 percent or more has increased to twelve states in 2010 from nine in 2009.[6] Meanwhile, portion sizes have exploded and the types of things we eat more of are worse for us: fats, oils, sugars, sweeteners. The average American eats fifteen more pounds of sugar a year today than in 1970, for example.[7] For one of three Americans, this often spells high blood pressure, heart disease, strokes, type 2 diabetes, or cancer. Obesity is a real issue, and it comes from an unhealthy habit of overindulging in food.

Merriam Webster defines gluttony as "excess in eating or drinking," and the Bible defines it as a sin (see for example Prov. 23:2, 20–21; 28:7). Moreover, Scripture implores us to exercise restraint and self-control in the use of our bodies (see Gal. 5:22–23; 2 Peter 1:5–6), which are to be viewed as temples of the Holy Spirit (see 1 Cor. 6:19–20). The early church fathers elaborated on this and made a point to include gluttony on lists of vices to be avoided. For centuries the Christian church regarded gluttony as one of the gravest sins, listing it—along with pride, covetousness, lust, envy, anger, and sloth—as one of the "seven deadly sins."

The real problem with gluttony, notes theologian Dennis Okholm, is not the food itself or our physical need for it, "but in how we go about our eating and in the thought (or lack of thought) we give to our eating. Ultimately, gluttony refers to a desire or a longing that seeks filling."[8]

As with the "food as escapism" approach, overeating is very much a self-centered activity of seeking fulfillment in something other than God. It's a misplaced longing and inordinate desire, something we do because we aren't satisfied elsewhere. It has to do with the fact that we've become persuaded that "ours is a world of scarcity, and thus we think we have to grab the goodies before they are gone."[9]

But do we? Perhaps instead of eating indulgently as a way to fulfill a longing, we should think about eating instead as a means of learning to long after God more, resting in his abundance and consuming in moderation.

Opportunity #2: Eat with Restraint

The "manna and quail" episode from Exodus 16 offers a great lesson about the virtues of restraint and reliance on God in our eating habits. When the Israelites were hungry and desperate in the desert, God provided manna, a layer of it each morning, white like coriander seed and tasting like honey-sweet wafers. Each day they were given just enough for that day; extra was not to be hoarded and kept for the future.

Naturally, some Israelites disobeyed and saved extra manna for the next day, but it spoiled and was filled with maggots. God was making a point to his people: get out of the scarcity mentality and rest in my abundance. The lesson was repeated in the New Testament with the feeding of the five thousand. God provides. The people of God are meant to eat not too little, nor too much, but just enough. And that takes trust in a provider God.

In the end, eating with restraint amplifies the joyful experience of food. Eating too much makes us feel gross and often brings feelings of shame. Eating just enough, however, can help us remember that what we do have is a gift from God we should savor in thanksgiving. It can also remind us of our brethren in other parts of the world for whom overeating isn't even an option. Hunger and malnutrition are very real, very widespread problems in the world, and the fact that one in seven human beings on this planet goes to bed hungry each night[10] should be a sobering wake-up call to those of us who regularly fill our bellies with more than they need.

One way we can exercise restraint in the way we approach food is through fasting, which has long been a key spiritual discipline within the Christian tradition. But "fasting" isn't just another way to say "dieting," notes Okholm:

> For the early church fathers, fasting was not what Jenny Craig and Slim Fast mean by dieting. There are some similarities . . . but motivation and goal especially make this discipline different: simply put, we fast to become healthy Christians who are able to love God and others. Dieting tends to put the focus on us (and on our appearance). While Christians might be appropriately concerned about fat, calories, weight, and appearance, we should be driven chiefly to develop attitudes of contentment, gratitude, trust, and patience. These are

the aims that radically distinguish the discipline the church has called "fasting" from what our culture calls "dieting."[11]

To go without food for a time, or to eat less of it than we could, is thus not something we should do primarily because we want a slimmer waistline, but rather something we may do because we want to tangibly express our trust and contentment in God. The countercultural nature of fasting reveals to the world a different set of priorities: where eating is an activity bigger than just me and my stomach or waistline and an expression of faith in a God who gives us our very life.

Caution #3: Food as Means to Control the Body

In America, the primary metaphor for food is fuel. It's a necessary substance to keep our machine bodies moving, a stimulant to give us energy when we pause long enough to gobble up a candy bar or throw back a Red Bull.

"Americans say 'I'm full' at the end of the meal because unconsciously they think of eating as refueling," writes Clotaire Rapaille, a cultural anthropologist who contrasts America's "fuel" approach to food to that of France, where "the purpose of food is pleasure, and even a home-cooked meal is something diners savor for a long period."[12] Rapaille finds it interesting, for example, that in America rest stops often combine gas stations and food courts: one-stop-shops where our car and our stomach "tanks" can get topped off.

Indeed, there is a sense in which, increasingly, we think of our bodies as machines that we can control and—through food, dietary supplements, medicine, surgery, exercise— optimize for maximum performance. Our gyms and health clubs are to our bodies what Jiffy Lubes are to our cars; power cleanses and plastic surgery are to our bodies what oil changes and tune-ups are to our cars. We've come to see the body as a thing to subdue, a mass of flesh to morph into whatever shape we'd like, "a problem to be monitored rather than a gift."[13] With this perspective, food "becomes merely functional—a matter to be approached guardedly and out of necessity, not something we anticipate and relish."[14]

It's a widespread mentality in our culture today: thinking of food as something we consume merely to keep our bodies under our control. This is why the diet and health food industries are booming; it's why eating disorders are so widespread. People desperate to get their body image in line with a perceived "ideal" have turned to hyper-regulated food intake and obsessive calorie counting, because it's one way we can exert control over our bodies.

But is this really how we should approach food? Is food merely fuel we consume for the purposes of building a more well-oiled machine of a body? Is food a mercenary we can put to work for us to whatever end we seek, be it gaining muscle mass or losing weight? Yes, food can be these things. And certainly we can be thankful for the way that food does sustain us and give us the power to run, grow, and exert energy. But we shouldn't look at food *only* in this way.

Opportunity #3: Eat for Wellness

Part of the problem of the "food as control" approach is that it amplifies our pride and leads to a Gnostic sense of separation from and mastery over our bodies. One of the purposes of food is "to express our dependence on God," notes Chester, but sometimes "we use food to express our independence *from* God."[15] Such a posture causes us to deny our dependency and dishonor our bodies, writes Jung:

We seek to deny vulnerability, to appear strong and self-reliant, to operate from a position of superiority. We dishonor our bodies when we seek to manage them as though they were foreign to us. . . . To honor our bodies means to respect them, to see them more as friend than enemy. To honor our bodies means that we trust them, not in such a way that we act on every impulse, but that we get in touch with who we are and what we are feeling.[16]

Instead of forcing our bodies into superhuman feats of strength or eating food as fuel to build up unnaturally machine-like bodies, we should recognize the limitations of our bodies and respect them for what they can and cannot do. We should eat to sustain our bodies and to keep them healthy, recognizing our inherent fragility and aspiring for wellness and normal functionality. Being healthy is a good thing, of course, but it shouldn't be a mark of pride (look at my great body!) as much as a way for us to honor the gift that God has given us by stewarding it well.

Tips for Learning to Appreciate Good Food

- Watch *Chopped*, *Top Chef*, or any other of the many great chef reality competitions.
- Visit local farms.
- Learn about the seasons of your local community's produce. Cook with seasonal ingredients.
- Go wine tasting.
- Go to farmers' markets.
- Visit a developing country.
- Take factory tours to see how your food is made.
- Seek out and support great local restaurants. Compliment the chef.
- Take a cooking class.
- Prepare your own food.

Caution #4: Food as Status Symbol

Do you scoff at those who feed their children McDonald's and shop for groceries at Walmart? Do you turn up your nose at microwave dinners, Velveeta cheese, and iceberg lettuce? Do you find yourself frequently talking about how much you like free-range brisket *sous-vide*, how a macaron is *not* the same thing as a macaroon, and how you'd prefer to eat exclusively local, raw, hormone-free, and/or gastro-molecular cuisine? If so, you might have a problem with using food as a status symbol—a means to demonstrate your enlightened, conscientious culinary sophistication.

But you aren't alone. The temptation to use food as a status marker is widespread. And it's easy to see why. These days, food is increasingly prone to social stratification. The requirements for "classy" eating are ever more complex and yet prohibitively expensive for all but the most resourced of classes: food must be "slow," locally grown (and preferably purchased at farmers' markets), "artisan," handmade, craft-brewed, organic, hormone-free, cage-free, grass-fed, and free of high fructose corn syrup, preservatives, or any chemical-sounding ingredient more than four syllables long.

All of these "requirements," though not bad in and of themselves, make it difficult to enter the club of conscientious eating, and thus an "in vs. out" snobbery is born. Food becomes less about the goodness of consuming and more about the pride that comes with showcasing one's morally superior eating habits. In this mode, eating is drained of joy and replaced with mathematical, ingredient-police precision and self-righteous condescension.

"Foodies have turned the dining room into a classroom and chewing into a means of sparking serious synaptical brain activity," writes Stephen Webb in his article "Against the Gourmands." "When we try to make meals a means of moralistic debate, we demean the gifted character of nature's provisions. . . . We inevitably take too much pleasure from our actions and mistake physical satisfaction for a sense of social accomplishment."[17]

In 2011, *New York Times* columnist Frank Bruni raised similar warnings against the dangers of "culinary elitism" when he took celebrity chef Anthony Bourdain to task for his snarky dismissal of populist cooking personality Paula Deen, whose buttery Southern cooking Bourdain suggested was a menace to America's health.

Bruni notes that there's a definite class component to the sort of snobbery exhibited by what Bourdain represents (the urbane, sophisticated, tiny-portions-created-by-hip-chefs foodie crowd) and what Deen represents (average America, the working class, large portions of down-home cooking):

> When Deen fries a chicken, many of us balk. When the Manhattan chefs David Chang or Andrew Carmenelli do, we grovel for reservations and swoon over the homey exhilaration of it all. Her strips of bacon, skirting pancakes, represent heedless gluttony. Chang's dominoes of pork belly, swaddled in an Asian bun, signify high art.[18]

The inconsistencies of this underscore the wrongheaded nature of the whole "food as status symbol" approach. When food is divorced from its more natural functions—for sustenance, to be enjoyed in community and savored with joy and thanksgiving—and instead turned into an edible version of a mink coat, it becomes something altogether distasteful.

Opportunity #4: Eat with Humility

Food as class warfare was an issue even for the New Testament church. In 1 Corinthians 11, Paul addressed the problems that had arisen in Corinth when the rich and poor came together for the Lord's Supper, with the wealthy Christians flaunting their status by feasting on their own private stash of food and humiliating their poorer, hungry counterparts.

Paul was adamant that class divisions and social posturing of this sort had no place at the Lord's table: "When you gather to eat, you should all eat together. Anyone who is hungry should eat something at home, so that when you meet together it may not result in judgment" (1 Cor. 11:33–34).

Reality Check: Sometimes We Only Have Time (and Money) for McDonald's

Fast food may not be ideal, but let's face it: sometimes it's our only option. For many people around the world, time and money are limited resources, and eating fast food saves both. It can be easy for those with expendable time and money to talk about the healthier, environmentally friendlier superiority of "slow food" and more natural, unprocessed food, but when you're a single mom struggling to pay rent and feed young children, fast food can be a lifesaver. Some fast-food chains are getting better about offering healthy options, but the fact is, most healthy food is not all that affordable or convenient for the majority of eaters around the world. As Lisa Graham McMinn and Megan Anna Neff note,

> If I live in an urban city's low-income housing and am dependent on public transportation, my closest grocer will supply me with my food. Even if I wanted to, I wouldn't have options to buy eggs from "happy" chickens, or fairly traded coffee and cocoa. If I live on a low income, Walmart allows my household budget dollars to go further than they would go at Whole Foods. . . . This question of food justice is part of a larger conversation about social justice.[19]

What can we do to make healthier food more accessible to all people? Until we address these issues, none of us should look down our noses at those who eat at McDonald's or shop at discount grocery stores. For many people, it's the best they can do.

The Eucharist was meant to be a meal of solemn gratitude for God's mercy and grace, not a showcase for social standing or elite culinary tastes. And likewise with any of our meals: eating should be an experience of humility and thanksgiving, not one of pride.

Webb gets it right when he says, "Frozen pizzas, canned vegetables, cheap hamburgers, and sugary beverages are not the enemy; we are, which suggests that junk food is not the real temptation: pride is."[20]

Instead of eating as a performance of moral superiority or eating as a self-righteous activity, we should instead strive to eat in a manner that is humble, quiet, and nondescript. It's fine—indeed, probably wise—to eat locally grown, organic food if we are able. But we should do it because it's a good thing, not because it *looks* good. And in the same vein, it's fine to eat gourmet foods if we are able, but we'd better eat them in a spirit of humility and thanksgiving; not everyone can afford fine foods, after all. It's a luxury and one we should never wear as a badge of honor.

Caution #5: Food as Injustice

Where does the food you eat come from? Are the farmers and food workers who cultivated the ingredients paid fairly? Are the animals treated inhumanely? How is the process of producing and transporting this food harming the environment? Do our eating habits hurt or harm the earth? These are questions that have been raised in the "food justice" movement led by authors like Michael Pollan (*Food Rules*), Eric Schlosser (*Fast Food Nation*), Wendell Berry (*Bringing It to the Table*), and documentaries like *Food, Inc.* They are questions that have situated our day-to-day eating habits within the interconnected web of globalization, reminding us that food choices in comfortable suburbia can have ripple effects all over the world.

Though it's easy to do, eating food without thinking about the bigger picture can be careless and un-Christian. Cheap and fast food may be convenient, but how often do we think about the fact that cheap food is frequently made possible because of low wages and less-than-fair trade prices? How often do we think about the hidden costs of low-cost food: suffering local farmers, farms being bought up by corporations, animal misery, unsustainable agricultural practices, inequitable land ownership, and unnatural chemical enhancements with attendant health problems?

As Christians, we can't ignore the fact that "our eating habits have ethical dimensions, and loving our neighbor requires us to eat intentionally."[21] Tom Beaudoin puts it even more strongly when, in the introduction to his book *Consuming Faith*, he says, "Christians cannot be Christians without making their economic involvements, local and global, a test of their faith."[22]

Opportunity #5: Eat with a Conscience

Eating more justly does not mean we should shun all corporations, disown fast food completely, or eat nothing but food grown in our local community. We don't have to turn into radicals, but we should try to eat with more of a conscience. We should consider the economics of the food industry and how our food purchases support not just the satiating of our own stomachs but the flourishing of all the earth.

What can we do to eat more justly and to more responsibly fulfill our roles as stewards of creation? The following are a few things Lisa McMinn and Megan Neff suggest in their book *Walking Gently on the Earth*:

Eat locally. Consider giving up one non-local food and adding a local one. Shop at farmers' markets or grow your own food.

Think globally. Educate yourself about global trade. Buy global food from sources that use fair trade practices, and look for direct trade products and practices.

Eat low on the food chain. Intentionally move down the food chain. Learn how to cook with fewer ingredients and especially fewer ingredients that required refrigeration or air-freight shipment.

Use your consumer power to pursue justice. Support just food merchants wherever you find them. If you discover a fair trade chocolate company or coffee company, give them your business.[23]

One of my favorite coffee shops, Intelligentsia, is a good example of this mindset. Intelligentsia develops relationships directly with farmers and pays them even more than fair trade. Direct trade also means faster shipping, which means fresher, better coffee for consumers. Intelligentsia cares about excellent tasting coffee—every drink is ground and brewed by the cup—but they also care about justice.

Elisha Witt, a twentysomething Christian and former barista at the Venice, California, location of Intelligentsia, said this about the process of making coffee there:

> As a barista for Intelligentsia, I feel like I am doing more than just brewing coffee for a customer, I'm representing all the hands that went into the careful skill of growing, processing, cupping, buying, roasting, shipping, training, and finally brewing. . . . As a Christian, I love God through my enjoyment of drinking coffee and appreciation for all the farmers and artisans involved.[24]

Drinking coffee or eating anything that has been prepared with such care and thought—with a consideration for the ethics of its origins—enhances our enjoyment of it and reinforces the message that food, when it is considerately consumed, can be healthy for individuals but also for society.

Toward a Christian Ethic of Eating Well

Eating food thoughtfully doesn't have to mean that we approach it hyper-analytically or in a way that strips the experience of joy. We don't have to worry about becoming gluttonous *every* time we eat a whoopie pie (unless we eat them regularly); we don't necessarily need to know the happy living conditions of the chickens we consume; we probably don't need to count the calories and examine the ingredient listings of every last beverage we drink.

But because eating is such a constant activity in our lives, and because our eating habits reveal a lot about our values in this world, we would do well to think about these things at least somewhat more than we already do.

Like most things, food can be consumed in good ways and bad ways; it can be approached recklessly or considerately, carelessly or discerningly. In the same way that we might consume alcohol in the wrong ways or for the wrong reasons (see chaps. 9–11), so also can the consumption of food become a mark on our witness.

On the other hand, if we consume food properly, healthily, unpretentiously, with restraint but also deep enjoyment—and above all, with gratitude to God—the world will take notice as we bear witness to a mode of consumption that is countercultural in a good way.

But what does this look like? The following are some reminders to help us think about a Christian ethic of eating well:

- *Slow down.* Try to find time to truly enjoy food. Prepare it yourself. Savor it.

- *Give thanks.* Be thankful for the food you have, for the hands that prepared it, for the land and animals it comes from; above all, for God the provider and sustainer of life.

- *Show hospitality.* Invite others to dine with you. Follow Jesus's example. Share food with strangers. Throw long dinner parties.

- *Eat in community.* Enjoy food with others. Let it be a unifying source of social pleasure.

- *Enjoy food.* Recognize that eating is "a sensuous activity that sparks enjoyments,"[25] and engage food with all your senses. Relish the fact that—thanks be to God—you have taste buds and food has spice.

- *Eat justly.* Recognize that your eating affects others. Try to support ethical and just practices in food making.

- *Fight global hunger.* Remember that nearly a billion people in the world do not have enough to eat, and you do. Keep that in perspective and do what you can to feed the hungry in your community and across the world.

- *Develop taste.* Expose yourself to new things and expand your palette. Learn to appreciate quality food, unique flavors, textures, and combinations.

- *Eat humbly.* Rather than eating food to show off your culinary sophistication, eat with humility and thanksgiving, awestruck by the beauty and goodness you are privileged to enjoy.

The Final Course

The way we eat matters. What we do culturally matters because, quite simply, we exist in a society where identity is largely expressed through the creation and consumption of culture. And if our identity is in Christ, how is this evidenced in our cultural engagements? As we move forward in this book to discuss other aspects of culture, this will be a central question. "Culture is critical in expressing our kingdom citizenship," writes T. M. Moore in *Culture Matters*:

> If all that we do is consciously designed to reflect the glory of God, and if we are consistently seeking the kingdom and his righteousness as our first priority in all things (Matt. 6:33), then our cultural activities, preferences, and practices will necessarily reveal us to be a people different from those around us in the world.[26]

Being different from those around us. Being set apart. This is a tricky idea that has led many Christians down the path of "Christ against culture" isolationism. But being different doesn't have to mean "either/or" extremism. Usually it's more complicated than that, more nuanced and gray. Sometimes it just means that we engage culture a little more thoughtfully, a little more deliberately, and a little more moderately than those around us. Sometimes it means we avoid what's clearly bad for us.

Always, though, it's a demonstration of our conviction that as ambassadors of Christ's kingdom and as children of light, we should strive to live in a manner worthy of our calling. We are to live in a manner that recalls Christ and anticipates his future reign—even in how we eat, drink, see, hear, observe, and make sense of the here and now.

PART 2

LISTENING

M usic. Who doesn't listen to and love it? Whether we prefer a classical symphony concert under the summer stars, a sweaty mosh pit at a hardcore rock show, or a jazz playlist on our iPod in the comfort of our living room, music is a part of all of our lives. It has been for as long as civilization has existed. Music is a cultural constant and yet constantly in flux, something mysterious and elemental that somehow connects with the deepest parts of the human soul.

Because we hold music so dear and recognize its power, it has also been the source of much strife, fear, and protest. Music has often become fodder for culture wars. Worship wars. Even Cold Wars. It's a powerful thing.

As Christians, how should we understand, engage, and appreciate music? If the answer to that were simple, we could stop this conversation right now, turn up the radio, and be on our merry way. But it's not simple. Music is complicated, and an edifying, healthy relationship with it requires thinking that goes beyond black-and-white simplicities.

In the chapters in this section, we'll take a look at what music has to offer the Christian life and how we might be better connoisseurs of it. Since the topic of music is so vast, we'll look specifically at the contemporary pop/rock genre (basically everything guitar-based from Elvis to Arcade Fire) as a case study of Christian engagement with music. Chapter 3 will recount the history of Christianity's relationship with rock music, while chapters 4 and 5 will explore specific ideas about discernment, taste, patronage, and community as they relate to music today.

* * * * * * * * * * *

Interlude

Music Means

* * * * * * * * * * *

At a conference in Oxford one summer, I listened to well-known pastor Rick Warren say, "There is no such thing as Christian music; only Christian lyrics." With all due respect to the amazing Mr. Warren, I totally disagree.

Words are the only thing that earn a song the distinction of being called "Christian"? What kind of words? Words about Jesus, God, doves, and waterfalls, and second person singular platitudes of affection directed at the Lord? So the lyrics of Handel's *Messiah* are the only Christian thing about that masterpiece? The minimalist sacred compositions of Arvo Pärt are secular if not for God-oriented choral lyrics? The sparkling guitar riffs of U2's "Where the Streets Have No Name" communicate nothing spiritual whatsoever?

My experience of music tells me that there can be something transcendent, something holy in music *itself*—the pleasing chords and harmonies, the dissonance giving way to resolution, the movements and crescendos, the energy of cacophonous sounds working together like color on a painter's canvas. Music *means*.

I didn't have to read the lyrics of Bon Iver's "Beth/Rest" to be totally devastated by it the first time I heard it, nor did I have to decipher Jónsi's jibberish in Sigur Rós songs to recognize the church-like power of it. I didn't have to know Italian to be moved to tears at the climax of Pavarotti's performance of "Nessun Dorma" at the 2006 Winter Olympics. And I didn't need to know Latin in order to worship God through the requiems of Rutter, Berlioz, or Brahms. The music itself is meaningful.

Thanks be to God that he created sounds, tones, voices, instruments, and all that goes into composing beautiful music: triads, intervals, rhythm, minor chords, time signatures, rests, dynamics, and so on. It's an amazing thing. Music communicates so much even when it doesn't say anything. Lyrics can add deeper layers of meaning to a composition, to be sure, but they are not the sole carrier of meaning, "Christian" or otherwise.

In his book *The Day Metallica Came to Church*, pastor John Van Sloten describes a Christmas sermon series he preached on Johann Sebastian Bach. At one point he stopped talking and let Bach's music do the preaching:

> We were trying to wrap our heads around the mysteries of Christ's incarnation—the idea that Jesus was fully God and fully human at the same time. I could have used words to try to explain it, but words didn't seem big enough. Better to let Bach's music—a different kind of language—preach the point. In his "Credo," where the words of the Nicene Creed affirm that Jesus is both God and human—Bach weaves two voices together, an alto and a soprano singing over and through and around each other, brilliantly depicting the true nature of Jesus's birth. That point could never have been made as eloquently with words. The mystery of the incarnation needed a different language—music, in this case.[1]

Music itself is a powerful, God-given gift of communication. We can't affirm something just because it has a lyric about "God" any more than we can disavow something because it doesn't. Music is more complicated than that, and we must open our minds and our ears if we really want to get the most out of it.

* * * * * * * * * *

3

Christians and "The Devil's Music"

* * * * * * * * * *

Somehow, I don't think I ever destroyed a single one of my secular CDs. For many of my fellow evangelical churchgoing youth in the 1980s and '90s, however, it was a common rite of passage: around a bonfire at camp or a trash can in the church parking lot, repentant kids dumping shoeboxes full of tapes, CDs, and records of unholy music. Led Zeppelin, Michael Jackson, Pink Floyd, Madonna, Beastie Boys, Korn, Metallica—all were kindle for the fires.

I don't know how I escaped it. Maybe I was too much of a rule-keeper to dare bring my secular music to camp or youth group events (though I do remember listening to Limp Bizkit on my friend's Discman in the youth group van). Some of my other friends weren't so lucky. A close friend in youth group once got caught with a Marilyn Manson CD at church camp, and a preacher attempted to exorcise him because of it. Perhaps unsurprisingly, that friend abandoned the faith a few years later.

Thankfully, you don't hear about too many secular music purgings around bonfires anymore. For evangelicals today,

Metallica is as likely to be a positive sermon illustration as it is kindling for a fire. Youth pastors are as likely to list The Smiths or Nirvana as "likes" on a Facebook wall as they are to denounce them from a pulpit. How did this happen?

Over the decades, a lot has changed in the way evangelicals have viewed secular pop/rock music. Sixty years ago it was largely a "hands off" evil, not to be engaged at all (except via protest) by Christians. Today it's mostly accepted as something Christians should not only engage but in many cases affirm. This chapter is about what happened between then and now.

Worse Than the Saloon!

One of rock music's important antecedents in the "slippery slope" from formal meter and dignified classicism to more chaotic, less predictable (and thereby dangerous!) styles is, of course, jazz. And jazz music—like its grandson, rock music—was perceived in its early years as a most undignified, dangerous threat.

At the time—roughly between 1917 and 1930—mass media was on the rise and popular music, as heard on the radio and played in clubs, was increasingly a force to be reckoned with. With the accompanying "problems" of increased leisure time, the growth of cities, and the general excesses of the Roaring Twenties, various coalitions of Victorian-minded moral crusaders branded jazz as case in point of how popular mass culture was eroding the foundations of a Christian society.

Anti-jazz magazine articles popped up with titles like "The Jazz Problem" or "Unspeakable Jazz Must Go," the latter being a 1921 critique in *Ladies' Home Journal* in which clergy and everyday citizens decried the perils of this popular new music form. Jazz is "worse than the saloon," one person remarked. It is "simply rotten. It belongs in the underworld." The instruments' broken, jerky rhythms have a "sensual appeal" that "call[s] out the low and rowdy instinct," making youth act "in a restless and rowdy manner."[1]

Critics suspected that jazz—with its improvised, unruly essence—tapped into the carnal nature of youth and fired up wayward proclivities; this concern would also come to define the early Christian resistance to rock music. Jazz, like rock, was seen as a gateway drug: a musical form that was primitive, evil, possibly pagan in origin, and certain to wreak havoc in civilized society if left unchecked.

As jazz, blues, country western, and R&B continued to win over youth on the radio in the 1930s to 1950s and coalesce in the clubs of Chicago and the recording studios of Memphis, rock 'n' roll was born. "Rock 'n' roll," like "jazz" before it, was originally black slang for sexual intercourse, a fact that didn't help its case among the straight-laced, frequently racist detractors who labeled it "jungle music." And so, when rock pioneers like Chuck Berry and Little Richard gave way to mid-1950s white rockers like Bill Haley, Buddy Holly, and Elvis Presley, the stage was set for an epic showdown between the burgeoning postwar youth culture of the Baby Boomers and that of their parents, who in some cases saw rock music as riot-inducing noise at best and an evil tool of Satan at worst.

The Devil's Music

From the first scandalous shakes of Elvis's hips and onward throughout its development, rock 'n' roll was associated with visions of riotous hellions run amok. Because parents couldn't stand it, kids loved it even more; playing rock music became an act of defiance for teenagers, and thus a rebellious youth culture formed around it, amplifying the fears of adults.[2]

One of the charges against rock that got a lot of traction during the Cold War was the notion that rock 'n' roll was a communist weapon to undermine the character of America's youth. Leading this charge was David A. Noebel, longtime Christian crusader against pop culture who kicked off a rather illustrious publishing career with the 1965 pamphlet "Communism, Hypnotism and The Beatles," followed by the 1966 tome *Rhythm, Riots and Revolution*, a sizable book in which dubious experts and "scientists" (with names like "Dr. Freedom") support the thesis that Communists used rock music to destroy the mental and emotional stability of America's youth.[3]

Like his "jazz music makes youth act rowdy" forebears, Noebel was of the opinion that this new form of music had the power to directly cause its listeners to do bad things.

"The music designed for high school students," writes Noebel, "is extremely effective in producing degrees of artificial neurosis and in preparing them for riot and ultimately revolution to destroy our American form of government and the basic Christian principles governing our way of life."[4]

Noebel characterizes the effects of rock music on youth as a sort of Pavlovian brainwashing in which just the sound of a George Harrison guitar riff could "make teenagers weep and wail, become uncontrollable and unruly, and take off their clothes and riot."[5]

Citing "laboratory tested" science, Noebel insists that Beatles-type rock music contains voodoo-inspired beats that synchronize with the body's natural rhythms and lull the unsuspecting listener into a state of hypnosis. He decries the fact that "today all major record companies are flooding our teenagers with a noise that is basically sexual, un-Christian, mentally unsettling, and riot-producing," the consequences of which are "staggering."[6]

Noebel wasn't alone in his alarmist views of rock 'n' roll's deleterious effects on youth. Bob Larson, DJ-turned-Christian-crusader against rock music, took a similar tack in his own prodigious output of "rock is of the devil" salvos, including books like *Rock & Roll: The Devil's Diversion* (1967), *Hippies, Hindus, and Rock & Roll* (1969), and *Rock and the Church* (1971). In the latter, Larson declares that "rock music is creating a crisis in the church"[7] because Christians are being too tolerant of rock as a ministry outreach for youth.

Larson's focus is less on Communism than the notion that rock 'n' roll is heathen and primitive, used by Satan to bring about evil and chaos. He takes aim specifically at the "beat" of rock music, a common target of early Christian critics of rock.

"The beat of rock is a force accommodating demonic possession," notes Larson, who connects (in an unabashedly racist way) rock music and dancing to "heathen tribal and voodoo rites" in Africa.[8] Larson doesn't let readers forget that "rock 'n' roll" actually means "promiscuous sexual relationship music," and he quotes Frank Zappa along these lines: "Rock music is sex. The big beat matches the body's rhythms."[9]

Larson represents a school of religious opposition to rock music based largely on fear of its *form*. The backbeat and screeching guitars were themselves evil. And so when Jesus Rock was born in the early 1970s and Christian versions of rock 'n' roll were debuted, Larson wrote books like *Rock and the Church* to expose the "false perspective of Christian rock" and lay out a clear call for Christians to maintain a hard divide between the sacred (traditional church music) and the secular (rock style).

"Any fusion of secular methods with sacred intentions is in danger of becoming a truce with the world," wrote Larson. "A clean break must be made with the works of darkness."[10]

Kick Off Your Sunday Shoes! A Brief History of Christians and Dancing

For many of the same reasons rock 'n' roll was feared and opposed by many conservative Christians, dancing—at concerts, in jazz clubs, in *Footloose* scenarios—has also been historically frowned upon by evangelicals. In the same way that jazz and later rock music was seen as dangerously unwieldy and heathen, dancing was often viewed as an out-of-control activity that could easily lead unsuspecting youth down a path of moral destruction.

"There is no difference between the repetitive movements of witch doctors and tribal dancers and the dances of American teen-agers," wrote Bob Larson. "The same coarse bodily motions which lead African dancers into a state of uncontrolled frenzy are present in modern dances."[11]

This "uncontrolled frenzy" idea was central in anti-dance rhetoric even from the Puritans in America, who associated the disorderly movement of dancers with a temptation to sexual immorality, due to the absence of reason and the rule of passion. These ideas go back even further: Petrarch made the point in the fourteenth century that uncontrolled movements and roving eyes bespoke an inner lack of control. Cicero famously said, "No man danced unless he was either drunk or mad." In the Elizabethan era, the importance of displaying inner as well as outward control became paramount in the ideals conceived to define the gentleman and the Christian.

Much of the Christian skepticism about dance has centered upon the fear of dance as a potential gateway to immoral behavior with members of the opposite sex. It wasn't that dancing in itself was evil. (This argument was hard to make given the many positive mentions

Dancing with the Devil

In spite of the assertions of folks like Noebel and Larson that the very style of rock music was irredeemably secular and shouldn't be flirted with by Christians, Christian rock flourished in the 1970s and 1980s. An entire industry—Contemporary Christian of dancing in the Old Testament.) It was that dancing—particularly face-to-face dancing between man and woman—often accompanied temptation to lust and frequently led to a whole range of other vices, from prostitution to divorce and even murder.

Throughout the eighteenth and nineteenth century in America, concerns about dancing included everything from the close ties of dancing to drinking and the effeminate connotations of men dancing to the sexualizing of women, the sanitation of dance halls, and poor stewardship of time, health, and money.

There were also questions of piety: eighteenth century evangelists and clergy preached during the Great Awakening that Christians should be so transformed by their personal conversion experience that they wouldn't even desire amusements like dancing. Dancing was seen as something that had no place in the moral landscape of right Christian living.

Yet in the eighteenth and nineteenth centuries, dance became one of the most fashionable amusements of the day, and with the onset of jazz and rock in the twentieth century, it became even more a part of the fabric of popular culture. For many Christians, dancing thus became a symbol of "worldliness" and abstaining from it a mark of being set apart. That's why many American evangelical universities established "no dancing" policies on their campuses (many still have them).

In recent years, however, Christian opinions about dance have loosened a bit. My own evangelical alma mater, Wheaton College, ended its dancing ban in 2003, and other Christian universities followed suit. Many churches have started dance ministries, and several professional Christian dance companies have gained notoriety (London-based Springs Dance Company and Houston-based Ad Deum being two examples).

Music (CCM)—was born, offering Christianized (i.e., lyrically pure) alternatives that sounded like secular rock but didn't lead listeners straight to hell.

Champions of Christian rock like Dan and Steve Peters (authors of books including *Why Knock Rock?* and *What about Christian Rock?*) were still largely suspicious of secular rock music, but not so much for its sound as for its lyrical content and the poor lifestyle modeling of its rock stars. The Peters brothers, who toured the country in the eighties speaking about the dangers of secular music and the merits of CCM, pointed out in great detail the worrisome role-modeling of rock stars. In chapter 2 ("The Rock-Hard Facts") of *What about Christian Rock?*, they share lurid vignettes about contemporary rock stars, such as: a quote of Jon Bon Jovi recalling a "drinking jag" while on tour with Mötley Crüe (involving three bottles of Jack Daniel's and a trip to a neighborhood whorehouse); the sexualized lyrics of Prince, Madonna, Duran Duran, and even Olivia Newton-John; the drug habits of Boy George; the "pro-masturbation" songs of Cyndi Lauper; and the "pro marital-infidelity" songs of Whitney Houston.[12]

For the Peters brothers, the single most troubling thing about secular music was its lyrics, which they said promoted "rebellion and violence, hedonism, drug and alcohol abuse, despondency, suicide, satanism/occultism, secular human-ism, and worldly commercialism."[13] An easy fix, then, was to suggest Christian rock alternatives that had similar sounds but totally different lyrical content. In *Christian Rock?* the Peters brothers suggest, for example, "alternatives" like Ken Medema (a sort of Christian Stevie Wonder), Jerusalem ("CCM's answer to Scorpion"), In 3D ("reminiscent of The Police"), Silverwind ("Abba sound-alike"), and John Michael Talbot ("Gordon Lightfoot-like"). This sort of "if you like Pearl Jam, try Audio Adrenaline" comparison approach be-came a fairly common posture in the CCM era. Essentially it was an assessment of rock music on an almost exclusively lyrical plane. If lyrics were "Christian" (not always an easy determination, as it turns out), the music—everything from heavy metal (Stryper, Jerusalem) to folk rock (Children of the Day, Mark Heard)—was acceptable.

As CCM grew into a booming business in the eighties and nineties—and with it grew all manner of "Christian-friendly" copycat hair metal, grunge, shoegaze, even boy bands (Plus One)—the gradual effect was that Christian audiences were conditioned to like the *sounds* of secular rock music (if not the lyrics). The Noebel/Larson claims that rock music was *in its very form* evil became increasingly antiquated.

In books like *Rock Reconsidered* and *Rock of This Age*, author Steve Lawhead (former manager of DeGarmo & Key) debunks the Noebel/Larson suggestions of subliminal messaging via the evils of syncopation. "Rock music is not hypnotic," writes Lawhead. "People are not emotionally or psychologically damaged by exposure to rock beats."[14]

Lawhead represents a Christian position vis-a-vis rock music that allows more room for individual discernment and discounts the "magic bullet" theory of media that songs (or movies, or television) directly and irresistibly shape the opinions and actions of impotent consumers. "Young people are not exactly powerless pawns of pop culture," notes Lawhead. "By their acceptance or rejection of various elements, they continually transform the culture that surrounds them."[15]

Lawhead's approach still acknowledges that rock music isn't for everyone and that we should be sympathetic toward "our weaker brothers," but his more open-minded position toward rock was certainly ahead of its time. In *Rock of This Age*, Lawhead cites Titus 1:15 ("To the pure, all things are pure") to suggest that a healthy Christian approach to rock music depends not on avoiding all things secular but on the listener having the right intentions and discernment:

> Notice he did not say, "To the pure some things are pure" or "most things are pure." He said *all* things, extending the boundaries quite far indeed, opening the door for a more

liberated approach. For if our attitudes and intentions are pure, how can the object of our desire be otherwise?[16]

By shifting concern away from a big, amorphous, ill-defined blob of "secular culture" to the responsibility of the discerning individual, Lawhead foreshadowed a helpful shift in evangelical thinking about pop culture. And yet as we will see, an emphasis on subjective discernment comes with its own set of challenges.

What Makes Music "Christian"?

As CCM continued to grow and eventually peak in the late nineties, the question of what exactly made Christian music *Christian* became ever more complex. When Christian pop singer Amy Grant's album *Heart in Motion* became a bona fide hit on the secular charts in 1991, many wondered what was Christian about "Baby Baby." Later, as more and more Christian artists (Switchfoot, P.O.D., Sixpence None the Richer, etc.) found crossover success, the questions for CCM became even more pressing. What makes one lyric "Christian" and another not? If a musician professes Christian faith, is any song they create thereby Christian? Why would a Christian college gym refuse to play U2 songs over the sound system (too secular) but happily play P.O.D.'s version of U2's "Bullet the Blue Sky"?[17]

Charlie Peacock addresses many of these questions in his book *At the Crossroads: An Insider's Look at the Past, Present, and Future of Contemporary Christian Music*, a 1999 call for reform from one of CCM's central players (Peacock worked as producer with artists like The 77s, Al Green, Michael Card, and Rich Mullins). Peacock critiques CCM for not sufficiently reflecting the full scope of the Christian mission and encourages readers "to approach music, ministry, and the music industry in a more comprehensive and faithful manner, one that is informed by the whole of Scripture and the evidence of creation."[18]

Peacock's critique presciently observes the identity crisis of CCM, noting that while most forms of popular music are named according to their musical style (jazz, blues, classical, folk, rap, rock), CCM has to tie its identity to the lyrics or to a profession of faith by the artists. But Peacock warns that "getting listeners to recognize Christian music does not ensure that they will engage the music and lyric with the depth of interest they need to derive some spiritual, emotional, or intellectual benefit from them."[19] Peacock argues that unless listeners can appreciate the *music* on some level—melody, rhythm, style, production—they "will receive little perceivable benefit from an easily recognizable Christian lyric."[20]

The major oversight of CCM, argues Peacock, is the lack of a "comprehensive theology of music in general."[21] He takes issue with the position that music is only valuable for Christians when it serves some "holier" purpose (like worship, evangelism, or discipleship).

> God saw fit to include music in the totality of his creation and as such it needs no further justification. This is the starting place for thinking about music, period, full stop, end of report. . . . Creation is useful because it is good. It is not good just because it is useful.[22]

Peacock believes that Christians aren't called to a narrow-minded, simplistic, or easy ("let's just label what we do 'Christian'!") music-making, but rather to "music which favors a comprehensive and diverse picture of musical faithfulness."[23] He believes that Christians should worry less about labeling the things they do "Christian" and worry more about creating music that is the best, most creative around. "Christians who own a coffee house should be known for serving the best coffee in town at a great price," he notes, "not for having 'Christian' on their sign in the parking lot."[24]

Peacock's critiques must have resonated, because as 1999 gave way to the twenty-first century, the hard line between CCM and "secular" music became fuzzier as more and more Christian artists crossed over to the mainstream and other Christian artists began their careers outside of CCM altogether. Christian consumers of music, it seemed, joined Peacock in the hunger for meatier music—music that explored all areas of life and sought excellence and beauty above all.

Good Music Is Good Music

In the same year that Charlie Peacock wrote about CCM in *At the Crossroads*, Jay Howard and John Streck released *Apostles of Rock*, a scholarly study of CCM that attempted to make sense of the different approaches Christians had taken toward rock/pop over the last half century. In their assessment, CCM has been characterized by three approaches that roughly correspond to Richard Niebuhr's paradigms of Christ and culture: separational (Christ against culture), integrational (Christ of culture), and transformational (Christ transforming culture). They define the three approaches in this way:

> For the separational artist, music is ministry and the ever-present danger of the commercial system is the risk of becoming too much like the world—in more religious terminology, of the salt losing its saltiness (*see* Matt. 5:13 NIV). For the integrational artist, music is entertainment and such dangers do not exist. Offering a positive alternative to the hedonism generally found in mainstream pop music—even when the

music is only marginally different from standard pop fare—
is an acceptable, appropriate role for CCM. Finally, for the
transformational artist, music is believed to be a form of
artistic expression. Rooted in a vocabulary of "truth," "honesty," and "reality," transformational CCM demands that the
artist and audience enter into what are perceived to be the
painful and broken experiences of life, seeking to transform
them in the light of Christ's restoration.[25]

Using these categories, we could see the Noebel/Larson
"secular rock is of the devil!" arguments as reflecting the
"separational" approach, while the Peters brothers and CCM
pioneers might reflect the "integrational" approach, looking
at CCM as a wholesome alternative to mainstream rock. The
"transformational" approach is the type of music-making
Charlie Peacock favors: music that seeks not to withdraw
from culture but to transform it; music deemed valuable not
because of its utility but because it manifests truth and quality. In this approach, music is seen as an art form rather than
an evangelistic tool.

I believe the transformational approach is more and more
common among Christian artists today. The last decade or so
has seen a gradual shrinking of the CCM industry and an increase in Christian artists who seek to create music not under
the banner of any label but simply with the object of creating
art. Artists of faith like Sufjan Stevens, Cold War Kids, Foster
the People, My Brightest Diamond, Thrice, Mindy Smith,
Over the Rhine, David Bazan, Sleeping at Last, Rosie Thomas,
Damien Jurado, The Civil Wars, and many others have gone
about their art largely outside of the world of CCM, in many
cases specifically avoiding association with it.

Meanwhile, on the receiving end of music, Christians have
increasingly looked beyond the "Christian" label in their
assessment of the good, true, and beautiful in music. *CCM*

Magazine ended its monthly print run in 2008, after thirty years, and other Christian magazines like *Relevant* gained traction by focusing their music coverage on any and all kinds of secular music, including cover stories on Kanye West, Jack White, Wilco, Ben Harper, Bob Dylan, Ben Folds, and Muse. *Paste Magazine*, founded by a Christian (Josh Jackson), is another example of the shift in Christian consumption of music toward a broader appreciation of quality. *Paste*, with the tagline "Signs of Life in Music, Film & Culture," doesn't define itself as a religious publication and focuses on well-written critical engagement with the best that culture has to offer.

Many churches and Christian institutions have also adopted a broader approach to appreciating and valuing music. During my research for *Hipster Christianity*, I attended several churches where high quality secular music was played over the sound system before the service (Radiohead, Bon Iver, Fleet Foxes). Pastors like John Van Sloten of Calgary's New Hope Church, believing that God speaks to us through any and everything in creation, regularly preach sermons on secular artists like Coldplay and Metallica (yes, Metallica). Christian universities like Calvin College have translated this sort of broad-minded appreciation of secular music into an enviable concert roster that yearly draws some of the most acclaimed secular artists of the moment: Cut Copy, Washed Out, Sigur Rós, Blitzen Trapper, Fleet Foxes, Broken Social Scene, Lupe Fiasco, Neko Case, and many more. Even stalwart evangelical flagship Wheaton College hosted The Decemberists for a concert on campus in 2008.

Along with this shift toward a more open-arms approach to secular music came a sort of rediscovery of secular music of the past, formerly devalued within Christendom. Spirituality was there all along, it seemed. Faith-oriented artists like

88

Johnny Cash, U2, and Bob Dylan were all but declared saints by many evangelicals, who churned out books with titles like *Restless Pilgrim: The Spiritual Journey of Bob Dylan* (2002), *The Gospel According to Bob Dylan* (2011), and *Walk On: The Spiritual Journey of U2* (2005). Music producer Mark Joseph wrote books like *Rock and Roll Rebellion* (1999) and *Faith, God, and Rock & Roll* (2003) in which he asserts that spirituality in pop music hasn't been limited to CCM and shouldn't be.

The increasingly dominant Christian view of pop music, it seems, is that there is goodness, truth, and transcendence to be found even in the most remote secular corners. Many agree with music journalist Steve Turner when he writes, "The best rock 'n roll is itself a crying out for an experience of transcendence that the modern secular world doesn't offer. . . . There will continue to be a search for redemption in rock 'n roll, if only because the creation of music seems to provoke musicians into asking questions about the ultimate source of creativity."[26]

We've Come Far, but Is It Too Far?

A lot has changed since the days of "devil music" protests and secular CD burnings. For the average Christian teenager today, the very idea of secular and Christian music being separate, oppositional categories is increasingly nonsensical. This isn't to say there aren't still vocal detractors in the Christian community speaking out against rock 'n' roll. As recently as 2001, Chuck Colson and Nancy Pearcey wrote this about rock music:

> The sheer energy of rock—the pounding beat, the screams, the spectacle—is intended to bypass the mind and appeal directly to the sensations and feelings. Thus rock music, by

its very form, encourages a mentality that is subjective, emotional, and sensual—no matter what the lyrics may say.[27]

To be fair, Colson and Pearcey aren't quite retreading the Bob Larson arguments here; they are speaking about the importance of taking *form* (not just content) into account when assessing pop culture. "The danger," they say, "is that Christian popular culture may mimic mainstream culture in style, while changing only the content,"[28] which is a statement Charlie Peacock and the critics of CCM's "lyrics only" distinctiveness would probably agree with.

Indeed, the shift from "rock music is evil" to "rock music is perfectly fine!" within evangelical Christianity becomes problematic if the cultural meaning of "rock music" is downplayed or disregarded completely. After all, "rock" carries with it cultural baggage that cannot easily be shaken, even if Christian lyrics are added, as Howard and Streck write:

> The meaning of rock is not to be found in the sonic waveforms, nor is it to be found in lyrics transcribed and analyzed. Rock and roll is a form of music that must be understood in situ and furthermore is one that comes with a significant measure of cultural baggage. So, while it may be true that there are no inherent meanings in a syncopated beat or a I-IV-V chord progression, to strap on a Stratocaster and climb on stage is necessarily to evoke the presence of Elvis Presley, The Beatles, Jimi Hendrix, The Rolling Stones, most of those who followed, and all the meanings that have come to be attached to them.[29]

The point here is that in the Christian assessment of pop music, it's never as easy as saying "it's all good" or "it's all bad." Much must be considered, including the cultural baggage and meanings communicated in the very form. Colson and Pearcey may sound stodgy in their assessment of the "pounding beat, the screams, the spectacle" of rock music, but their intentions in cultural critique are valid. Their position—that music isn't inherently bad or good but can take on meanings at odds with a Christian worldview—reflects the thinking of a hero of theirs, Francis Schaeffer.

Schaeffer, like Abraham Kuyper before him, believed that every aspect of culture, art, and entertainment fell under the lordship of Christ and could thus honor him. However, "the problem is that everything can also be misused."

> They are not automatically good; they are neutral in the sense that they can be made good or bad. . . . So the arts can be used in a destructive way. But that is different from the concept that art as art is destructive in itself.[30]

And so, in the ongoing story of Christianity's relationship with popular music, questions remain, as indeed they should. Have we gone too far in the opposite direction from "that's evil!" legalism to the point that any and all music is now deemed acceptable? Have Christians uncritically embraced music that has no real value or place in the life of a follower of Christ? How can we be better, more thoughtful consumers of music, unsatisfied with simplistic rubrics and assessments of merit and yet still willing to discern between the good and the bad, the worthy and the toxic? These are the questions we'll tackle in the next two chapters.

* * * * * * * * * *

Interlude

Is Smoking Pot Okay for Christians?

* * * * * * * * * *

It was my sophomore year in college and I was at a Doves concert in downtown Chicago with a group of students from my dorm. At some point during the concert, several of the (evangelical Christian) college students I was with started smoking, and one of them offered me a joint. Having never smoked anything in my life, I declined and continued to enjoy the show. But I started thinking: Do lots of evangelical college students smoke marijuana? Is weed really a necessary supplement to the enjoyment of music like this? Can't Christians enjoy secular music without adopting the shadier habits of concert-going culture? I guess I was sort of naïve to be troubled by this event, sheltered nineteen-year-old evangelical that I was. But the questions it raised in my mind are important and I think still warrant some discussion.

Several years later I attended the Festival of Faith and Music at Calvin College and had the fascinating pleasure of listening to Muslim rapper Lupe Fiasco play a show in the Calvin College fieldhouse. He's a good musician and I liked the show, but the thick stench of weed in the air reminded me of the same questions I'd wondered about years before at the Doves concert in Chicago. Do pot and Christianity really mix well?

In their efforts to be more open-minded and plugged in to the world of secular culture, have Christians lost a real sense of what it means to be in the world—engaging, appreciating—but not *of* it? Is it possible to engage the secular world without accommodating every aspect of it, to maintain a distinctive, set-apart Christian identity even while we actively consume a variety of secular cultural items surrounding us in this world?

Is smoking pot ever okay for Christians? It's easy to answer "no" when smoking pot is against the law of the land (as it still is in most places). But what if one day it is made totally legal? Some might justify it by saying it's part of our cultural "witness" to engage in practices that are deeply ingrained in the worlds we seek to influence (the world of rock music, perhaps). But where does that logic stop? Should Christians become avid gamblers in order to better infiltrate Las Vegas culture? Should they frequent strip clubs in order to strike up missional friendships with that crowd?

Others justify it by arguing that it's harmless and pleasurable, relaxing and community-building. But what does it do to our Christian witness? Are the cultural connotations associated with pot smoking things we'd want people to associate with following Christ? Weed brings to mind the "stoner" or "slacker" culture—zoned out, disengaged, pleasure-seeking rebels always in search of a high. The image of those who smoke pot is one of laziness, irresponsibility, mischief. Given these connotations, Christians should be cautious about using marijuana. Christians are called to be above reproach, "without blemish in the midst of a crooked and twisted generation," shining "as lights in the world" (Phil. 2:15 ESV), keeping our conduct honorable, so unbelievers "may see your good deeds and glorify God on the day of visitation" (1 Peter 2:12 ESV).

Aside from the fact that in most US states it is illegal, there are other concerns one might raise against Christians smoking pot (the health effects, the mind-altering aspect of it, etc.) that I won't address in detail here. This issue warrants more space than this brief "Interlude" discussion; the important point is that we continue to think about these questions, discuss them in community, and mull over the implications.

* * * * * * * * * *

4

What Are You Listening To?

* * * * * * * * * * *

It's rare anymore to hear the popular music press discussing music that "crosses the line." After all, in terms of transgressive content, our culture has pushed through envelope after envelope: Madonna's sexually suggestive music, videos, and *Sex* book; Eminem and his championing of spousal abuse; Marilyn Manson's ordination into the Church of Satan; The Prodigy's "Smack My B---- Up"; Lady Gaga's "Judas"; Ozzy Osbourne biting off a bat's head on stage, and so on. Our pop music culture has seen it all and—in the name of free speech—tolerated most of it. And yet from time to time the discussion gets churned up again: Is there a "too far" line?

Such was the discussion in 2011 surrounding Los Angeles rap collective Odd Future and especially their leader, "Tyler, the Creator" (Tyler Okonma), who makes Eminem's brand of misogyny seem harmless by comparison. Tyler and Odd Future regularly rap about rape, violence against women, drugs, and murder fantasies; they employ offensive language with nearly every lyric, using the *f*-word 204 times in the 73 minutes of Tyler's 2011 album *Goblin*, for example.[1]

The controversy surrounding Odd Future's shocking lyrical content includes some defenders, such as *Pitchfork*, the indie music authority who called Tyler, the Creator's *Bastard* "a minor masterpiece of shock art and teenage spleen-vent," noting that "morally, it's repugnant, but the pure shocking force of it is so raw and distilled that it carries a certain appeal of its own."[2] Even politically correct NPR gave Odd Future their stamp of approval in an article entitled "Why You Should Listen to the Rap Group Odd Future, Even Though It's Hard," writing:

> They're loud. They're lewd, nihilistic, and disrespectful. The group raps about rape frequently. They give all of their music away for free. They curse constantly and use every slur you can think of. . . . If you're over forty; have kids and are white, they don't like you. . . . You know what else? They're really good. Especially their ringleader, called Tyler The Creator.[3]

But even some who acknowledge the musical merits and creativity of Odd Future feel conflicted about their morally repugnant lyrics. On his blog, *New York Magazine* music critic Nitsuh Abebe writes about the difficulty of trying to appreciate Odd Future's talents when their lyrics make light of marginalized groups.

"It bums me out that I can love so much about a few of these tracks, but wouldn't put them on a mixtape for a lot of people I care about," he writes, later describing the lyrical problem in a way that feels reminiscent of the "weaker brother" arguments of Romans 14:

> For those who can bracket it and enjoy the many amazing things about the music, it's one of the least interesting things about the group—misogyny and homophobia are everywhere,

but music this vital is not, necessarily. But if you, or truths you care about, are on the business end of those taunts, it's an incredibly significant deal; it might as well be a picket line you're crossing. This, in the end, is the hopelessly selfish complaint I'm making: I wish I could embrace the pleasure I get from this music without feeling like a scab, without knowing I can bracket things and include myself in a way that's not so possible for others around me. And I say that as someone with pretty highly developed bracketing skills.[4]

Abebe's conflicted response to Odd Future suggests that even for secular ears—even those with "highly developed bracketing skills"—there is sometimes a point where music can go too far in the quest for transgressive shock. It can occasionally be impossible to defend, even under the banner of art and "saying something important." This point seems especially crucial for Christians to remember, especially as we compensate for our regrettable history of ignoring secular music by opening up our arms wider and wider to any and all of it.

On the positive journey toward a wider appreciation of culture, Christians shouldn't forget that—as Odd Future reminds us—not everything that is artistic, "real," or forward thinking is *good for us*. Discernment is necessary. Can Christians support the music of Kanye West, even while he raps repeatedly about how he's a "muthaf---ing monster"? Should Christians affirm the edgy, racy, and obscene in music, if it's "art"? These are tricky questions.

Is the Profane Holy?

One of the tensions that has long informed the Christian critique of culture is that of God's immanence vs. transcendence. Is God present here, in all things, infusing even culture with his goodness ("God in all")? Or is he distant from the fallen things below, a "wholly other" Being whose character does not manifest itself in the cultural works of sinful, estranged humanity ("God above all")?

One's approach to the question of how Christians relate to culture is likely influenced by what side of the transcendence-immanence continuum one tends to favor. Protestant theologian Paul Tillich, for example, favored the "transcendent" view and thus rejected most popular culture as being a thoroughly secular impediment to spiritual growth. On the "immanent" side, an example might be Roman Catholic theologian Hans Urs von Balthasar, who had a more positive view of human creativity and culture and felt that it could stir up a yearning in humans for God. Tillich "was inclined to see ordinary reality as desacralized," while Balthasar "was more ready to sacralize it—to treat it not as something empty or fallen, but as something that, at least in part, is 'holy.'"[5]

The latter seems to be the perspective of more and more evangelical Christians, who perhaps were raised with a view closer to the "pop culture is a spiritual impediment" approach but have come to favor a more sacramental view of reality.

More and more Christians seem to advocate the idea that, as one blogging pastor put it, "All truth is inspired by the Holy Spirit no matter where it is found."[6] Because God reigns over all things and has dominion over all creation, who's to say we can't find redeemable goodness, truth, or beauty in a Jay-Z or Ben Folds song? Does it even make sense to talk about the "sacred" as opposed to the "secular"?

This way of thinking has drawn upon, in part, the works of Dutch Reformed theologian Abraham Kuyper, who denied a sacred-secular dichotomy and argued that Christians should not separate from but rather should engage all areas of culture. Why? Because God is sovereign over every corner of culture—every "sphere," says Kuyper, who famously suggested that "there is not a square inch in the whole domain of our human existence over which Christ, who is Sovereign over *all*, does not cry: 'Mine!'"[7]

Kuyper is increasingly popular among Christians today because of his strong affirmation of the "cultural mandate" for Christians to work, create, and develop culture to exhibit the glory of God. But he's also popular because of his thoughts on "common grace," the idea that by God's grace there is residual good in the world (beyond the "particular grace" of salvation) that infuses all things and causes even unregenerate humanity to potentially grasp truth and reflect the glory of God. Common grace, writes Kuyper, "relaxes the curse which rests upon it, arrests its process of corruption, and thus allows the untrammeled development of our life in which to glorify Himself as Creator."[8]

The concept is similar to Calvin's notion of *sensus divinitatis* (a sense of the divine), the idea that God implanted an inherent understanding of himself in each person, which complements the revelation of creation in which God "speaks to us everywhere." Calvin believed that "the mind of man, though fallen and perverted from its wholeness, is nevertheless clothed and ornamented with God's excellent gifts," and that there are many gifts "the Lord left to human nature even after it was despoiled of its true good."[9]

One doesn't have to attend many hip churches—where secular music is proudly played and sermons are often inspired by Christopher Nolan films—to see that Calvin's *sensus divinitatis* and Kuyper's common grace have caught on in evangelical Christianity. John Van Sloten, who regularly preaches sermons on things like Neil Young, *The Simpsons*, or Texas hold 'em, is certainly with Calvin on *sensus divinitatis*:

So when we fall in love with a new Coldplay song or with a venerable Rodin sculpture, when we're deeply moved by a great film, we can thank God for that. God made us to be moved in these ways. God made what's moving us. And once we've tasted God's truth in any of these inspired places—again, knowingly or not—we find ourselves seeking to repeat the experience.[10]

The thinking of Calvin, Kuyper, and even von Balthasar has contributed much to a healthy Christian approach to culture—one that acknowledges the transcendence of God over all creation but also his immanence through the Spirit's common grace infiltration of everyday life.

Yet in the midst of this upsurge in appreciating common grace, there's a real danger that we'll get a bit too carried away in "finding God" in places where he just isn't there. There's the potential that we'll forgo discernment and simply give the "sacred" stamp of approval to every created thing because it contains some spark of common grace within it.

Kuyper's dislike of the sacred-secular dichotomy wasn't his way of saying that everything is sacred; rather, it was an attempt to show that all creation *had the potential* to serve the purposes of God's kingdom and reflect his glory. Common grace may extend to all, but not everyone embraces it or responds to God in the same way. And indeed, Kuyper's concept of *antithesis*—that there is a fundamental conflict between faith and unbelief, between the Christian and non-Christian worldview—indicates that there is still quite a bit of distance between those who exist solely with common grace (everyone) and those who have both common and special grace (Christians). Kuyper's point is not that Christians should remove themselves from the world and create a separate culture, but neither is it that Christians should acquiesce to the world and accept everything within it. Rather, his call is that Christians should involve themselves in the project of redeeming every sphere of creation—whether chemistry, politics, painting, or farming. As Philip Ryken reminds us, common grace "is not saving grace. . . . Nevertheless, there is something gracious about it,"[11] something for which we should have ears to hear.

Thus when it comes to how Christians should engage something like pop music, we should remember that while it is good to have ears to hear the voice of God everywhere, we must be cautious to not use the "but it's common grace!" argument to condone *everything*. Can the profane communicate truth? Sure. Can the rough lyrics of "parental advisory" music grasp something transcendent? Of course. But for every nugget of truth in a Lil Wayne song, every spark of God's glory on display in a Nine Inch Nails album, there is also a lot in that music that is outside the scope of what Christians are told in Philippians 4:8 to dwell on: whatever is true, noble, right, pure, lovely, admirable, excellent, or praiseworthy.

Of course, at this point things get immensely more complicated, because determinations of what is or isn't true, noble, or right are often highly subjective. If Metallica can be more of a worshipful experience to one pastor than a Michael Card concert might be, who's to say that for another Christian, God might not be encountered in the music of Led Zeppelin or Arcade Fire more presently than he is encountered in the music of Matt Redman? Are there any limits to where and how we should seek God in popular culture, or is anything and everything fair game?

The Lines and Limits of "Christian Liberty"

One of the fuzzy areas in any discussion of Christian engagement with culture is the question of Christian liberty. As opposed to offering a clear set of "dos and don'ts" in all

Should Christians Care about Cussing?

Invariably one of the things that comes up in discussions of Christian engagement with contemporary popular music is the prevalence of obscene language in much of it. Should Christians subject themselves to music full of profanity? Rap music is the most obvious flashpoint for this discussion, given how ubiquitous f-bombs, b--ches, n---as and other such words are in this genre. But defenders, including many Christian fans, are quick to point out that this language is simply the accepted parlance of rap: the genre, the community, the culture.

It's true: language is culturally relative, and curse words connote different meanings and relative levels of taboo in various contexts and cultures. In some Asian cultures, for example, "sh-t" is not taboo at all. My saintly Malaysian Christian friend Sue Lee, for example, once referred to the early morning crusties in her eyes as "eye sh-t," and was surprised that we gasped when she said it.

But the fact that explicit language is culturally relative should not, I believe, justify its usage or our claims that it is innocuous. It doesn't follow that because the s-word is not profane in one culture, it is thereby inoffensive in all cultures. We exist in a particular cultural context, and it is within that context that we must evaluate the sort of language that is offensive, profane, or unseemly.

It may seem to go without saying, but words are not just words. They carry meaning. And in America in the twenty-first century, certain "curse" words still carry a meaning that connotes extreme anger, an intention to degrade, or simply an expression of transgression. Certain

areas of culture, Scripture instead emphasizes our freedom in Christ and leaves a great many cultural matters open to our own individual consciences. Christians have the "right" to consume all sorts of things, though we are told not everything is beneficial or constructive (see 1 Cor. 10:23). Rather, we are instructed, "whether you eat or drink or whatever you do, do it all for the glory of God" (1 Cor. 10:31) and "do not cause anyone to stumble" (v. 32).

words are still bleeped on network television; certain words still earn films an R rating; we are still protecting our children from hearing certain words. As long as there are words that parents chastise little ten-year-old Johnny for uttering, no one can argue that "taboo" language doesn't exist.

Even though cussing may be the norm in some genres of music, I find it hard to believe that such explicit language, however ubiquitous, is *not* intended to shock, provoke, and offend. Rappers aren't using that language in the way they use words like *sick* or *shawty* (i.e., simply slang); they're using it because they know those words are loaded with transgressive cultural meaning. And we are incredibly naïve if we think otherwise.

Is it possible that someday language will change and words now deemed profane will be entirely acceptable? Sure. But inevitably new curse words will be introduced, because fallen humans will always feel the need to be obscene and to express their emotions through verbal interjections. In the meantime, though, our culture still defines certain language as inappropriate, profane, and offensive. And as long as such language exists, Christians should be cautious about letting it slip regularly into their vocabulary. Should we avoid listening to any music that contains any profane language? No. But we *should* take language into account in our overall evaluation of the merits of something we might consume, and we should take seriously the biblical calls to rid ourselves of "obscene talk" (Col. 3:8 ESV) and "corrupting talk" (Eph. 4:29 ESV). There's no need to get legalistic about it, but yes, we should care about cussing.

This last part is key, something the apostle Paul routinely emphasized (especially in Romans and 1 Corinthians). Because it is true that Christians have differing tolerances ("One person's faith allows them to eat anything, but another, whose faith is weak, eats only vegetables," Rom. 14:2), we should not pass judgment on or treat with contempt those with different liberties than us.

"Nowhere in Scripture does it say that another person's

Christian liberty choices must be your own," notes Rex Rogers in *Christian Liberty*, though it does say we should "allow room for others to exercise their Christian liberty before God, fully persuaded in their own minds."[12]

While the question of liberty is very much guided by personal conscience, it must also be considered in the context of community. I may not have a problem listening to a certain style of music, for example, but if others in my community do, I should take that into account. In the "food sacrificed to idols" discussion of 1 Corinthians 8, Paul tells us to be careful "that the exercise of your rights does not become a stumbling block to the weak" (v. 9). In other words, a Christian who isn't offended by rough language should not insist on listening to obscenity-laden music in the car with friends or relatives.

But how do we determine our own personal liberty in the first place? Is it just an "as long as my conscience doesn't tell me it's wrong" free-for-all? How do we know when or if our liberty has gone too far?

One of the important things we must learn is the difference between *convictions* and *preferences*, notes Rogers. Convictions are the "nonnegotiables" of our faith—the essential, moral issues based on biblical principles (Rogers calls it "God's holy list")—while preferences are nonessential things neither forbidden nor commanded by God. Holding preferences is not wrong, "if and only if one's preferences do not themselves violate the revealed moral will of God," notes Rogers. "God gives us Christian liberty to develop our list beyond God's list, but our list must never contradict or otherwise undermine God's list of moral principles for our lives."[13]

Part of the beauty of the Bible is that much of what it sets out are *principles* of moral living (which tend to be timeless and relevant in a diversity of contexts) rather than *rules* (which can be quickly time-bound or irrelevant in their cultural specificity). Responsible Christians should steadfastly apply these principles to their decision making in the "gray matters" of freedom and conscience.

In making those decisions, we should remember that not everything that is permissible is beneficial. Christian liberty may permit me to listen to the harsh raps of Tyler, the Creator, but is it beneficial? Or am I using my Christian liberty to indulge my sinful desires (see Gal. 5:13)? Though Christian liberty doesn't look the same for everyone, it's still something guided by core principles revealed to us by God in Scripture, which means that there probably *are* some things that are not expressly forbidden in the Bible but should nevertheless be avoided. Determining just what those things are is the tricky part, and it requires the development of discernment.

Five Discerning Questions

When you're at the record store—well, digital music store—contemplating which music to buy, what exactly does "Christian discernment" look like? The following are a few questions to help guide us in the gray areas of cultural consumption (by the way, these principles are applicable to cultural items beyond only music):

1. *Does it point me toward God?* Every moment of our lives should be an opportunity to worship God. In whatever we eat, drink, watch, play, or listen to, we should strive to do it to the glory of God. It doesn't have to be "churchy" to be worship, and it doesn't have to be a praise song to be God-honoring, but given all the things we could spend our time enjoying or consuming, why not choose that which points us toward God? Often this simply requires a shift in our thinking—to start

approaching music consumption actively rather than passively, seeking out the goodness and truth within music rather than taking it at face value. When we start listening in a deeper way, the bounds of what can facilitate our worship are greatly expanded.

2. *Would Jesus listen to it?* Okay, I know the WWJD thing is overplayed, but if as Christians we are called to follow after Christ and "be imitators" (Eph. 5:1 ESV) of him, I think it's an appropriate question to ask. And it's not about whether we can envision Jesus putting on headphones and enjoying Beyoncé (though I think he might) as much as whether we would feel ashamed if Jesus took a gander at our iTunes libraries. After all, our ears and our bodies are not our own; they were bought at a price. They belong to Jesus. We are called to be "a living sacrifice, holy and acceptable to God," not conformed to this world but transformed by the renewing of our minds (Rom. 12:1–2 ESV). Would Jesus recognize that transformation in the music we choose to listen to?

3. *What would my community say?* Discernment in our cultural habits should include a consideration of those around us. We don't want to offend those around us with things that we are free to consume but that might be a frustrating stumbling block to them. Also, it's simply a wise thing to consider the counsel of others rather than relying solely on one's own judgment. As Proverbs 18:2 says, "Fools find no pleasure in understanding but delight in airing their own opinions." We shouldn't isolate ourselves and privilege our own opinions about things. If others around us have thoughts about why something is or is not appropriate, maybe we should listen.

4. *Is it of good quality?* If we're going to be spending money, time, and energy listening to music, why not

focus on the highest quality we can find? Sure, there's a time and a place for "escapist" pop fare, but a diet of one hundred percent Katy Perry and Three Doors Down does *not* do a body good. We'll talk more about the question of who determines "good quality" in the next chapter, but I'm convinced that a key aspect of a healthy Christian consumption is the ability to recognize and then support the most excellent and creative content we can find. Discernment is not just about avoiding too many *f*-words or overly nihilistic themes; it's also about avoiding the trite, cheap, and clichéd and instead seeking out the best.

5. *Is it edifying?* This sounds like something Focus on the Family might ask, but it's a solid question. Paul tells Christians to rid themselves of "anger, rage, malice, slander, and filthy language from your lips" (Col. 3:8), which isn't to say we should avoid any media that depicts such things, just that we should beware of such influences tarnishing our character and eroding our witness as God's chosen people. We are to set our hearts and minds "on things above, not on earthly things" (Col. 3:2) and to dwell on whatever is true, noble, right, pure, lovely, admirable, excellent, or praiseworthy (see Phil. 4:8). If we can't find any of those redeemable attributes in the music we are consuming, we should question whether it's worthwhile.

Discernment Isn't Easy

Reading culture critically is a task that is as active as creating it well. Discernment is never as easy as a checklist and cannot abide a simple rubric. Rather, it requires us to respect the inherent "gray area" complexity of culture and thus to engage it smartly, through a lens of sound biblical thinking. Sometimes we'll evaluate a thing and determine it to be at odds with biblical values. If we are unable to do that—to discern the world's values versus God's—then we will "irresponsibly acquiesce to ideas and positions totally incongruent with who and what we are as Christians."[14]

We have to be able and willing to call a spade a spade, though it's easier said than done. Discerning the good from the bad in music is forever problematic, but "as with all questions in life, the key to determining acceptability for the Christian is whether the music directly violates Scripture or whether the music falls within the infinite realm of choice that God has given us."[15] When something "directly violates Scripture," it's an easy choice to avoid it. But it's within that "infinite realm of choice" where things get complicated and we must employ our creative, imaginative faculties of discernment.

Indeed, as discerning consumers of culture, we have the privilege of participating in the creative process of culture making by *creatively receiving* it. To investigate a work of culture (a rich, textured album like *The White Album*, for example) is to involve oneself as consumer in a way that is as active and vital as what happens on the production end. Deciphering meaning and knowing God more through art and culture is not easy, but it's what we were made to do. As Pastor John Van Sloten argues, "If creation is God's greatest piece of art, then perhaps we need to engage it as such, not always expecting only linear, rational, comprehensible revelation but also different, *unlike* ways of knowing. Perhaps we need to accept that knowing God is as much an art as it is a science."[16]

Poaching Pop Culture

Part of the "art" of knowing and appreciating the beauty of God's creation is the ability to exercise freedom of interpretation and, within reason, to read into a cultural text something that

19 "Secular" Songs with Sacred Potential

Sometimes secular songs don't lend themselves well to redemptive or worshipful experiences. Sometimes, regardless of what the artists behind them intended, they do. Here's a list of songs that are not "Christian" but might nevertheless be experienced by Christians in a worshipful way (at least they have been by me):

Jeff Buckley, "Hallelujah"
Mumford & Sons, "Awake My Soul"
Beach Boys, "God Only Knows"
Joni Mitchell, "Both Sides Now"
Simon & Garfunkel, "Bridge Over Troubled Water"
Louis Armstrong, "What a Wonderful World"
The Beatles, "Hey Jude"
Bon Iver, "Holocene"
Coldplay, "Clocks"
Sigur Rós, "Untitled 8"
Kanye West, "Lost in the World"
Explosions in the Sky, "Your Hand in Mine"
Trespassers William, "Vapour Trail"
Fleet Foxes, "Helplessness Blues"
Interpol, "NYC"
U2, "Where the Streets Have No Name"
The Cure, "Pictures of You"
Bob Dylan, "Blowing in the Wind"
Sam Cooke, "A Change Is Gonna Come"

may or may not have been the creator's intention. Of course, we don't want to get carried away with this. Some Christians try a little too hard to find Christ figures in movies, and although it's probably been attempted by one or another youth pastor, I'm not sure that a Ke$ha lyric can be turned into a sermon illustration. Making secular cultural texts say "Christian" things often looks foolish and cheap, especially when we don't do the work of understanding the intended meaning first.

It is important for Christians to engage culture on its own terms and "go the extra hermeneutical mile to make sure they do not simply project their own interests onto cultural texts." But it's also important for Christians not to be "helpless victims of popular culture" but rather to "make their own cultural statements out of whatever the culture industries produce,"[17] something Kevin Vanhoozer eloquently champions:

> Christian cultural agency is the art of being "in between" Christ and everyday culture. It is the art of making Christian "space" in the dominant "places" that make up our cultural landscape. . . . Christian cultural agents recognize cultural hegemony when they see it and take counter-hegemonic measures in response. Indeed, the church itself is a kind of counter-cultural industry, concerned not with making products for consumption (and worldly gain) but with cultivating certain practices: the practices of the kingdom of God.[18]

Vanhoozer advocates an informed Christian cultural literacy in which Christians can locate within pop culture the elements that can be redeemed and taken captive for the cause of Christ. He cites French cultural critic Michel de Certeau's model of "poaching" cultural texts—the idea that an audience can appropriate a text for its own purposes, transforming its meaning to better fit one's own perspective or goal. This becomes a sort of countercultural form of consumption—an active pursuit of not just the meaning and merits of a cultural text (a song, for example) but those parts of it that can be reinterpreted through a Christian lens. If, as Kuyper argued, all spheres of culture are ultimately under the sovereign rule of God and have the potential to be redeemed and give glory to God, shouldn't Christians actively be scanning the horizons of culture for anything and everything that might speak to the majesty of the Creator?

In terms of music, what does this countercultural Christian "poaching" look like? Perhaps it is playing a Sigur Rós or Explosions in the Sky song—wordless but majestic post-rock anthems—in a worship service. Maybe it's just listening to Radiohead's "Everything in Its Right Place" and meditating on it in a liturgical way, as if it were a prayer of thanksgiving or lament. Or maybe, for you, it's simply listening to Cole Porter, Richard Wagner, or Woody Guthrie and praising God through the artistry of their songs. It will look different for everyone.

Music is a subjective thing, no doubt about it. We all have our tastes, and different music moves us in different ways. But maybe this isn't a problem as much as it is God's way of engaging each individual's tastes, wherever they are. As Van Sloten suggests, "What if we're experiencing God's manifold brilliance when he disperses truth in this very subjective way? . . . In this way, God's voice, God's truth, is magnified rather than merely atomized or relativized."[19]

Music is big enough to be interpreted in nearly limitless ways. The disparity of human engagement with music— across genres, cultures, tastes, and so on—is reason enough to give glory to the God whose creation in its variety expresses the Creator's manifold brilliance.

Of course, not everything out there sings the praises of God, and not everything is worthy of our redemptive "poaching" consumption. But enough of it—perhaps *most* of it—is. And as Christians seeking to hear God's voice more clearly in creation and to glorify him in as many of our activities as possible, we should be on the lookout and ready, with open ears and a discerning mind, seeking out the melodies of heaven wherever they can be heard on earth.

* * * * * * * * * *

Interlude

Eight Transcendent Music Moments In My Life

* * * * * * * * * *

Singing hymns in King's College Chapel: At the conclusion of the Oxbridge 2005 conference, in the magnificent King's College Chapel in Cambridge (UK), four hundred or so of us belted out centuries-old hymns, accompanied by pipe organ, as afternoon sunlight glistened in the tall stained glass windows. It was as I imagine heaven might be.

Over the Rhine concert at Schubas: It was a fall concert in 2003, some months after the Iraq War began. Over the Rhine was on their "Changes Come" tour, playing songs from their masterpiece, *Ohio*. I was having a crazy stressful fall semester of my junior year. Fall was in the air. It was Schubas Tavern in Chicago. Broken bottles of beer, candles, incense, Karin Bergquist's voice, friends. Catharsis.

Singing Bob Dylan songs late into the night with Malcolm Guite at Williams College: Do you know Malcolm Guite? He's a charming, Hobbit-esque poet and chaplain from Cambridge. He also plays music, and one late night at a C. S. Lewis Summer Institute conference at Williams College, I joined a small group of friends in a singalong to Dylan classics, with Malcolm on acoustic guitar. We weren't singing hymns, but on a humid summer night in the Appalachian Berkshires with a handful of friends and fellow believers, "Blowin' in the Wind" was its own sort of liturgy.

Singing worship songs in multiple languages at L'Abri: There was a moment during my stay at Swiss L'Abri, on a misty mountain afternoon, when I sat down with a girl from Spain and a guy from South Korea, who joined me in spontaneously singing familiar praise choruses, together yet each in our own language. I was tired and jet-lagged, but it was something I'll never forget: a trio of greatly diverse people, quietly singing in three languages, praising the Creator of the green meadows and craggy snow-capped peaks outside our chalet.

Singing "May the Mind of Christ, My Savior" at Wheaton commencement: This song has always meant so much to me, but never more so than on the day I graduated from college. I had tears in my eyes singing it—the unofficial Wheaton College hymn—on that day, as so many memories and emotions of four years came rushing forth amid thankfulness and praise. "May the Word of Christ dwell richly / In my heart from hour to hour, / So that all may see I triumph / Only through His pow'r."

Singing Scottish songs with the McCrackens: Growing up, whenever the extended McCracken family got together, my grandmother—who was enormously proud of our family's Scottish heritage, though herself a Swede—insisted on having a singalong to Scottish folk songs. She'd pass around lyrics and take her position at the piano, and we'd all joyously sing songs like "A Scottish Soldier" and "These Are My Mountains." When I think of my family, my childhood, and my ancestors, I think of these songs.

"O Holy Night" on Christmas Eve: My mom plays the violin, and for most Christmas Eve candlelight services when I was growing up, she would play a violin solo of "O Holy Night" (accompanied by my sister on piano) as the candlelight gradually enveloped the room. The stirring simplicity of that melody, straining to make sense of the incarnation on such a sacred night, always moved me.

Explosions in the Sky concert in Hollywood Forever Cemetery: Who knew concerts in cemeteries could be so moving? It's easy to imagine when the band is Explosions in the Sky—instrumental post-rock epicness—and the setting is a windy, cool summer night in Hollywood in an iconic old cemetery. As I lay on my back in the grass, looking up at the palm trees swaying and the stars beyond, I couldn't help but feel a bit of transcendence.

* * * * * * * * * *

5

A Christian Approach
to Music Appreciation

* * * * * * * * * *

For most of the significant music experiences of my life, I can remember who I experienced them alongside. The same can't be said for the most significant movie experiences of my life, for example, or the most illuminating intellectual epiphanies I've had, or the best books I've read. But there's something about music that is fundamentally about more than just me. It's about me plus others. It's about my sister beside me at Red Rocks amphitheater, watching Coldplay perform "Clocks" on a rainy Rocky Mountain night. It's about sitting in a college dorm room listening to two copies of Radiohead's *Kid A* album played simultaneously, four seconds apart (try it). It's about all those memories I described in the Interlude.

Deciding what's worthy, appropriate, and good to listen to is only part of the equation of music appreciation. There's a lot more to it that goes beyond just the cerebral cloisters between two ear buds. Music appreciation is also about community, artists, critics, tradition, and the development of taste. It's not just about avoiding the bad and the unhealthy; it's about energetically educating ourselves to better pursue the good.

It's Better with Friends

One of the keys to being a better consumer of culture is realizing that we frequently engage culture within a web of connections and community. It's rarely just me and the song. We understand culture, we discover and share it, we parse the meaning of it, with others.

This is especially true in the world of music, where communities often form around a certain artist or genre and entire vocabularies and cultural practices are created around shared musical interests. Think about the entire *world* of culture associated with, say, rap music: a way of speaking, a manner of dressing, bling, swagger, basketball, certain forms of liquor. Or country music: pickup trucks, beer, patriotism, NASCAR. Music has a way of creating and defining communities.

Community is a crucial part of healthier cultural consumption. Whether we're talking about enjoying food together (see chap. 2), discussing a film we just saw (see chap. 8), or having a celebratory toast with friends and family on some occasion of joy (see chap. 11), fellowship is almost always an enriching key to appreciating and expressing culture. In describing the attributes of good "leisurers," Miroslav Volf says that the ability to enjoy "fellowship with one another" and "delight in the communion with God" are key, and that such communion anticipates our future enjoyment of God in

4 Ways Community Enhances the Experience of Music

How does community add to the experience and appreciation of music? Here are four ways:

1. *Sharing*: What a joy it is to share music with others! Who doesn't love making a mix CD for a special someone? There's something about enjoying music fully that simply requires us to share it with others, to recommend it and praise it publicly. As C. S. Lewis says, "Praise not merely expresses but completes the enjoyment; it is its appointed consummation."[1]

2. *Discovery*: A corollary to sharing is discovery, because the flip side of sharing what we know with others is that they'll share what they've found—and then everyone comes away with something new! There's too much music in the world for us to know about all of it, but thankfully, if we know enough people who love and appreciate music, we'll hear about a lot of it eventually.

3. *Education*: From others we not only learn about new music but also learn to see and hear things about music we may not have seen or heard before. We might listen to a song with a friend who's a drummer and be awakened to the intricacies of creative drumbeats and rhythmic patterns. We might learn about the cultural background of a particular genre because a friend in our group grew up in that context.

4. *Enjoyment*: Enjoying music together is simply more fun. There's a reason we'd rather go to a concert with friends than on our own and that we like to have music playing when we throw a party. Music and crowds were made to go together. We celebrate and rejoice in community in a lot of ways, but music is almost always a part of it.

the new creation.[2] We are made to be in community, to reflect the trinitarian communion of our Creator. It's our purpose, our destiny, our DNA. No wonder it makes our experience of culture all the more beautiful.

Church Worship Wars: Music in Community Isn't Always Easy

Anyone who has stood in a church and sung a song with hundreds of fellow believers in unified praise knows the power of music in community. There's something moving, something wonderful about hearing the voices of those around you singing, along with your own, in praise of the God we collectively call Father.

And yet, as most of us familiar with church life know, worship music can also become an unfortunate source of strife. "Worship wars" have long plagued evangelical church culture, but especially during the transition in the twentieth century from "traditional" music styles (organs, hymns, choirs) to "contemporary" worship styles (guitar, drums, praise choruses). My grandmother spoke for many (including me) when she lamented her church's removal of the organ and campaigned to bring it back. She didn't like the loud rock music and "7/11" choruses (7 words repeated 11 times), just like the baby boomer pastors didn't like her "outdated" hymns and classical preferences.

People of different backgrounds often have vastly different tastes in music, so it's natural that problems may arise when a disparate church community makes decisions about music styles. Yet these differences of tastes don't necessarily *need* to breed disharmony in the church; on the contrary, they can actually provide opportunities for stronger unity.

Music in the church can unite us if we are willing to move away from the "me" mentality and humbly place the community above ourselves, notes Andrew Braine, a teacher in Biola University's Music in Worship program.

"It gives us an opportunity for humility, because I'm not going to hear what I think I want to hear all the time, and that's fine," said Braine. "The community should come before my own individual preferences, and we should take delight in seeing others enjoy a song even if we don't."[3] Braine's point hints at a larger truth about the power of music in community: it can be an opportunity to grow in humility and learn from one another. If I put aside my pride for a minute and take joy in watching others enjoy their preferred style of music, it can be a teaching moment and a reminder that music isn't just about me. What does music do for others? Can I learn to appreciate an "alien" genre of music simply because my neighbor is loving it? If we're going to be better connoisseurs of music, we should ask these sorts of questions.

Patronage

Part of consuming music well is recognizing that the creators of much of the music we listen to are trying to make a living from it. For the culture makers, there are economic realities at play and livelihoods at stake. As appreciators and supporters of culture, our responsibility is not just to celebrate or praise culture but also to support it financially.

Artists need their fans to buy their albums, purchase tickets to their films, acquire their paintings, and eat at their restaurants. Many times they also need investors who see potential and are willing to advance funds to make the creation of the work even possible. Culture making and culture funding are inextricably linked, and the latter is an activity fundamental to a healthy posture of cultural consumption.

Because we usually pay money for the product we consume (CD, book, film ticket, cup of coffee), our role as consumer is decidedly economic. So we're always funding culture—well, unless we aren't, which is unfortunately common in this age of rampant piracy. Thus, we should start here: pay for the things you consume. In the case of music, where you might already have a lot that you didn't pay for (e.g., albums burned from a friend), you should find another way to support the artist financially. Buy one of their previous albums. Go to their concert, and bring a friend. Buy merchandise. Get the vinyl. If you really love an artist, prove it with your wallet. Money talks, and it says a lot about who we are if we're actually willing to give artists their due for the work we enjoy from them.

According to my brother-in-law Brett, who has worked in the music industry for a decade and has managed bands like Foster the People and Cold War Kids, touring and merchandise are and probably forever will be the primary revenue generators for musical artists. But what if we don't have the money to attend concerts and buy shirts from our favorite bands? There are a few other things we can do, according to Brett.

The first is that we can support our favorite artists by spreading the news about them. "If you think that an artist makes great art, my opinion is that the most important thing you can do as a consumer is tell people about it," said Brett. "Word of mouth is the way bands make more money, by converting fans and then those fans telling ten people about their experience."

A second way we can support them is by being okay with our favorite artists allowing movies, television shows, and brands to use their music. "I can understand that you don't want your mom to tell you she heard your favorite song in a shampoo commercial," said Brett, "but fans need to realize that this is an amazing way for the songwriters to make up for the money that is being stolen from them by illegal downloads."

Increasingly, another way to support artists is to contribute funds directly to them as investors. The internet has revolutionized the potential here, as the "middlemen" (labels, studios, etc.) are increasingly irrelevant and artists can receive funding from and deliver the product directly to their audiences. Websites like Kickstarter have brought "crowdfunding" to the mainstream, allowing artists of all sorts the chance to mount grassroots online fundraising campaigns to make possible things like album recordings and movie shoots by soliciting fan support directly. Though not always successful—unworthy and unproven artists still have a hard time raising funds—Kickstarter has been a win for some musicians, like Massachusetts singer-songwriter Marissa Nadler, who in 2010 raised $17,000 to help fund the recording of her new full-length album.[4]

In 2010, one of my favorite bands, Over the Rhine, set out to record their new album, *The Long Surrender*, relying on the donations of their small but dedicated fan base. In a letter to fans announcing the project, Linford Detweiler and Karin Bergquist wrote this:

> In 2010, there is no middleman. It's just us and you. So, for the first time in our career, we are simply going to appeal directly to you, the people who care about Over the Rhine's music, and ask if you will partner directly with us in making this new record.[5]

The letter goes on to ask fans to donate $15 in advance to help fund the record, with the promise that an autographed album would be shipped to them upon completion, as well as three bonus tracks and a personal thank-you. I donated and received the album as a download several months before it officially came out—as well as MP3 demo versions of all the album's songs. The whole process felt wonderfully personal, as if I were part of the creative process right there with Over the Rhine.

Patronage like this can be a wonderful way not only to express appreciation for the good work of your favorite artists but also to tangibly contribute to the process of creation. Once again: culture making is nothing without culture funding. Money is the point at which creators and consumers connect, vulgar as that may sound. It's one of the areas where a culture *receiver* functions as something of a *maker* as well.

There's a great tradition of cultural patronage within Christianity; the church has been ground zero for some of the most magnificent art commissions in history (e.g., Michelangelo's ceiling in the Sistine Chapel). I say let's revive our heritage of being leaders in patronage. Let's support artists, paying for them to flourish and create more good work. Let's fund legitimate artistic creation within our sacred spaces. More than just *saying* we are pro-art, we should let our money talk: fund forward-thinking architecture; commission stained glass artists, sculptors, and painters for works inside our churches; pay the aspiring chef in our congregation to cater a meal for the community.

And let's not limit it to "Christian" artists either. We should fund whoever is worthy, whoever out there has the potential to create the best albums, the most visionary visual art, the most significant films. This sort of patronage will make the secular world take notice. Why are Christians caring so much for the arts and the livelihood of artists? Because such things have a place in the extravagant, abundant landscape of the new creation, and the world needs reminders of the flourishing and shalom to come.

Refining Taste in Music

Every year, thousands of CDs are released; twenty million songs are available to purchase on iTunes. Many of us are not lacking in friends who recommend music to us. We're bombarded by options, which makes it all the more useful for us to hone our own taste and preferences. It's practical to be particular; it narrows things down.

Having stylistic preferences or favorite genres still only gets us so far, however. Say we like folk music. There is still a *ton* of folk music released every year, not to mention the massive amount released in the past that we can also choose from. How on earth do we know what's worth spending our time and money on? Clearly at some point evaluation of quality comes into play. But how do we know what is the best?

Preferences are one thing, notes Christian art theorist Hans Rookmaaker, but "even if our preferences cannot be discussed, our choices can, since quality and content are not just a matter of taste, but a matter of norms. If we talk about portraits, some are more, some are less beautiful, of a higher or a lower artistic quality."[6]

At this point we must talk about the notion of "having good taste." Is it even sensible to talk in objective terms about such a thing? Many people would say no. "Good quality" is subjectively defined from culture to culture, class to class, they would say; there's no such thing as objective good taste. And to a point I agree. I'm not sure an ironclad, universal formula for "good" art or "proper" taste exists. But I do think that within a given culture—and especially within a given style or genre—objective assessments of quality are valid.

During my trombone-playing days in high school, I yearly performed for solo contests and auditioned for state band. I knew that the results of such performances were quantifiable. I would play the music either well or poorly. In these cases, the existence of objective "good" and "bad" in music is obvious. But quality also encompasses more intangible things than simply playing the notes on pitch. It's also about how those notes are written in the first place. Is the music dynamic, interesting, layered, emotional? Does it stir the soul? Evaluation on these points allows us to declare, for example, that Bach is more masterful than Holst, though both are certainly masters.

Much of it has to do with critical consensus and the test of time. Do critics agree on what is the best among a certain genre? What sticks? The Beatles are objectively better than the Monkees for a lot of reasons, but in no small part because a half century later, no critic would say the Monkees are better. This is not to say that the Monkees are bad; just that the Beatles are better, and the vast majority can agree on that fact.

When I asked my friend Laura, a music critic who writes for publications like *Under the Radar* and *Filter*, what constitutes "objective good" in music, she said that it existed in different forms within each genre, but that one "universal" marker of good was whether an artist believes in the story they are telling. "I need to feel some emotional truth they are exploring, some honesty," she said. "You can be authentic in any genre, but it's all about whether an artist is attempting to tell a story that is true."

Laura noted that the "easy to swallow" music that tends to appeal to the masses often is created with mass appeal in mind as opposed to authentic truth-telling. Music that is authentic and true is often more difficult and requires more work, she said. "The best stuff isn't always the easiest. We need to ask ourselves, 'Are we feeding ourselves McDonald's or are we going to a four-star restaurant?'"

Developing taste is important because it allows us to enter into a positive critical discourse that has as its goal the discovery and enjoyment of the best that is out there. In his book *Good Taste, Bad Taste, and Christian Taste*, Frank Burch Brown argues that "taste is essential to the enjoyment of those special works of art that help connect us with all we perceive to be holy"[7] and that Christians shouldn't treat it as irrelevant to their faith. He writes:

> The evidence of scripture, tradition, and experience all suggest that art can sometimes mediate not only a sense of life but also a sense of grace and of the mystery that we call God. And since art cannot mediate without the aid of aesthetic imagination, response, and judgment—without taste, in short—we must consider the perhaps surprising possibility that taste at its most encompassing is no less crucial to religious life and faith than is intellectual understanding and moral commitment.[8]

For Brown, taste is not something to be arrogantly flaunted or wielded over others but rather a means to humbly develop perception and cultivate discernment that allows us to "enter into the sense of God and the sense of good."[9]

But our understanding and pursuit of taste should also be charitable and "ecumenical," argues Brown. It should allow for differences of opinion and be understood more as a fluid conversation rather than a unilateral, once-and-for-all decree. Taste should not be treated as a "nonessential" that favors complete liberty and disregards the importance of aesthetic judgments in religious life, he notes. But treating taste as "essential" has problems of its own:

> It has too often resulted in attempts to regularize taste by decree, privileging the tastes of one group, silencing the voices of others, banning indigenous or local styles, or arbitrarily prohibiting instruments such as piano or guitar—and all without any attempt to engage in dialogue.[10]

The key here is indeed dialogue. Discerning taste does not exist in a vacuum, after all, but within an ongoing conversation.

Christians should recognize that taste has both subjective and objective elements; it includes both our individual resonances with a work and also the larger community of interpretation and evaluation. It is something we have inherently but also something that must be developed and informed. Good taste is not simply pointing to one's record collection and declaring it tasteful; good taste is being willing to expand one's horizons, hear what others have to say, and seek a more thorough understanding of how a work of art can be better perceived, enjoyed, and evaluated. For Christians seeking to be better consumers of culture, the value of developing a more discerning taste is vital.

Tips for Better Music Appreciation

From Laura Studarus, Christian and music critic for publications such as *Under the Radar*, *Filter*, *Relevant*, and *Pitchfork*.

- Think about a music artist you like and try to understand what aspects of their music you like best. Try to find those qualities in other music. Branch out.
- Check yourself. Am I interested in this music because I want to be part of the *scene*, or am I genuinely interested or moved by it?
- Slow down and take time to digest an album. Don't judge or move on from something too quickly.
- Don't be afraid of the grittier content, but don't dwell there.
- Strike a balance between being true to your own personal tastes and also listening to what critics say.
- Try to be aware of the emotions that music stirs within you.
- Have a good knowledge base of music (genres, history, what's come before), but don't feel like you have to be a walking music encyclopedia.
- Music is not like taking your SATs. At the end of the day, it's about enjoyment.

The Danger of Music Snobbery

We all have friends who are music snobs. They are the people always declaring bands that no one else has heard of to be the best thing ever. They are the ones who refuse to publicly endorse a band that is popular on Top 40 radio. They go out of their way to claim they never liked Coldplay. They are physically sickened by bands like Nickleback and Maroon 5. For them, anything outside their very limited and educated opinion of "good" is laughable, and they let you know it.

This is the dangerous side of developing good taste: sometimes we let it become a badge of honor. We sometimes exert our taste as a public sign of esteem rather than a humble means of exploration and discovery. In contrast to the "ecumenical taste" that Brown describes, taste can often become narrow and snobbish—a status symbol less about loving music than showing that we know more about it than you do.

For Christians, this must be aggressively avoided. Pride and snobbery have no place in a healthy Christian appreciation of culture. We must develop our taste humbly, being open-minded to what others enjoy and why they do. We should "learn to discern, as an act of love, what others find delightful and meaningful in art that has little appeal to oneself or one's own group."[11]

The key to good taste is being open to things not immediately attractive or resonant. There are many things I didn't like at first but now have come to absolutely love: Jim Jarmusch films, brussel sprouts, Sufjan Stevens's *Age of Adz*, Twitter. In many cases, it takes us being willing to listen to the opinions of others to truly come to appreciate something. I didn't come to love Emily Dickinson poetry until I took a class on her with the wonderful Dr. Roger Lundin, one of the world's foremost Dickinson scholars. Likewise with C. S. Lewis's *Till We Have Faces*. Only through the poetic explications of people like Andrew Lazo and Jerry Root (both Lewis experts) did I come to see this book as the masterpiece that it is.

Here again we see that having a humble attitude—being willing to learn, seeking the opinions of others, not resting on first impressions—yields more lasting rewards. Being snobbish about one's "advanced" taste is not only a bad witness; it's a refusal to grow. The pursuit of a more discerning, well-rounded taste is never finished. It's a process. And it should never be about me, at least primarily. It should be about God: hearing him, honoring him, celebrating his truth and beauty in ever more perceptive ways.

Conclusion: Toward a More Mature Music Consumption

With music, as with any area of culture we consume as Christians, we must remember that we have a choice as to where we spend our time and money, and we ought to choose wisely. *Consumer* doesn't have to be a derogatory term. If we are discerning, thoughtful, passionate consumers of music, driven not by status or fashion but by a sincere desire to encounter beauty and honor creativity, consuming can become a God-glorifying action.

As Tom Beaudoin writes in *Consuming Faith*, "There is nothing wrong with buying, nothing wrong with the existence of brands." But Christians must be mature and responsible in their consumption, to the point that it becomes a positive witness to the secular world. Christians must realize that "we each have some freedom to accept God's gifting us with life, by becoming someone who stewards more life for others."

> In that work, God's gift of life becomes more believable to others, and awareness of and responsible relationship to God

spreads through our use of our resources, through consciousness about those affected by our purchases.[12]

As we've seen in our discussion of food and now music, the consumer end of culture is crucial for Christians to get right. Will we be apathetic separatists who cede appreciation of culture to "the world"? Will we, as another extreme, be uncritical and careless in our accepting of any and every bit of culture at our disposal? Or will we do the work it takes to thrive somewhere in the "gray" middle—Christian consumers not in a zone of compromise but in a space of flourishing and worship? That is the space within which I aspire to exist.

PART 3

WATCHING

Of all the areas of culture that have elicited passionate and wide-ranging responses from Christians, cinema is perhaps the most contentious.

As a film critic for much of the last decade, writing for Christian publications like *Relevant* and *Christianity Today*, I've seen the diversity of Christian approaches to film firsthand. Some Christians see Hollywood as a malevolent propaganda machine, churning out smut for the masses. They cut off from it completely. Others see some value in film, but only insofar as it is family friendly or espouses a positive or Christian message. Then there are the Christians—mostly in younger generations—who accept or are open to pretty much all films, prioritizing artistic merit or entertainment value over evaluation of a film's moral content.

There are a multitude of opinions and arguments surrounding the question of how a Christian should approach film-watching. And the debates often get heated. But is there a *best* approach to appreciating and engaging with film?

The chapters in this section explore some issues related to the consumption of film (with a brief foray into television), including: how Christians have historically related to film (chap. 6), whether there is a discerning "line" of what is or isn't edifying (chap. 7) and how we can better appreciate both the art and entertainment of movie-watching. These chapters will build on the general principles developed thus far and continue expanding upon the seven key themes of Christian cultural consumption (see pp. 21–22).

****

Interlude

Four Christian Approaches to Film

****

Jack Hafer has been a Christian working in the film industry since the 1980s (you may have seen his 2001 film *To End All Wars*). He's also the current chair of the film department at Biola University, an evangelical college with an impressive track record for producing graduates who find success in Hollywood. I asked Hafer to categorize different approaches Christians have taken to film and filmmaking, and he described three. Below I've summarized his three approaches, plus a fourth that I have personally observed:

1. *Message-centric*: Some Christians are only interested in films insofar as they explicitly preach the gospel or relay an unmistakably biblical message. This approach typically downplays aesthetics in favor of unmissable morals, preferring didactic directness over subtlety. Good films are evangelistic films. Examples: *A Thief in the Night*; *Fireproof*.

2. *For the common good*: This approach doesn't focus on evangelism as much as whether or not a film has overall positive values for the common good. "In Hollywood it's easy to make temptation look enticing but challenging to make goodness look attractive," notes Hafer, but "that's a challenge this approach takes on." These are films not made for the church but for wide audiences, espousing

broad but generally Judeo-Christian values, where good triumphs over evil. Examples: *Indiana Jones*; *The Blind Side*.

3. *Religious in content*: This approach favors films that feature religious elements or plots: movies about Christians, preachers, nuns, monks, Joan of Arc, etc. It sees value in films that make religious sentiments look attractive or films that create a sense of awe, longing, and wonder about the transcendent. These films need not be preachy, but often compellingly portray stories of faith. Examples: *The Way*; *Diary of a Country Priest*.

4. *Aesthetically transcendent*: In this approach, "sacred" films are those that—through exceptional artistry and powerful narrative—evoke feelings of transcendental longing akin to what Germans call *Sehnsucht*. They are films so beautiful that the viewer is brought to a place of stasis or spiritual contemplation. Christians who favor this approach are less interested in specifically Christian messages or plotlines than they are in true, powerful portrayals of beauty and longing. Examples: *Tokyo Story*; *The Tree of Life*.

* * * * * * * * * *

6

A Brief History of Christians and Movies

It was move-in day at Wheaton College, the evangelical flagship institution where I was beginning my freshman year. As I settled into my room, unpacking my rather nascent DVD collection—a predictable assortment for a budding evangelical cinephile (*Gladiator*, *American Beauty*, *The Thin Red Line*, *Braveheart*)—I began chatting with my roommate, whom I had just met. While unpacking his CDs (one hundred percent Christian), he looked curiously upon my movie tower. I asked him what his favorite films were. He said he couldn't think of one.

"I don't watch many movies," he said. In fact, he had never been to a movie theater. Not once. In his life. His family saw movie theaters as mostly dens of iniquity. They stayed away.

I cringed. How was I going to get along with this guy? I didn't just tolerate movies; I *loved* them. Within weeks of moving in I began writing movie reviews for *The Wheaton Record*, and my ambition was to either make films or review them, Roger Ebert style. I wondered if my roommate would judge me and forever associate me with the slippery slope of worldliness.

In the end, my roommate turned out to be great, and though I never did get him to come to a movie theater with me, he respected my interests. But that doesn't mean I didn't receive flak from many other directions. My time at Wheaton, writing film reviews for sometimes controversial R-rated films like *Million Dollar Baby*, was not always an easy road. But most of the time it was rich. There was a lot of support for intelligent, discerning Christian engagement with secular film, even while there were (and still are) some vocal Christians who disapproved entirely.

The relationship between Christians and Hollywood (film, but also television) has been, and is, complex. It's been a sometimes mutually respectful but most of the time uneasy or downright contentious relationship. In this chapter we'll take a brief look at the history of the dynamic, understanding the context of how Christians have historically engaged cinema, how the relationship is changing, and what it all teaches us about how to be better consumers today.

Movies and Fear

From the get-go, and for much of the narrative of Christian consumption of cinema in America, "the movies" were often seen as a threat and a vice. Born in the early twentieth century and quickly rising to become one of the most popular amusements of the day, the movies were a child of modernism and mass culture—both things Christians didn't particularly trust. Modernism was shaking the foundations of faith, just as mass culture and urbanization were introducing new amusements and dubious ethics into a culture with ever more leisure time at its disposal.

Until at least the 1960s (and for some, even until today), mass media like film, radio, and television were looked upon through a "media effects" lens: as powerful, propagandistic tools with the power to brainwash consumers or at least cause them to react in a certain way (watching a villain in a film rob a bank, for example, causes the viewer to then want to go do the same thing). We see echoes of this even today, such as when the Columbine killers were said to have been inspired by *The Matrix*, trench coats and all.

Film was thought to be particularly dangerous. Its visceral, escapist nature—presenting glittering moving pictures of actual bodies, engaging in what appear to be actual vices, to cavernous dark theaters of inert, seemingly passive consumers—made film an obvious culprit for all manner of bad behavior in culture. "The movies made me do it!" was not a joke in 1915. It was how people thought, particularly Christians and the old guard vestiges of Victorian culture. Movies were especially menacing in the effects they were thought to have on young people, the very demographic so attracted to the novelty of nickelodeons showing thrilling narratives of train robberies and caped crusaders.

Suspicions of the ill effects of movies on children were later "confirmed" by publications such as *Our Movie Made Children* by Henry James Forman, a 1933 summary of twelve separate investigations into the influence of movies on children. This publication argued that psychological science proved that the emotional enticements of films and their "propaganda" were impossible for children to resist and that indeed, films "encouraged many children to delinquency and crimes, both by having stimulated desires for luxury and leisure, and by giving instruction in methods of 'petting' and techniques in committing crimes."[1]

Fears of the power of cinema to lead people into sin were only exacerbated by sordid tales of the lifestyles of film stars, such as Roscoe "Fatty" Arbuckle, who in 1921 was embroiled in a murder trial that became one of the biggest tabloid scandals of the decade. The perception was that Hollywood stars were bootleggers and drug traffickers, sex-crazed flappers and lechers who married and divorced in rapid fashion. In a culture rapidly changing, where religion was increasingly relegated to the defensive margins, the movies were a lightning rod, a scapegoat cause for the perceived erosion of morality. And Christians were leading the choir of voices crying foul.

Early Cinema and Censorship

Early on, one of the things that defined the relationship between Christianity and Hollywood was censorship. Following the Supreme Court's decision in the *Mutual Film Corporation v. Ohio Industrial Commission* case of 1915 that cinema was not protected under the First Amendment, censorship became a fact of life on the state and local levels. Towns across the country established local censorship boards that ruled on what was or wasn't allowed in their community's movie houses. This was an annoyance for the film industry, but the threat of federal censorship was a much more frightening prospect. To ward that off, the industry established a facade of disciplined self-regulation, in which the concerns of everyone from Main Street to Madison Avenue regarding film content were supposedly heard and heeded.

In 1922, Hollywood studio heads formed the Motion Pictures Producers and Distributors Association of America (MPPDA), headed by Will H. Hays, a Presbyterian from

Indiana who was "the ideal man to reassure the hometown critics that one of their own would be riding herd on the untrustworthy aliens who ran the movie business."[2]

As liaison between the film industry and religious reform groups angry about immoral content coming out of Hollywood, Hays formed the Studio Relations Committee in 1926, which came up with the "Don'ts and Be Carefuls" list, adopted by the Association of Motion Picture Producers (AMPP) on June 8, 1927.

This list broadly outlined eleven things that "shall not" appear in motion pictures (ill-defined things like "any inference of sex perversion") and twenty-five "special care must be exercised" elements (such as "sympathy for criminals").[3] Intended to appease the church's calls for stricter moral standards in Hollywood, the "Don'ts" were little more than a PR move and were largely disregarded by filmmakers. More than anything, Hays's office was one of preemptive damage control to ward off negative publicity and, above all, federal censorship.

Catholics and the Hollywood Production Code

By the late 1920s, it became clear that Hays's office was not making Hollywood any more moral, and pressure from Christians to clean up filthy films only increased. Desperate to appease faith-based critics of Hollywood and avoid federal censorship, the industry agreed to a new "Motion Picture Production Code" in 1930, a philosophical document written by Catholics to outline acceptable movie content. Father Daniel Lord, a Jesuit who served as accompanist for silent pictures while in seminary, authored the code, which emphasized that films coming out of Hollywood should portray good as good and evil as evil. Films that glamorized gangsters and made sin look enticing were not to be approved under the new code.

Though the Hollywood studios signed their agreement to abide by the Production Code, the content of their films didn't become any cleaner. In the 1930s, as films became more violent and sexual and seductive vamps like Mae West rose to superstar status, Christians became more outraged than ever.

Enraged Catholics unleashed their wrath in the form of the Legion of Decency. Formed by the United States Conference of Catholic Bishops on April 28, 1934, and with the firm endorsement (imperative, even) of Rome,[4] the Legion spread rapidly and impacted the box office almost immediately. Upwards of eleven million people eventually signed the Legion of Decency Oath,[5] and not just Catholics.

The unleashed fury of an organized Christian coalition prompted Hollywood to form the Production Code Administration (PCA) and place Catholic Joseph Breen as its head. The PCA was made sole arbiter—with Breen as "umpire"—of a film's compliance with the Code, with a $25,000 fine for films that went forward without PCA approval.

From 1934 to 1954, roughly corresponding to the time of Hollywood's "Golden Age," Breen held an unprecedented position of authority over the film industry, as arbiter and enforcer of the moral standards for pictures as outlined in the Production Code. He was more than just a bureaucrat charged with cleaning up the dirtied industry; he was a missionary of the Catholic Church, entrusted to standardize the Code (a document "deeply Catholic in tone and outlook"[6]) that had been written by his Jesuit brethren four years earlier.

The Hollywood film industry had suffered financially during the Great Depression, but after 1934, when the Code began to be enforced in earnest, it began a period of growth that would last until the coming of television. As it turned out, more wholesome fare met with big box-office results (such as Shirley Temple and Frank Capra films). Within months of the PCA's formation, Catholic watchdog groups were reporting up to 90 percent approval of the movies they screened.[7]

The climate of the country in 1934 was ready for cleaner, more family-friendly cinema. Jack Vizzard, a longtime official of the PCA, described the mood of these times as "one of severe backlash." After the flappers, speakeasies, and moral ambiguity of the Jazz Age, "an enormous sense of guilt set in" with the stock market crash of 1929.[8] And whereas pre-Code Hollywood vented the "disorientations and despair" of America in the Depression through angst-ridden, envelope-pushing films, "Hollywood after 1934 reflected the restoration of cultural equilibrium under FDR."[9]

Protestant Abandonment of Hollywood

As Catholics became more influential in the filmmaking industry (especially the enforcement of its morality—at least until Breen's retirement in 1954), Protestants more or less gave up on Hollywood.

The rise of modernism in the 1920s and disillusionment of the subsequent Depression took a heavy toll on Protestant authority, unanimity, and self-confidence. Modernism brought many problems to "Old" Protestantism, including the secularization of American universities, the elevation of science and impact of evolutionary debate (i.e., the Scopes trial), and the undermining of belief in an inerrant Bible. The question of how best to deal with modernism sparked contentious division between moderate, mainline denominations and the more conservative fundamentalists—a rift that would become, as Mark Noll points out, "a permanent feature of the religious landscape" and "one of the key factors that ended the Protestant hegemony."[10]

What had come out of the twenties was a "deeply, permanently divided Protestantism," according to historian Martin Marty, one which "no longer presented a single front" and was "ever less prepared to hold its place of dominance in American culture in the decades to come."[11] As the liberal Protestants went one way, fundamentalism went another. And for fundamentalists, this meant that pop culture was either avoided completely or looked upon with extreme skepticism. Evangelicalism had no place for the temptations and distractions of secular art and popular culture. Movies were all but relinquished to the secularists, and movie theaters came to be regarded as "the devil's house."

Despite a brief period of relatively "clean" Hollywood output under the watchful, empowered eye of the Catholic-run PCA, Hollywood gradually regained its reputation as peddler of glitzy vice from the 1940s through 1960s. Film noir ushered

Christianity and Hollywood: 20 Moments of Tension

Films that angered or were protested/boycotted by Christians:

King of Kings (1926)
The Callahans and the Murphys (1927)
Sign of the Cross (1932)
Gone with the Wind (1939)
The Miracle (1948)
Lolita (1962)
A Clockwork Orange (1971)
Jesus Christ Superstar (1973)
The Exorcist (1973)
Jesus of Nazareth (1977)

Monty Python's Life of Brian (1979)
Hail Mary (1985)
The Last Temptation of Christ (1988)
Kids (1995)
Dogma (1999)
The Passion of the Christ (2004)
Saved! (2004)
Million Dollar Baby (2004)
The Da Vinci Code (2006)
Religulous (2008)

in a new era of "gray area" moral ambiguity in the movies, where upstanding protagonists seemed harder to come by; James Dean popularized rebellion and Marilyn Monroe redefined sex appeal on the big screen. New competition from television led filmmakers to push the envelope to keep audiences coming back. Foreign films from Europe brought entirely new (and scandalizing) sensibilities to American screens. For many Christians—particularly fundamentalist Protestants—all of this proved their point that Hollywood was of the devil.

The Culture Wars

One of the pivotal moments in the Christian relationship with Hollywood came with events surrounding the American debut of Roberto Rosselini's *The Miracle* (1948), a foreign art film that the Legion of Decency condemned as "a sacrilegious and blasphemous mockery of Christian and religious truth,"[12] but which nevertheless made its way to some American screens. Widespread boycotts and calls for censorship eventually led to a landmark Supreme Court case, *Joseph Burstyn, Inc. v. Wilson*, which in 1952 determined that film was indeed an art form worthy of First Amendment protection and that accusations of "sacrilegious" content could not warrant censorship. The decision signaled the death knell for film censorship and significantly weakened the power of religious protest groups like the Legion of Decency to keep offensive films from the public.

This didn't deter religious fervor against the worst of Hollywood's output, however; in fact, it likely exacerbated the growing divide between Hollywood and the church. By the 1970s, the "Religious Right," emboldened by the rise of the Moral Majority, "came to view campaigns against movies as extensions of their broader activism on life-style and other issues."[13] Dustups over films like Franco Zeffirelli's *Jesus of Nazareth* (1977) and *Monty Python's Life of Brian* (1979) resulted in protests and boycotts led by the likes of Bob Jones III. In 1985, Jean-Luc Godard's *Hail Mary* drew protests from religious groups concerned about the film's portrayal of the Virgin Mary as well as its full-frontal nudity. But the granddaddy of Christian protesting came in 1988 with Martin Scorsese's *The Last Temptation of Christ*, a film that sparked an explosive controversy encapsulating the larger battles of the culture wars.

The *Last Temptation* confrontation is perhaps the single biggest clash between Christians and Hollywood in the history of cinema. In the weeks leading up to *Temptation*'s release, more than 1,200 Christian radio stations in California alone denounced the film—which depicts Jesus as fantasizing about Mary Magdalene—as blasphemy; leaders such as Bill Bright, Pat Robertson, Jerry Falwell, and James Dobson condemned it and urged their audiences to boycott products from the film's parent company, MCA. It all came to a head on August 12, 1988, when about 25,000 Christians marched on Universal Studios in Los Angeles, carrying Bibles and wooden crucifixes, chanting "Jesus, Jesus, Jesus."[14]

Curse Counting

In 1968, the Production Code was officially replaced by the Motion Picture Association of America's voluntary movie classification system, which assigned a rating (in their current form: G, PG, PG-13, R, or NC-17) to films based on content. The big difference here was that the MPAA was not a "gate-keeper" that could approve or disapprove of a film based on content (like the PCA); it was merely a rating body, issuing a certificate number with one of its classifications that each film had to display in its credits and advertising materials. It was less an "endorsement" than a cautionary guide for viewers and parents.

For Christians concerned about film content, this shift complicated things a bit. Was an R rating an immediate and in-all-cases marker of inappropriateness? Are PG-13 films okay for Christian teens? In some cases yes; in some cases no. The ambiguities and arbitrariness of the rating system necessitated more sophisticated tools for Christian assessment of secular cinema.

This gave rise to publications like Focus on the Family's *Plugged In* magazine, now a website that offers reviews of films (as well as music and television) for evangelical parents. Designed "to shine a light on the world of popular entertainment while giving families the essential tools they need to understand, navigate, and impact the culture in which they live,"[15] Plugged In includes eyebrow-raising discussions of a film's "positive elements," "spiritual content," "nudity and sexual content," "violent content," "crude or profane language," "drug and alcohol content," and "other negative elements." Reviews are exhaustive in their detail, with vivid overviews of sexual content ("A teen girl strips down to her panties in Jim's room and touches herself."[16]) as well as exact counts of *f*-words and cautions that, "Unfortunately, the Lord's name is abused 15 times ('Jesus' and 'Christ' are used six times; 'g--d--n' six times)."[17]

This curse-counting approach was "perfected" in Ted Baehr's Movieguide, "The family guide to movies and entertainment." Movieguide offers "quality ratings" on a 4-star scale, but also "acceptability ratings" on a scale of -4 ("Abhorrent") to +4 ("Exemplary"), and gives special attention to whether the film presents a positive worldview (biblical/

moral/Christian) or a negative worldview (humanism, romanticism, paganism). Liam Neeson's 2012 action film *The Grey*, for example, received a 3-star ("Good") quality rating from Movieguide but a -3 ("Excessive") acceptability rating for content that includes a "strong Nihilistic, Humanist worldview" and "a pagan use of abundant foul language and some anti-religious comments by two humanists/atheists in debates over God and religion and man."[18]

More than just a resource for Christian families to know what their children are watching, Movieguide has an agenda to prove to Hollywood that the most conservative, redemptive, family-friendly and pro-capitalist (yes, pro-capitalist!) movies earn the most money at the box office. In a 2009 *Wall Street Journal* op-ed, Movieguide's Ted Baehr and Tom Snyder argued that "films with strong pro-capitalist content—extolling free-market principles or containing positive portrayals of real or fictional businessmen and entrepreneurs—tended to make the most money."[19] They attributed the success of top box office moneymakers *The Dark Knight* and *Iron Man*, for example, to their featuring billionaire protagonists—capitalists whom audiences want to celebrate. Around the same time, the pair made their case in the *Washington Post*, where they wrote:

> Contrary to popular opinion, 2008 was the year that obscenity, sex, and nudity didn't sell—again. In fact, movies with no foul language, no sex, and no explicit nudity earned much more money on average than movies with some foul language, sex, and explicit nudity, or a lot of it, by 2 to 1 or more![20]

Movieguide makes a point to claim perhaps more influence on Hollywood than they deserve. Their website notes, "When we started in 1985, only 6 percent of the movies were aimed at families; by 2008, 45 percent of the movies released in theaters were aimed at families," while the number of R-rated films has also decreased during Movieguide's existence: "In 1985, 81 percent of the movies were rated R, but since 2001, less than 40 percent of the major movies released theatrically were R-rated." Their conclusion is that the cumulative activities of Movieguide "have led to a significant increase in the number of family-friendly and Christian-friendly movies over the past 21 years."[21]

I'll leave you to assess the trustworthiness of Movieguide's logic.

Toward a More Nuanced Christian Approach to Film

Not every Christian film critic ascribes to Ted Baehr's methods of evaluating movies, however, and increasingly, Christian approaches to engaging film are going beyond "curse counting" and "family friendliness" rubrics as methods of evaluating film. "Parents' guides" are still going strong, of course, but more and more Christians seem to be opening up to a relationship with cinema that is less about culture war defensiveness and more about thoughtful engagement.

Christian magazines like *Christianity Today*, *World*, and *Relevant* have for many years now been offering thoughtful reviews of all sorts of films, engaging with them not exclusively on the curse-counting content level but holistically, as works of art deserving a more balanced assessment. In general, Christian film criticism seems to be increasingly appreciative of quality filmmaking and narrative depth as opposed to questions of moral offensiveness. Websites like Patheos.com's Christ and Pop Culture channel, *The Other Journal*'s blog *Filmwell* and *Image* journal's "Arts and Faith" forum are evidence of the growing interest in a more intellectually robust Christian engagement with film.

If in the past, Christian approaches to film honed in on its portrayals of vice or virtue, today it seems that more and more Christians are focusing on whether or not a film is a truth-telling, honest work of art. In *Christianity Today*'s list of the ten "Most Redeeming" films of 2010—defined as "the year's best movies that include stories of redemption"— for example, three R-rated movies made the list: *The King's Speech*, *Winter's Bone*, and *The Fighter*.[22]

The 2011 Arts and Faith Top 100 Films list[23] is a good barometer of an increasing sophistication in the way Christians value and engage cinema. The list, voted on by sixty-five professional film writers and lecturers, lifelong cinephiles, seminary students, and ordinary movie fans, celebrates films with overt religious themes (*Jesus of Montreal*, *The Apostle*, *A Man for All Seasons*) but also films with "sublime expression of humane values" (*Tokyo Story*, *Bicycle Thieves*), "populist favorites" (*It's a Wonderful Life*), and "dreamy arthouse tone poems" (*Wings of Desire*).[24] It's telling that the list is made up of nearly two-thirds foreign language films with only a handful of films from the last ten years. Christians are increasingly exploring the history and aesthetic accomplishments of cinema, finding in secular and world cinema great truth and beauty with incredible relevance to the life of faith.

Too Far?

Though I applaud the positive advances that have been made in Christian approaches to cinema, I have wondered in recent years if there might be a danger of going too far. That is, in the movement away from legalistic and curse-counting approaches, have we gone too far in the other direction, embracing and affirming films too readily and indiscriminately?

Were the pangs of fundamentalist guilt that plagued my heart when I watched Kubrick's *Eyes Wide Shut* in my college dorm room as a freshman, or when I viewed Bertolucci's NC-17 *The Dreamers*, really such a bad thing? Or is it really okay for a Christian—in the name of artistic appreciation—to view pretty much anything?

What are we to make of churches that host screenings of R-rated films, or Christian websites and magazines that give 3-star reviews to films that are full of sex and nudity (full disclosure: I have written 3-star reviews of films like this for *Christianity Today*)? At what point should Christian viewers put on the brakes and say, "I'm sorry, but it's just not edifying to be viewing these images"?

This is a tricky question, complicated by all sorts of questions about subjective experience, Christian freedom, and "weaker/stronger brother" considerations. It's a question that vividly reveals the larger tension between legalism and license that evangelicals are continually dealing with. As Matthew Lee Anderson puts it:

> [Evangelicals] alternate between playing the legalist card when people attempt to draw lines about how Christians should or should not act, and playing the libertine card when others sanction their immoral actions with the gospel. We either have cheap grace or it doesn't exist at all. . . . We need to guard against conflating our understanding of Christian freedom with our culture's premise that freedom is our absolute right to do whatever we want without harming others.[25]

The question of Christian freedom, as it pertains to movies (among many other areas of culture), is a huge one. It's a big enough question that we must tackle it at length in the next chapter.

As we've seen, the consumer relationship between Christianity and movies has covered a broad spectrum in the last century: from censorship, protest, and cinephobia to curse-counting, criticism, and cinephilia. But within this vast spectrum, what sort of relationship with cinema should Christians strive for? What does it look like to be a Christ-following filmgoer?

* * * * * * * * * * *

Interlude

Comments on My Film Reviews

* * * * * * * * * * *

Writing film reviews for *Christianity Today*—"A Magazine of Evangelical Conviction"—has been a great experience for me over the years. Occasionally, however, and especially when I write a review of an R-rated film, my reviews (posted online) receive harsh comments from Christians wondering why such "filth" would even be viewed by a *CT* reviewer. Below is a sampling of some actual comments my reviews of R-rated films have received over the years (original grammar and punctuation preserved). These don't necessarily represent the majority opinion, mind you, but they do demonstrate that for many Christians even today, movies occupy very dangerous moral territory.

Revolutionary Road (2009)

"How can *CT* rate a film with 3 or 4 stars that will stumble people with female breast nudity. Then also to go on and have discussions starters."

Love and Other Drugs (2010)

"Shouldn't a Christian be Christlike? How/why does a Christian reviewer sit through this? You don't have to view the movie to know it is not going to give glory to God."

Taking Woodstock (2010)

"I think that No True Christian should be looking at any of these type of movies because it is anti-Christ, nothing of it is good and there is nothing good can come from it."

Black Swan (2010)

"Have no desire to see this movie. Why is *CT* recommending, even in a qualified way, something that sounds like absolute filth?"

The Girl with the Dragon Tattoo (2011)

"How can a Christian magazine recommend this movie? The preview I saw, and your review, reveal a very interesting plot, but rape, sex, nudity, etc., are not necessary except to arouse the senses in a very ungodly way. Shame on you for presenting this as something acceptable."

(On the other side of the spectrum): "I am so proud of *Christianity Today* for carefully, appropriately, and wisely appreciating this film. Way to go. Thanks for not being afraid to engage the edgy stuff. Well done."

* * * * * * * * * *

7

Where Do We Draw the Line?

* * * * * * * * * * *

A few years back I was traveling in Europe and happened to be in Paris for a few days on my own. One afternoon while strolling the Left Bank, I decided to take in a film: *Antichrist*, a new release from art-house director Lars von Trier. The movie was full of disturbing images that made anything from *The Exorcist* look saintly by comparison. When the lead actress (Charlotte Gainsbourg) drills a hole in Willem Dafoe's leg and puts in a big bolt with a millstone, it's one thing; when she takes scissors to her own sex organs, it's just too much. I walked out of the theater and have yet to see the ending of the film.

As a film critic, I see a lot of movies that are not necessarily pleasant to sit through. And indeed, a lot of my favorite films would hardly be categorized as "pleasant" viewing experiences. Films like *Breaking the Waves*, *Requiem for a Dream*, or a number of films by David Lynch or Quentin Tarantino, are, in my view, works of art, deeply disturbing though they may be.

But sometimes it's a fine line between "just far enough to make an impact" and "too far." Whether it's brutal violence, explicit sex, language, or just a general thematic fixation on nihilism, there is certainly a line that can be crossed—a line Christians must take seriously and seek to understand in mature and nuanced ways.

Christians have come a long way since the days of outright avoidance or censorship of cinema on account of its depictions of immoral behavior, yet we shouldn't go so far in the libertine direction that we deny that a "too far" might exist. Film is a medium too powerful to be approached flippantly or simplistically, from one direction or another. It deserves to be reckoned with in a deeper and more thoughtful way, and with a conscience.

This chapter is about giving Christians some tools to reckon with film in all of its gray-area glory—tools to make prudent choices about what to see (or not see) and how best to make sense of the "line."

From Avoidance to Divine Encounter

In his seminal book *Reel Spirituality: Theology and Film in Dialogue*, Robert K. Johnston organizes the narrative of Christian approaches to cinema along a continuum that reflects the chronology we observed in the previous chapter. Johnston describes five Christian approaches to film, from avoidance and caution (the early days of cinema) to dialogue, appropriation, and "divine encounter" (more recent)[1]:

> *Avoidance*: The boycott mentality. Movies are largely moral stumbling blocks for Christians; frequent moviegoing inhibits the spiritual impact of a believer. Abstinence is the best policy.

Caution: Christian viewers can watch movies, but they should do so carefully and with great caution and discernment, with evaluative attention focused on the ethical, religious, and moral content of films.

Dialogue: This approach attempts to bring film and theology into a two-way conversation. It emphasizes thoughtful consideration of film and resists snap judgments or dismissals of film based solely on objectionable moral content.

Appropriation: Recognizes that movies can offer insights for the Christian life. More than just being willing to "dialogue," this approach calls for Christian viewers to be open to encountering spiritual truth through film, letting a film enlarge our theological understanding.

Divine Encounter: The notion that movies can at times have "a sacramental capacity to provide the viewer an experience of transcendence."[2] This approach focuses on aesthetic beauty and believes that even if a filmmaker doesn't intend it to be, a film can be a celebration of grace.

Johnston's five approaches chart a gradual shift in focus for Christians in how they have encountered cinema: from primarily moral evaluation in the beginning to a more aesthetic evaluation today (though Johnston notes that all five approaches can still be found in various corners of Christianity).

Though some may see it as progress that Christians have moved beyond moral criticism and have placed larger emphasis on aesthetic criticism, I think it's important to note that there is value in *both* approaches. Certainly at times a film *can* provide "divine encounter," but at times there are also films that should be cleanly avoided. A healthy Christian approach to consuming film, I think, includes *both* moral and aesthetic considerations; indeed, they often inform each other and work together in one's overall assessment of a film.

Discernment in film-viewing is not an either-or proposition of focusing entirely on the number of sex scenes and f-bombs on one hand or the excellent cinematography and stellar acting performances on the other. We need to consider all of it. Discernment is a tricky business, much more complicated than a checklist or matrix of black-and-white criteria. And it begins on the inside, with an awareness that while discernment is a virtue we should all aspire to, it doesn't look exactly the same for all of us.

Discernment from the Inside Out

As we saw in the last chapter, one of the reasons movies have been feared, protested, or boycotted by Christians has been the perception that film is a powerful medium—that it can harm the psyche of passive consumers, inject torrid images into their memory banks, or cause people to mimic bad behavior. It's the idea that in the consumer-movie relationship, movies hold most of the influencing power.

In his book *The Seductive Image*, K. L. Billingsley notes that the content of movies is largely "nihilistic from the standpoint of belief, immoral from the standpoint of behavior, trash from the standpoint of art, and incompetent from the standpoint of craftsmanship," and that indeed, "films are powerful and influence behavior, especially that of young people, who possess great powers of imitation." And yet, Billingsley notes, "myriads of people, young and old, who regularly attend movies are relatively unaffected by them. . . . To assume that everyone will imitate what they see is practically to deny free will, spiritual discernment, or moral courage."[3]

Billingsley is wise to recognize that while it is true that film is often riddled with unseemly elements and hazardous depictions of sin, this doesn't mean that watching them will necessarily lead Christians astray. It's all about *how* we go about watching film. The burden is on us. There is no religious case against the movies themselves, notes Billingsley, "only against the abuse and misuse of them."[4]

Sex, Nudity, Violence, or Language: What's Worst?

When it comes to R-rated film content, is there a hierarchy of offensiveness? For Christians, it does seem like sex and nudity are seen as more problematic than violence or language. Überviolent films like *The Passion of the Christ*, *Saving Private Ryan*, and *Braveheart* are celebrated by many evangelicals, despite their arguably excessive violence. Offensive language also seems to generally be on the "less problematic" end of the spectrum. In the comments section of my review of Clint Eastwood's *Gran Torino*—an R-rated film containing numerous racial epithets and more than 70 f-words—readers on *Christianity Today's* website praised the film as "most excellent," "classic," and "the best Christian film I've seen this year." Only a few commenters even mentioned the foul language, with the consensus being that "the story of redemption and sacrifice outweighed the language or racial slurs."[5]

Meanwhile, any film with significant amounts of sex or nudity is typically seen as inappropriate for Christian viewers. The one comment posted on my review of *Taking Woodstock*—an R-rated film containing a fair amount of sex and nudity—read in part, "I think that No True Christian should be looking at any of these type of movies."[6] Part of this makes sense, given that sexual temptation often hits closer to home for most people than does the temptation to violence. As film critic Justin Chang notes, "It's a lot harder to uphold the biblical commandment to not lust or commit adultery than it is to not kill."[7] However, we must be careful to not universalize this. I know many people for whom blood and guts on screen affects them far more than sex or nudity. It seems that once again, the maxim "know your own weaknesses" applies here as well. Which is the worst? Only you can say.

Indeed, as with food, music, alcohol, tobacco, and pretty much everything else in culture that we might consume, movies are rarely inherently bad things. But they can *become* bad if we consume them recklessly or in an undiscerning manner.

And even if we go into a theater or put in a DVD in the most thoughtful, careful, discerning frame of mind, sometimes a film just goes too far. Sometimes the best thing to do is just press Stop or leave the theater. That's what happened when I saw *Antichrist*. It's essential that as Christians we recognize (1) that a line of "too far" *does* exist, and (2) that the line is different for everyone. There are some things we should just not be watching, but those pressure points are different for each of us.

Finding the Line: Five Considerations

How does one assess where "the line" exists for them? It's something I've thought about quite a bit on my own journey as a film critic, wondering if it's "worth" watching a brutal film for the sake of art, for example. The following are five practical considerations that I think can help make the question of "how far is too far?" a bit more manageable.

What Is Your Weakness?

The first thing to consider when trying to determine what's "too far" is to take stock of your own weaknesses and propensities. Where does sin strike you the hardest? In her article "Christians and Movies: Recognizing the Danger Within, Not Without," Christian film critic Rebecca Cusey hammers this home. "We must each do the hard work of recognizing our own weaknesses," she writes. "For some, it may be that sexual content does indeed feed a weakness within. Others may revel in the dark side of violence or evilly enjoy gruesome

158

scenes. For many women, the danger is a false depiction of romance, as in *Titanic*, which feeds the selfish dissatisfaction in our hearts with our spouses and families."[8] We all know our own weaknesses, and we must be real with ourselves when we consider whether or not to watch a film that dwells in the spaces of our struggles. Do you struggle with pornography? If so, it's probably a good idea to avoid films that contain explicit sex or nudity, no matter how artistic they may be.

What Are the Weaknesses in Your Community?

It's essential that the "what's appropriate" question be considered in terms of community. Moviegoing, after all, is typically something we do with others. What are the weaknesses of those around you? Maybe you don't struggle with lust when watching a film like *Mulholland Drive*; it's still probably not a good idea to show the film in the lounge of a college dorm, full of eighteen-year-old freshman boys. Be mindful of those around you and their struggles. Paul instructs Christians in 1 Corinthians 8–9 to bear with one another in love and not partake in something if it will make another "stumble" (8:13 ESV). In our moviegoing, we shouldn't dismiss someone who isn't "up to our level," who might not appreciate *Eyes Wide Shut* the way we do. We should respect those who decide to stay away from certain media and perhaps check ourselves in the process. Likewise for the abstainers: they shouldn't judge the "stronger brother" for what he can consume in good conscience.

Is It Beneficial?

In 1 Corinthians 6:12, Paul says "'I have the right to do anything,' you say—but not everything is beneficial." There is a "but" there, and it invites an active consideration of just what makes something "worth it," even if it's tough to watch. "I think this verse affirms the power of an informed faith to 'keep your foot from evil' (Prov. 4:27)," notes cultural critic Bill Romanowski. And yet "considering the biblical mandate to be 'in the world but not of it,' I also understand it to mean that we should establish habits and practices that support a fitting role for popular culture in our lives and society."[9] Thus, when we decide what among the infinite "permissible" items in pop culture to consume, we should think about this question of what is "beneficial." Would my time be better spent doing something else? Will the artistic benefit outweigh the rough content? Sometimes it's hard to know before you see a film. That's why reading critics and doing some homework beforehand can help. Have the previous films by the filmmaker been valuable, or have they been exploitative? Do the reviews mention that the film is "gratuitously raunchy"? If so, that might be a red flag.

Has the Filmmaker Earned the Right?

The "too far" question is moral but also aesthetic. This is something my film critic friend Justin Chang pointed to when I asked him how he determines the "line." Does a film's violence, nudity, or sex serve a necessary purpose in the story? Has the filmmaker earned the right? Chang—who writes film reviews for *Variety* and is a Christian—believes that when Christians evaluate the presence of gritty elements in film, they should consider the aesthetic purposes that content might serve. "I really liked *Irreversible*," notes Chang, "and it shows some of the most hideous imagery you'll ever see. But I think it also has a lot going on philosophically, and it leaves you feeling that rape and violence toward women are to be absolutely abhorred."[10] But if a filmmaker is simply showcasing explicit sex or violence to be provocative or push our buttons, or seems to be celebrating vice in some way, it's a different story. As Cusey points out, there is "a huge difference between an explicit movie with something to say (like *Knocked Up*) and one made purely for titillation."[11]

Have You Prayed about It?

Actually, this should probably be the first question you ask yourself. Have you *prayerfully* taken into account the questions above? Prayer is essential for any question of discernment or evaluation of a "gray area," something noted by Rebecca Ver Straten-McSparran, who helps Christian undergraduates think through these questions at the Los Angeles Film Studies Center. "Everything that is debatable or questionable must be taken first to prayer," she notes. "What is right or wrong has much more to do with a growing intimacy with God than rules that we follow out of guilt or choices made that are culturally comfortable," she adds. This means we must "thoughtfully search Scripture and make space and time to *listen* to what God is saying."[12]

Is There Value in Being Exposed to the Darkness?

At the heart of this discussion of "the line" is the question of what purpose darkness and evil might serve in art. It would be easy to just avoid art that is difficult, risqué, or R-rated, but something about the way the world is (that is, difficult, risqué, R-rated) tells us that to be truthful, art must grapple with the darkness of the world. As filmmaker Akira Kurosawa once said, "The artist is the one who does not look away."

There is truth to be found—sometimes most clearly—in the midst of, or on account of, darkness. Should we wallow in it? No. Should we seek it out? Surely not. But should we bear with it to some extent, toward the end of experiencing art? Probably.

It's very tempting to ignore difficult truth, or at least to hide from any of the truths that don't line up in the comfortable, familiar ways we want them to. But art has the ability to shake us out of our comfort zones and show us the realities of existence—both beautiful and ugly—we might otherwise look past or ignore.

We should also be open to the possibility that darkness is itself beauty, that there is "a potent and necessary dark side to God's beauty," and that it also reveals his truth—something Ver Straten-McSparran points out in a Princeton lecture on "The Dark Side of Beauty."[13]

In her lecture, Ver Straten-McSparran calls for a vision of the sublime in art that includes the dark side of beauty—"that combination of beauty, terror, and grandeur." She argues that "holy" cinema is not that which inspires us through superb acting, beautiful cinematography, and an inspiring story (*The King's Speech* is her example) but is that which truly "peels" us and jolts us: "The truly holy requires us to pay attention, to struggle to grasp hold of it. It is difficult. It may be disturbing. It requires, oh dear . . . suffering?"[14]

In depicting realistic darkness, art not only "peels" but can also serve as a vivid reminder of the world that ought to be. Darkness makes the light shine all the brighter, illuminating our eschatological hope. As Greg Wolfe has pointed out, "What is broken can still remind us of the need for wholeness."[15]

When it comes to hard-to-watch content in movies, then, we should always think in these "truth" terms. Hard to watch? For sure. But worth watching? In many cases, yes. We need to consider the aesthetic value of darkness, particularly in juxtaposition with the light. But we also shouldn't get too comfortable with the darkness. Darkness has its place and its purpose—and can in some cases even be beautiful—but it is not where we are meant to stay.

Worldliness vs. Holiness

Even if it may be artistic and "true," how does a Christian reconcile watching an R-rated, sex-filled film with the holiness they are called to ("Be holy, becase I am holy," 1 Peter 1:16)? The question raises valid concerns. Doesn't the regular viewing of immoral, titillating, explicitly violent cinema erode one's witness and impair one's path to holiness? Doesn't it numb and desensitize us?

Quite possibly. But the thing about holiness is that the point of it is not to steer clear of all that is unholy; it's not about retreating from "the world" and existing in some perfect space untainted by temptations and immoral sights and sounds. The point of holiness is positive: to live *in* the world, reflecting Christ and his holiness in the way that we live our lives. Holiness is more complicated than just abstaining from a checklist of vices. Does holiness require us to avoid certain activities? Certainly. But fleeing from potential hazards is only part of the story.

Likewise, "worldliness" is not as simple as engaging in a list of taboo activities: watching sketchy movies, gambling, dancing, or drinking. Rather, as K. L. Billingsley puts it, "the essence of worldliness is hubris, holding an inflated view of oneself or exalting oneself above others. Preventing that condition is a much trickier business than refusing to see *Ghostbusters* and chiding those who do."[16]

Should there be a noticeable difference between Christians and "the world"? Yes. Christians are called to be holy, set apart, sojourners and exiles in this world, bearing witness to the gospel through the way they live. But the difference between the church and culture is not a "hard" difference, notes Miroslav Volf in his analysis of 1 Peter (a key text on the nature of Christian difference).

163

For Christians, the distance from society that comes from the new birth in Christ is not meant to isolate from society, notes Volf, but rather serves the mission: "Without distance, churches can only give speeches that others have written for them and only go places where others lead them. To make a difference, one must be different."

Volf goes on to describe this "missionary distance" in 1 Peter as "soft difference," which is not to say weak difference:

> It is strong, but it is not hard. Fear for oneself and one's identity creates hardness. . . . In the mission to the world, hard difference operates with open or hidden pressures, manipulation, and threats. A decision for soft difference, on the other hand, presupposes a fearlessness which 1 Peter repeatedly encourages his readers to assume (3:14; 3:6). People who are secure in themselves—more accurately, who are secure in their God—are able to live the soft difference without fear. They have no need either to subordinate or damn others, but can allow others space to be themselves. For people who live the soft difference, mission fundamentally takes the form of witness and invitation. They seek to win others without pressure or manipulation, sometimes even "without a word" (3:1).[17]

Rather than holding an embattled, separatist, or hard-line "holiness vs. worldiness" approach to culture, I think Christians would do well to adopt Volf's "soft difference" mindset. Again, this is not to say the church should deny *any* difference from the world, or that it should be tepid or weak in its differentness; it's just to say that we shouldn't wield our difference as a weapon in a culture war, attacking the world for its worldliness and positioning ourselves arrogantly and with an oppositional attitude. Rather, our differentness should be positive, attractive, desirable. It should be conversational, relational. It's about witness. We should keep our conduct "honorable" for a missional purpose: so the world would "glorify God" (1 Peter 2:12 ESV).

For the sake of Christlike holiness, it may very well be the honorable thing for a Christian to not see a certain film. But those choices should be lived out as a positive affirmation of one's convictions rather than a negative chastisement of others, or of the film itself. Insofar as Christian identity is different from that of the surrounding culture (and it should be), it is a difference that is "constructed along the lines of its own internal vision of wholeness before God, and not through a negative process of rejecting outsiders."[18]

The Power of the Unseen

It has become popular for my generation of Christians to say things like "Christians should be known more for what they are *for* than for what they are against," and certainly this reflects an important truth. Our identity *should* radiate from an intrinsic, positive affirmation of the kingdom of God and the transforming work of the Holy Spirit in our lives, helping us to be holy as Christ is holy. But I think it's important to remember that the nature of our positive identity in Christ necessarily includes *some* negations—namely, avoiding sin. As new creations, we are to "put off your old self" (Eph. 4:22), avoiding a whole litany of vices mentioned throughout the Bible: sexual immorality, drunkenness, slander, adultery, deceit, greed, malice, envy, lust, and pride, to name just a few.

Thus, while our identity doesn't *derive* from our avoidance of certain things, it certainly should compel us to avoid certain things. Negation/avoidance of some things should be a natural outgrowth of the positive life in the Spirit. There's a witness in what we avoid. People notice when someone, as a matter of conviction, says no to something. It can be a very positive testimony.

When we're talking about how Christians should relate to the "world," I think it's useful to think about a distinction between "structure" and "direction." In *Desiring the Kingdom*, James Smith notes that on one hand, "the Scriptures affirm that the world as *structure* (as a given reality) is created by God and, as such, is fundamentally good. On the other hand, *world* is sometimes a sort of name given to human society that has taken the world (as structure) in the wrong *direction*."[19]

While Smith affirms that Christians should consider abstaining from certain cultural practices that might be considered normal by others, he argues that we shouldn't abstain from culture *as such* (the "structure"), but from its wrong directions. In this way, abstention "is a retreat not to weakness but to a different kind of power, the weak power of witness, the sort of strange power exerted by martyrs."[20]

For Christians engaging culture, there is certainly a time and place for selective abstinence. In the realm of moviegoing, if you know your weaknesses and your "line," then it follows that there will be certain films you will avoid. We shouldn't be ashamed to walk out of a theater if that line is crossed, or to not walk into a theater in the first place if we know the line will be crossed. But there's a good and a bad way to go about it. One can be thoughtful, quiet, well-informed, and—if asked—articulate in their reasoning to not see a film. Or one can be legalistic, loud, defensive, and simpleminded in their abstinence. In the latter case—a Christian refusing to see *Harry Potter* because it "promotes witchcraft," perhaps—the witness is a bad one for Christianity. But in the former case—a Christian humbly opting out of a screening of *American Pie* because for them, scenes of topless women

Above and Below the Line

Two films that hover around my own personal "line":

Shame: I was very conflicted about Steve McQueen's 2011, NC-17–rated film about sex addiction. It was being hailed by critics, and Michael Fassbender's performance as a struggling sex addict was praised as one of the year's best. Yet it was a film with quite a bit of explicit sexual content and nudity; hence its NC-17 rating. Ultimately I decided to see it, because I was a huge fan of director Steve McQueen's earlier film *Hunger* and wondered if *Shame* would equal its aesthetic depth. Was it worth it? For a one-time viewing, I would say yes. This is not to say I'd recommend it to anyone; I wouldn't and haven't. But it was artfully made and quite powerful; difficult, harrowing, but not exploitative; and artistically significant. Fassbender's performance was in my opinion the best of that year. For me, this film hovers above the "line" because it has such a serious, important exploration at its heart—the relational and spiritual deprivations of sex addiction—and probes it in a powerful, sobering manner.

Salò: Though banned in several countries upon its release in 1975, this controversial film from director Pier Paolo Pasolini—set in Mussolini's fascist regime—has been hailed as an important film by critics and historians and was released in 2008 by the Criterion Collection (which describes the film as "a masterpiece"). For these reasons, I rented it one day. As a film critic and scholar myself (I had just gone through a graduate program in film studies), I felt like it was a good idea to give it a try. I only made it about a third of the way through before ejecting the DVD. The images of sadism, abuse, and grotesque brutality were too much for me. Whatever social commentary or aesthetic goals the film possessed were for me overpowered by the unrelenting excess of obscenity on display. Though the shock value of the film's explicit imagery served a purpose, it was for me too far. I put *Salò* on the other side of my "too far" line from *Shame*, with the difference being that the latter had restraint and didn't go any further than it needed to.

are a stumbling block—the act of saying no can be a positive testimony.

In the art of filmmaking, the "unseen" is sometimes more powerful than the seen. What's happening off-camera, just beyond the frame? Alfred Hitchcock was a filmmaker who knew the power of the unseen very well. For Christians too, there is power in the unseen. There's value in leaving some things unwatched, some music unlistened to, some beverages unconsumed. We mustn't be afraid of saying no. We mustn't worry about being labeled prudes, cultural philistines, or legalists. Rather, we must focus on being more thoughtful, discerning consumers, willing to go deeper in our engagement and appreciation of the gray areas of culture, while also knowing our own limits and keeping our compass pointed in the direction of holiness.

* * * * * * * * * *

Interlude

*Thirty-three Films
That Take Faith Seriously*

* * * * * * * * * *

Christian moviegoers sometimes lament the dearth of good, positive, realistic portrayals of faith in film. If Christians are portrayed in film, they point out, it's usually as right-wing zealots (*Citizen Ruth*), scary Pentecostals (*Jesus Camp*), or psychotic killers (*Night of the Hunter*). Or faith is reduced to schmaltzy simplicity, as in most "Christian films" (*Facing the Giants, The Grace Card*). But many movies throughout film history have actually provided rich, artful portraits of faith. The following is a list of thirty-three films that take faith seriously—films I believe every Christian should make a point to see.

> *The Passion of Joan of Arc* (Carl Dreyer, 1928)
> *Diary of a Country Priest* (Robert Bresson, 1951)
> *Ordet* (Carl Dreyer, 1955)
> *Becket* (Peter Glenville, 1964)
> *The Sound of Music* (Robert Wise, 1965)
> *A Man For All Seasons* (Fred Zinnemann, 1966)
> *Brother Sun, Sister Moon* (Franco Zeffirelli, 1972)
> *Andrei Rublev* (Andrei Tarkovsky, 1973)
> *Chariots of Fire* (Hugh Hudson, 1981)

Tender Mercies (Bruce Beresford, 1983)
Amadeus (Milos Forman, 1984)
The Mission (Roland Joffé, 1986)
Babette's Feast (Gabriel Axel, 1987)
Jesus of Montreal (Denys Arcand, 1989)
The Decalogue (Krzysztof Kieslowski, 1989)
Shadowlands (Richard Attenborough, 1993)
Dead Man Walking (Tim Robbins, 1995)
The Apostle (Robert Duvall, 1997)
Central Station (Walter Salles, 1998)
Signs (M. Night Shyamalan, 2002)
Luther (Eric Till, 2003)
Land of Plenty (Wim Wenders, 2004)
Sophie Scholl: The Final Days (Marc Rothemund, 2005)
Into Great Silence (Philip Gröning, 2005)
Amazing Grace (Michael Apted, 2007)
Secret Sunshine (Lee Chang-dong, 2007)
A Serious Man (Joel and Ethan Coen, 2009)
Get Low (Aaron Schneider, 2009)
Letters to Father Jacob (Klaus Härö, 2009)
Of Gods and Men (Xavier Beauvois, 2011)
The Way (Emilio Estevez, 2011)
The Tree of Life (Terrence Malick, 2011)
Higher Ground (Vera Farmiga, 2011)

* * * * * * * * * *

8

The Art and Pleasure of Moviegoing

* * * * * * * * * *

I've been a moviegoer my whole life (like most people of my generation) and a film critic for the last ten years. When I was younger, I was a big fan of Steven Spielberg films (like everyone else in their youth). I remember seeing *Indiana Jones and the Last Crusade*, *Hook*, and *Jurassic Park* in the theater as a kid. In my adulthood, I've not abandoned Spielberg (I loved *A.I.* and *Lincoln*), but my tastes have become somewhat less mainstream. The reclusive Terrence Malick (*The Tree of Life*) is now my favorite filmmaker, and has been since *The Thin Red Line* changed the way I thought about cinema when I was a freshman in high school. I also like the films of "art house" directors Jim Jarmusch, Sofia Coppola, David Lynch, and the Dardenne Brothers. I love foreign films, read indie film blogs, attend film festivals, and host film screenings/discussions on occasion. When Malick's *The Tree of Life* came out in May 2011, I dedicated my blog to Malick for the whole month and hosted an after-party in Hollywood for thirty friends on opening night. Yes, I am a film nerd.

I'd say filmgoing is, from time to time, a worshipful experience for me. It doesn't take the place of church, of course, but in a very real sense it can be an experience quite similar to church: a quiet, large room, filled with a wide swath of humanity immersed in an often very emotional, engrossing, powerful narrative. It's no wonder movie theaters have been called "the church of the masses."

Like church, an experience in a movie theater can be as shallow or as meaningful as you make it. Movies are sometimes (perhaps most of the time) merely an easy, diversionary amusement. We leave the theater unchanged. But movies can also be quite profound, even life changing. They can enhance communities and spark lively conversation; they can show us things we've never seen and confront us with truth in jarring ways. And perhaps most vitally for the Christian consumer, a movie can most certainly bear witness to the majesty of God and the beautiful complexity of his creation.

Once we've decided to watch a film (having gone through the discernment questions discussed in the previous chapter), what can we do to make sure we're making the most of the experience? As someone whose faith has been enriched by this area of culture above all others, I'm passionate about this question. But before we get to some specific suggestions for maximizing our moviegoing, let's take a moment to reflect on the tension between art and entertainment—a dialectic that is present in most areas of culture but perhaps most vividly in the world of cinema.

Are Movies Art or Entertainment?

Short answer: the best ones are both. But of course the discussion goes further than that. It's complicated.

"Film as art" is an idea resisted by many, in part because from its inception film has been a "popular" or "mass" amusement—cheap and accessible to wider swaths of humanity than, say, the opera. In its relatively young history (barely a century old), cinema has been quite commercially lucrative and more associated with "fun" diversions like amusement park rides or baseball games than "serious" activities like reading or visiting an art museum. If one considers a given art form along the "high" versus "low" continuum, cinema has been mostly associated with the lower end. But what does that actually mean?

In his book *Art Needs No Justification*, Hans Rookmaaker suggests that the division between "high" and "low" art ultimately causes all art to suffer:

> High Art has shunned all practical demands, such as decoration, entertainment or in fact any role that might smack of involvement in real life. Yet this type of art inevitably attracts almost everybody who has some talent. . . . But inevitably the "low" arts have suffered also. They became the "popular" arts, sometimes called "commercial." It is art in the service of Mammon. As all genuinely talented people tend to shun this field, its quality has deteriorated, and too often what is produced lacks all imagination or quality.[1]

I agree with Rookmaaker that this division has unfortunately produced a needlessly simplistic binary, pitting the "commercial" against the "artistic," as if something cannot ever be both. Thus, because movies are so commercially minded (by necessity of the high costs involved in film production, distribution, and exhibition, they must make money and be subject to the market), they have sometimes had a difficult time being taken seriously as an art form.

The result of cinema's commercial/mass/low culture reputation is that audiences tend not to expect to be intellectually challenged by an experience in the movie theater. "It's only a movie. Why should I have to think?" is a fairly common sentiment. People go into a theater with a different frame of mind from the way they might go into a museum. In the latter case, they're looking to be educated or challenged; in the former, to be entertained.

But can't it be both? Can't we think of a movie as something wholly entertaining but also as intelligent, challenging, and artistic? Part of what I want to argue in this chapter is that

Rethinking "High" and "Low" Culture

I'd like to reimagine "high" and "low" culture not in terms of their old stereotypes—aristocratic vs. plebeian tastes, opera boxes vs. reality television—but in terms of how high or low something takes us in the upward path toward sublime epiphany. In this way, high and low would look more like this:

High culture: That which reaches for greater heights of transcendence and truth, seeking to reveal—often in pleasurable and entertaining fashion—beauty and goodness honestly and with excellence. Pays attention to craft, believes in meaning, and exudes humility.

Low culture: That which hovers closer to the base or surface, incurious and uninterested in truly wrestling with truth or achieving the sublime/transcendent. It is indulgent and undisciplined, more interested in esoteric obfuscation than true discovery.

In this new understanding, a work of art could be considered high culture even if viewed by millions on YouTube each week, and plenty of contemporary art on the walls of prestigious New York galleries could be considered low culture. This new understanding requires us to think more critically, beyond the simplistic associations (summer blockbusters equal low culture; foreign language films equal high culture) and with deeper considerations of what a work is actually contributing to culture.

a better form of consumption—when it comes to movies but also music, food, and so on—is a consumption that doesn't operate in the oppositional terms of "art vs. entertainment" or "high culture vs. low culture." Because the truth is, not all "high culture" or "art" is good quality, just as not all pop culture or entertainment is superficial. Those categories aren't usually the most helpful; they tend to reinforce problematic hierarchies of class and taste more than they improve the overall experience and appreciation of goodness, truth, or beauty.

Indeed, we must be open to seeing value in art *and* entertainment, broadening our definitions of both and recognizing that they aren't mutually exclusive. Very entertaining things can also be artfully made and profound; and the artsiest of artsy things can also—that's right—be pleasurable.

What Do the Critics Know?

Because film has been viewed primarily as a populist medium for "the masses," the masses in turn feel like they can assess a film's merits without any guidance from the critics. Everyone has an opinion about movies, and critics whose opinions are out of step with the common man's views are often derided as elitist.

As a critic myself, I know we can sometimes make the problem worse by endlessly praising art films that few people have heard of while dismissing the mainstream fare that audiences turn out for in great numbers. It's important that critics, like everyone else, resist the "art vs. entertainment" binary and adopt an openness to giving praise where it's due (even if it's a Michael Bay blockbuster or Will Ferrell comedy). That said, I believe there is value in analysis by film critics who know what they're talking about and can help viewers process the merits of a film. Rather than seeing a film critic's praise of art films as elitist, I would hope that one could see it as a beneficial service in bringing to light quality films and helping audiences understand the context and nuances of a film's achievements.

As Justin Chang points out, "Nobody calls the ballet critic or literary critic an elitist, but movie critics are elitist because they're trying to hold the medium to something higher," which is something audiences frequently resist. They want their movies to be simple, direct. But that approach misses out on the layers of depth that can be uncovered if one opens up to the possibility of film as art.

Good film criticism is "looking beyond the surface of things," notes Chang. "And film, above all mediums, is *so* much about surfaces. Looking beneath it is kind of necessary."

Chang is saddened by what he calls the "small-minded allergy to the idea that cinema is worth talking about as an art form," something that he encountered in conversations he had with readers about *The Tree of Life*. Several people complained to Chang that Malick's film didn't make its points fast enough, to which Chang responded by saying that "it's a film, not a PowerPoint presentation."

People tend to want a film's points made quickly and its pleasures immediate, observes Chang. "The idea that you might sit in a movie and have a meditative or spiritual experience is seen as a little weird," notes Chang, who also heard one person comment that *The Tree of Life* felt like it should have been shown at a museum rather than a movie theater.

These sentiments underscore the difficulty people have in conceiving of film as a serious art form and enjoying it on that level. That's something critics like Chang and myself would like to see change.

Going to the Movies to Think: Not Such a Bad Thing

How many times have you heard someone say, "Oh no, is this one of those *thinking* movies?" I wince every time I hear it. Is having to think during a movie really such a bad thing? It doesn't have to feel like going to the dentist. On the contrary, being able to think critically while watching a film can enhance rather than detract from the pleasures of the experience. For Christians, approaching film in a thinking way also shows the world that we care: not just to be amused and entertained, but to glean all the value out of a film that we can. It shows that we care to explore all that a filmmaker wants to show us and that we respect the creator of the work enough to do a little interpretive work.

Like myself, my friend Eugene Suen—a filmmaker of faith and former co-director of the Reel Spirituality Institute at Fuller Seminary—bristles at the unwillingness of Christian audiences to experience films that are challenging or slow or which contain an unorthodox narrative structure (like *The Tree of Life*).

"It's a shame when anything that even remotely deviates from traditional narrative ('acceptable') cinema is seen as alienating, boring, and pretentious," notes Suen. He sees this as symptomatic of a fundamental lack of openness, "an openness that we need as human beings—indeed, as Christians—in order to enlarge ourselves and arrive at a genuine understanding of others."

Cinema is a complex, fluid, fascinating art form, notes Suen, and Christians should adopt a more open-minded attitude toward it. He says:

> If Christians can work up the same kind of empathy and openness towards films (of whatever forms and styles) that

they exhibit towards people they are trying to reach and
help, they would be deeply enriched, and we would not have
the kind of unnecessary dichotomies (film as art vs. film as
entertainment, film as education vs. film as escapism) that
seem to plague our understanding of cinema and the arts at
large. How we encounter a work of art is but an aspect of
how we need to live.[2]

The value we derive from something is directly propor-
tional to the effort we put forth to engage it. Whether we're
talking about relationships, jobs, cooking, painting, or par-
enting, we derive the most pleasure from that which we work
the hardest at. A passive consumer, who sits back and takes
something in without much thought or interpretive effort,
is not going to have as full or invested an experience as the
consumer who takes a more active interpretive role.

When you meet a filmmaker halfway, doing some of the
work of interpretation rather than just sitting back passively,
you often admire a film all the more. You take more ownership for it, becoming—in a way—a creative force as crucial
as the artist who actually made the work. This goes for other
aspects of culture too: if you do the work of learning the
nuances of wine varietals, you'll likely enjoy wine tasting
more; if you do the work of researching the historical and
aesthetic context of painting, your experience of a gallery
will be more satisfying.

Of course there are also pleasures more immediate and
visceral in art and culture, which we shouldn't discount. A
Monet painting or salted caramel chocolate torte are pleasing
to the eye and the tongue, respectively, regardless of whether
one has any knowledge of Impressionism or *Fleur de sel*. But
the point is: knowledge rarely *detracts* from our experience
of culture; it enhances it.

Television Can Be Art Too!

Early in its history, American television was described as a "vast wasteland" by FCC Chairman Newton Minow,[3] and for much of its history television has had a hard time shedding that reputation. It has largely been perceived as populist, mindless amusement for the slovenly masses —"the boob tube"—with little or no nutritional value and nary a shred of artistic dignity. But television *can* be art too, and the last decade has made this exceedingly clear with shows like *The Sopranos*, *Mad Men*, *Breaking Bad*, *Friday Night Lights*, *Arrested Development*, *The West Wing*, *The Wire*, and others that match or surpass the quality of the best cinema or theater out there. The shift happened largely in the 2000s, "the first decade when television became recognizable as art, great art: collectible and life-changing and transformative and lasting."[4] Sure, television is still rife with brain-dulling content—reality dating shows and Kardashian spinoffs are still ubiquitous—but there is also a lot of very enriching material to be found, and television can be an edifying experience if approached in the right way.

Popular, *Escapist*, and *Pleasurable* Are Not Four-Letter Words

Is it okay to laugh at an Adam Sandler joke? What if I actually loved *Anchorman*? Sometimes you hear "sophisticated" film connoisseurs whispering about such things, as if they'd lose all credibility if they dared enjoy a popular film. But they need to loosen up. One of the reasons many people are leery of critics is precisely because so many of them come across as cynical, stuffy, disconnected, and bored by anything remotely resembling popular escapism, as if entertainment should never be fun. But such critics are missing the point. Escapism isn't automatically a bad thing. One shouldn't feel shame for embracing the lightness and triviality of entertainment.

One could argue, actually, that all art is escapist—insofar

as it puts parentheses on our everyday life, gives us a Sabbath-like reprieve from time, and transports us to another place, through "windows" onto the world provided by a film frame, a picture frame, a theater stage, or an orchestra hall. *Toy Story* and *Avatar* are escapist, but so is a film like *The Tree of Life*, which may be more difficult and artistic but is no less escapist in the sense that it sucks you in and transports you to another place. Indeed, we should not evaluate a film on whether or not it is escapist—because most films, by definition, are—but rather by how it engages us in that escapism: Does it heighten or sharpen our senses, or does it dull them? Does it involve our emotions in a truthful, honest manner, or does it cheaply manipulate them? Is the world it shows us true? Some of the greatest "crowd-pleasing" films—*The Lord of the Rings*, *Harry Potter*, the Dark Knight films, and so on—are escapist in the most positive sense and shouldn't be scoffed at.

We must be open to the idea that something that is escapist, entertaining, or pleasurable can also be artful and excellent. As Hans Rookmaaker states,

> In a way all art is entertainment, the God-given opportunity to relax with good music, with good art, a fine book. And there is nothing wrong with a ballad, with dance music (Mozart made quite a bit of it), or with making cartoons, posters, illustrations. But whatever one does, it has to have quality.[5]

We must be wary of approaching the arts from an aloof posture that devalues pleasure. Various approaches to (over) analysis and deconstruction of cultural texts admittedly suck all the joy out of the experience. And that's unfortunate, because fundamental to art and culture is joy. As Dana Gioia recently said in a lecture at Biola University, "The good thing about the arts is that they lead by pleasure. . . . One must begin in joy."[6]

Indeed, Alan Jacobs's advice for readers of books could apply, I think, to enjoyers of any of the arts. "Read what gives you delight—at least most of the time—and do so without shame," he writes, adding that one shouldn't make "the Great

12 Ways to Be a Better Television Viewer

- Don't watch too much television alone. That can be a dangerous habit.
- Don't watch an entire season of a television series in one weekend binge (on Netflix, DVD, etc.). Spread it out!
- Talk about television shows with others. Find friends in your workplace with whom you can have watercooler chats.
- Read "episode recaps" and reviews after you watch something. You can find some great writing about television these days.
- Apply the same discernment principles to television as you'd apply to movies (see chap. 7).
- Be extra careful with shows rated "TV-MA." It doesn't necessarily mean you shouldn't watch them. Just be careful.
- Be present. Don't write emails, surf the internet, or go overboard multitasking while also watching a show (except during a commercial break).
- Throw parties for "big event" television: live sports events, award shows, season finales, etc.
- Try to read as much as you watch television. Being conversant in literature helps one better appreciate television as art.
- Get outside or otherwise be physically active more than you're sitting in front of the TV.
- Recognize the unique advantages television storytelling has over movies, such as the ability to tell longer, more complex stories over the course of many seasons.
- Throw out your expectations of how television should be paced. Slow, subtle shows are sometimes the best ones.
- It's okay to have one or two "guilty pleasure" shows. But maybe just stay away from *The Bachelor*.

Books" one's "steady intellectual diet, any more than you would eat at the most elegant of restaurants every day. It would be too much."[7]

Far from a marker of "low" culture or mindless diversion, enjoyment is rightly fundamental to the experience of art. Anyone seeking to better appreciate a work of art therefore should not fear pleasure but should embrace it. Engagement with art and culture does frequently involve work, but it is work that should be joy-giving rather than tedious. And this goes for critics especially. The vocation of a critic should begin in love, not obligation, because when we love something, we hold it to a higher standard. Better criticism, better consumption, flows directly out of—not in opposition to—love, joy, and pleasure.

Getting More Out of Moviegoing: Three Suggestions

Moving beyond an allergy to "artsy" cinema is one thing; making the most of the moviegoing experience is another. How does one engage a film thoughtfully, maximizing not only the pleasure of the experience but also one's active intellectual engagement with it? The following are three suggestions I've found helpful in my own moviegoing life.

Appreciate Beauty

In their evaluation of culture—movies, music, paintings—Christians have in the past tended to emphasize content/message over aesthetics, which is a shame. Much joy can be found in an understanding of the stylistic particularities of a film and much beauty discovered. Christians of all people should place a high premium on beauty and artistry, even if it seems superfluous. Why? Because God seems to care about beauty, as Philip Ryken points out in *Art for God's*

Sake, where he describes the tabernacle, with its abundance of purely decorative elements, as something proving "that beauty has its own intrinsic value."[8] Recognizing and experiencing beauty can be a profound experience of worship as we glory in the creation God has given us, with all its attendant groanings, complexities, and "superfluous" grandeur. As Christians we should be keenly interested in humanity's mysterious penchant to identify something as beautiful and to be moved by it. The existence, recognition, and experience of beauty are indicators that there is something bigger afoot in this world. Being more attuned to beauty in the culture we encounter helps us to see it more clearly in the everyday, fixing our eyes more closely on the awe and wonder of God, the Creator and Artist behind all things.

Slow Down

These days we consume media at a breakneck pace: skimming articles on our Twitter feeds and Google Readers, listening to Pandora playlists on our headphones, squeezing in television episodes as we ride the subway to work—sometimes all of these at the same time. And when we're done with one bit of media, we quickly move on to the next. The downside of such a harried pace is that we often leave no room for *processing*. We may discuss a movie in the five minutes between leaving the theater and getting in the car, but often it stops there; we've moved on. Sometimes we don't even have that. The credits roll and we press Stop, open our laptops, and move on to another media encounter.

But taking time to slow down and digest something like a movie can really enrich the experience. Some of my favorite films only became my favorites after I revisited them for a second or third viewing, giving myself time and distance to consider them more fully. The same principle goes for other cultural experiences, like music. The richness and beauty of an album rarely reveals itself on the first listen; it takes multiple listens to learn to appreciate it. Coffee doesn't taste beautiful the first time one tries it. Nor does wine. The best things in life require more than just a passing assessment to be truly appreciated. As Alan Jacobs advises: "Slow down. . . . Chew the textual cud for a while before sending it to the further stomachs of your mind: you may well spare yourself a case of heartburn later."[9]

Develop Your Taste, but Also Humility

Everyone has their own tastes and preferences when it comes to movies (or any aspect of culture). And that's okay. I really like 1950s film noir, documentaries, and anything directed by David Fincher. Others might prefer Japanese anime or John Hughes comedies. It's valuable to recognize one's own tastes and preferences. But one should also be humble enough to listen to the opinions of others, read critics, and be open to venturing outside one's comfort zone. Sometimes developing taste begins with open-mindedness and intellectual humility, a willingness to try rather than dismiss that which is different. Having said that, you shouldn't feel obligated to fall in line with the critics or prevailing opinion about a work of art. It's okay to have a difference of opinion. As Chuck Klosterman says,

> If you really have integrity—if you truly live by your ideals, and those ideals dictate how you engage with the world at large—you will never feel betrayed by culture. You will simply enjoy culture more. You won't necessarily start watching syndicated episodes of *Everybody Loves Raymond*, but you will find it interesting that certain people do. You won't suddenly agree that *Amelie* was a more emotive movie than *Friday Night Lights*, but you won't feel alienated and offended

if every film critic you read tells you that it is. You will care, but you won't care.[10]

A Word about "Christian" Movies

Before moving on from our discussion of movies, let me say a few words about the "Christian" movie genre: films like *Blue Like Jazz* (2012), *Courageous* (2011), *Seven Days in Utopia* (2011), *To Save a Life* (2010), *Fireproof* (2008), *One Night With the King* (2006), and *Jonah: A VeggieTales Movie* (2002). They tend to be G- or PG-rated films—safe for the whole family—focused on promoting Christian values or a clear gospel message. End-times themes are also popular fodder (*The Omega Code*, *Left Behind*, etc.).

As Christians seeking to be more thoughtful consumers of film, what should we make of "Christian" movies? My short answer is that we should approach this genre of film in the same way we should approach any other, evaluating it with the same criteria we would evaluate anything. Unfortunately, most Christian filmmakers tend to suffer from the same problem that has plagued Christian *consumers* of film: a prioritizing of content over artistry and an emphasis on message over excellent craft. The result is often films that are preachy and moralizing, with filmmaking styles that are clichéd or antiquated, acting that is cheesy or overwrought, and an overarching style that is aesthetically uninteresting and sometimes distractingly bad.

But it's too easy to just harp on how terrible Christian films are. The bigger question is whether or not the genre is even necessary. What makes one film "Christian" and another not? If it contains a clear presentation of the gospel, is it automatically a "Christian" film? If the filmmakers are Christian, do we call their films "Christian films"? Or is the term perhaps only fitting for movies that are made by Christian churches?

It seems to me that we should think, once again, about common grace—the idea that "God in his infinite wisdom did not give all his gifts to Christians."[11]

The idea of common grace should enlarge our categories for what we deem "Christian" and "non-Christian." Bach's *St. Matthew Passion* is Christian, but so are his *Brandenburg Concertos*, notes Rookmaaker. "Not only the words or the cantatas are Christian, but also the instrumental parts of them."[12]

This is a key idea that Christian filmmakers have sometimes missed: the *form* of their films is just as or more important than the message. Making movies that are excellent, groundbreaking, and beautiful is absolutely vital. Works of art that focus on excellence are the ones that frequently have the most long-term kingdom impact. The priority in art-making shouldn't be overt evangelizing, notes Rookmaaker, but making beautiful art for the glory of God:

> Handel with his *Messiah*, Bach with his *Matthew Passion*, Rembrandt with his *Denial of St. Peter*, and the architects of those Cistercian churches were not evangelizing, nor making tools for evangelism; they worked to the glory of God. They did not compromise their art. They were not devising tools for religious propaganda or holy advertisement. And precisely because of that they were deep and important. Their works were not the means to an end, the winning of souls, but they were meaningful and an end in themselves, to God's glory, and showing forth something of the love that makes things warm and real. Art has too often become insincere and second-rate in its very effort to speak to all people, and to communicate a message that art was not meant to communicate.[13]

We should certainly support Christian filmmakers. But we shouldn't coddle them, and we shouldn't encourage low-quality work. We should hold them to a higher standard, spurring them on to excellence so that what they produce opens viewers' eyes to the magnificence of our gracious God. And as Christian consumers who care about honoring God through the arts, we should simply support *the best*—the most truthful, beautiful, God-glorifying—whether it is made by the hands of a Christian or a pagan.

Dangerous Beauty

As we've seen in this section, the relationship between Christians and cinema has been frequently rocky, fraught with plenty of perceived dangers both real and imaginary. Even as a verified cinephile and apologist for the form, I would be deceiving myself if I ignored or downplayed the very serious perils that can accompany a reckless, indiscriminate or excessive consumption of movies. Christians may have gone overboard in the past in their confrontational, separatist, hands-off approach to Hollywood, but it would be equally problematic to err on the other side—embracing cinema uncritically, without careful discernment. The reality is that cinema, like so many areas of culture, has the potential to be beautiful, life-giving, even transcendent, but it also has the potential to be degrading, exploitative, addictive, and desensitizing. Every good thing can become a bad thing if enlisted in the service of sinful desires.

Like so much beauty in the world, the beauty of film is dangerous. But that doesn't mean we should abandon it and hide away, just to be "safe" and untempted. If we do that, we're not only missing out on the opportunity to see the world more clearly through the lenses and frames of artists; we're also missing out on the chance to grow in faith and the knowledge of God.

PART 4

DRINKING

The fourth and final area of culture to be explored in this book is easily the most controversial: alcohol. It's a dicey, dangerous topic, one that has long divided Christians and is fiercely debated even today. Should Christians be okay with consuming alcoholic beverages? Is abstinence the most or only biblical approach? Solid believers stand on both sides of these questions. On any given Sunday, millions of Christians across the world imbibe wine as part of the Eucharist; some drink a beer together with fellow churchgoers at an afternoon potluck or sip a scotch while discussing deep theological matters with their pastor. Many other churchgoers gulp grape juice during communion in congregations where alcohol usage is frowned upon or banned completely.

The question of alcohol usage for Christians is an explosive one, in part because the stakes are so high. On the one hand, alcohol can be a deadly addiction and has, in many lives over many millennia, been a source of immense destruction. On the other hand, it can be a thing of great beauty: wine tasting with a loved one, sipping good bourbon on a porch with a close friend, enjoying a cold glass of beer with co-workers after a long day, and so on. But it can easily become something less than beautiful. Drunkenness is always an unflattering thing—ugly and unbecoming, especially for those supposedly representing Christ.

How *should* Christians consume alcohol? Is there a healthy, God-glorifying way to drink, avoiding abuse without having to abstain completely? The next three chapters will wrestle with these questions. Chapter 9 will consider what the Bible has to say about alcohol, while chapter 10 will summarize the history of Christianity's relationship with fermented beverages. Chapter 11 will then set forth some principles for a healthier Christian approach to the consumption of alcohol, bringing to bear many of the principles established in the earlier sections of this book and offering a climax of sorts for the vision of cultural consumption we've been developing.

* * * * * * * * * * *

Interlude

No Drinking Here!

M any evangelical colleges and universities require students to sign pledges to abstain from alcohol usage while they're enrolled. This was the case for me as an undergraduate at Wheaton College, and it's also the case for me now as a thirtysomething part-time seminary student at Talbot School of Theology (Biola University). Is it ridiculous to require people in their thirties to abstain from drinking alcohol while enrolled as graduate students? Some may think so, but I've made the choice to abide by the rule whenever I'm enrolled in a class.

For me it's not a matter of whether I believe it's an entirely sensible rule. It's not always our place to understand *why* a rule has been established. Personally, I think seminary would be a much more joyful experience if it included the occasional discussion of Christology over an oatmeal stout. But because the rule is in place and it is the *community* rule, I will abide by it and forgo the educational enhancements of brew. It's only for a short time, after all. When the semester ends, my fellow seminary abstainers and I usually celebrate the end of finals with a trip to a local pub.

Abstaining from something for the sake of the community is a very fine reason to abstain. From my perspective, drinking alcohol may be a perfectly biblical, perfectly Christian thing to do. But if for others in my community it is a hardship or a temptation, then by all means I will abstain. For Christians, the ascetic call to deny ourselves perfectly good things for the sake of a community or a commitment is a worthy pursuit. It's Christlike. Drinking alcohol can be a God-glorifying activity—just ask Martin Luther and John Calvin—but *not* drinking it can be too.

* * * * * * * * * * *

9

A Biblical History
of Intoxicating Beverages

* * * * * * * * * * *

To properly kick off our discussion of alcohol in the Christian life, we must begin with the Bible. Of course, the Bible doesn't have anything to say about craft beer, cocktails, tequila, or Heineken, but wine *did* exist in Bible times and was actually quite ubiquitous.

Does Scripture clearly prohibit the consumption of wine, or does it allow for moderate consumption (that is, drinking that doesn't lead to drunkenness)?

Biblical scholars have taken every position on this question. On one end of the spectrum you have folks like Stephen Reynolds (author of *The Biblical Approach to Alcohol*), who argues that the Bible teaches "an absolute prohibition against the beverage use of alcohol,"[1] and John MacArthur, who in a 2011 blog post on alcohol and Christianity said, "It is puerile and irresponsible for any pastor to encourage the recreational use of intoxicants."[2] Then there are those on the other end such as Scot McKnight, who maintains, "The Bible does not demand total abstinence from alcohol for all of God's people,"[3] and Kevin DeYoung, who says, "I don't believe you can condemn alcohol from the Bible."[4]

In the following chapter we'll take a look at how alcohol figures into the narrative of the Bible. Rather than methodically analyzing every pertinent text from Genesis to Revelation, we'll take a thematic approach, focusing on five big themes. But before we do, let me address a central question that tends to be one of the most hotly contested in any discussion of this sort.

Was the Wine Described in the Bible Really Intoxicating?

Central to the arguments of the prohibitionist approach (those who claim the Bible forbids the drinking of intoxicating beverages) is the claim that the most common words for wine in the Bible—the Hebrew *yayin* and the Greek *oinos*—do not necessarily refer to fermented, alcoholic wine. Reynolds, for example, argues that *yayin* and *oinos* should not be assumed to always mean "intoxicants."[5] This "two wine" approach suggests that when the Bible uses these terms in positive ways (associated with blessings and eschatological joy, for example), the wine in question is of the nonintoxicating kind, while the occasions in which it describes something negative (sin, judgment, drunkenness) refer to a different, fermented/intoxicating type of wine.[6] But many other scholars contest this, noting that there is no evidence in Scripture that the words *yayin* and *oinos* refer to different things at different times and that it is an unwarranted jump to read those distinctions into the text.

Kenneth Gentry says in *God Gave Wine*, "The Scripture itself never draws a distinction between 'safe' and 'unsafe' *yayin"* and "never commands us to avoid alcoholic *yayin* while encouraging us to consume only the non-alcoholic product of the grape."[7] Gentry notes that *yayin*—which is mentioned 144 times in the Old Testament—clearly refers to a fermented beverage, from its first mention (Noah becoming intoxicated by drinking it in Gen. 9:21) and throughout the Hebrew Scriptures, even when it is associated with joyful blessings (e.g., Ps. 104:14–15). Likewise *oinos*, the Greek equivalent to *yayin* that is referenced 33 times in the New Testament, also means fermented wine in all cases, argues Gentry. It is the word used by Paul in instructing Christians to not get drunk (see Eph. 5:18) as well as in the story of the wedding feast at Cana, when Jesus performs his first miracle by turning water into high-quality *oinos* (see John 2:1–11).

More could be said about the lexical analysis of the various words in Scripture referring to wine, but for the purposes of this book I am going to side with Gentry and the "one wine" approach, given that Scripture never clearly indicates otherwise. And if this is so, we can't get off the hook with a black-and-white understanding of alcohol—that it is either entirely prohibited or entirely permissible. As we will see in the five themes examined in the remainder of this chapter, alcohol in the Bible is more of a gray area than that. It's something good that can also become bad; a blessing that can also be a curse; a symbol of both worldliness and the kingdom of God.

Theme #1: Drunkenness Is a Sin

The Bible is extremely clear that *drunkenness* is a sin. Drinking to excess leads to bad things in the Bible. It wreaks havoc in the lives of Noah (see Gen. 9:20–28), Lot (see Gen. 19:30–38), Elah (see 1 Kings 16:8–10), and numerous other biblical figures. It elicits God's wrath (see Jer. 13:12–14; Lam. 4:21–22; Ezek. 23:28–33). It causes men to be "stubborn and rebellious" (Deut. 21:20), to "stagger" (Ps. 60:3), to be "inflamed" (Isa. 5:11), and to lose "understanding" (Hos. 4:11). The heavy drinker and glutton "will come to poverty" (Prov. 23:21 ESV), and the drunkard will not "inherit the kingdom of God" (1 Cor. 6:10). Those who are intoxicated by strong drink are "not wise" (Prov. 20:1).

Paul is especially clear on the condemnation of drunkenness. He instructs believers to "not get drunk on wine" (Eph. 5:18), to "behave decently as in the daytime, not in carousing and drunkenness" (Rom. 13:13), and to not even fellowship with drunkards (see 1 Cor. 5:11). Those who indulge "acts of the flesh" such as drunkenness "will not inherit the kingdom of God" (Gal. 5:19–21). The New Testament also forbids drunkenness on the basis that it impairs the believer's preparedness for the return of the Lord (see Luke 21:34; Rom. 13:11–14; 1 Thess. 5:6–8).

And this just scratches the surface. The Bible is clear that drunkenness is a sin leading to destruction and warranting the wrath of God; any Christian who willingly seeks out alcohol for the purposes of intoxication is living in blatant, sinful rebellion. But just because Scripture condemns the abuse, as Gentry says, "it does not necessarily follow that it also condemns moderate, occasional, and temperate drinking of alcoholic beverages,"[8] which we will see clearly as we further explore some of the other big themes of alcohol in the Bible.

Theme #2: Joy and Blessing

In contrast to the negative connotations associated with alcohol abuse is the biblical theme of wine as a symbol of joy and divine blessing. There are numerous places throughout

Scripture where wine is described as a symbol of joy and happiness: Psalm 4:7 ("You put more joy in my heart than they have when their grain and wine abound," ESV) and 104:15 ("wine to gladden the heart of man," ESV); Ecclesiastes 9:7 ("drink your wine with a joyful heart") and 10:19 ("wine makes life merry"), among others.

Wine is also commonly mentioned in the context of the blessings of the covenant, as in Deuteronomy 7:13 ("He will bless . . . the crops of your land—your grain, new wine, and olive oil"), Deuteronomy 33:28 ("Jacob secure in a land of grain and new wine, where the heavens drop dew"), Isaiah 36:17 ("until I come and take you to a land like your own—a land of grain and new wine"), and Hosea 2:8 ("She has not acknowledged that I was the one who gave her the grain, the new wine and oil"). In Genesis 14:18–20, Melchizedek— "priest of God Most High"—gives wine to Abraham "in the very context of divine blessing and without the least inkling of disapprobation."[9] In Isaiah 55:1, the bounty of God's mercy includes wine ("Come, buy wine and milk without money and without cost").

On the flip side, a shortage or absence of wine is associated with the curse of disobedience, as in Deuteronomy 28:39 ("you will not drink the wine or gather the grapes, because worms will eat them"); Jeremiah 48:33 ("I have stopped the flow of wine from the presses"); and Isaiah 16:10 ("no one sings or shouts in the vineyards; no one treads out wine at the presses, for I have put an end to the shouting").

Theme #3: Eschatological Symbol

Related to the theme of joy and blessing is the notion of wine as an eschatological symbol of the new creation's bounty. In the eschatological future, "the vats will overflow with new wine" (Joel 2:24) and "new wine will drip from the mountains and flow from all the hills" (Amos 9:13). Vineyards will be planted (see Ezek. 28:26) and farmers will "enjoy their fruit" (Jer. 31:5). "The Lord will reply to them: 'I am sending you grain, new wine and olive oil, enough to satisfy you fully; never again will I make you an object of scorn to the nations'" (Joel 2:19). In this glorious Messianic era, "the LORD Almighty will prepare a feast of rich food for all peoples, a banquet of aged wine—the best of meats and the finest of wines" (Isa. 25:6).

The Messianic connotations of wine also echo in the life and ministry of Jesus. His very first miracle involves making large amounts of wine from water at the wedding at Cana: turning a lack of wine into an abundance (120–180 gallons' worth!), even after the wedding guests had already had a lot to drink (see John 2:1–12). This act launched the kingdom of God in a manner that glimpses the fullness to come, when wine will flow abundantly from the mountains (see Amos 9:13).

Jesus's words at the Last Supper also evoke the "wine in the eschaton" motif. He tells his disciples, "I will not drink from this fruit of the vine from now on until that day when I drink it new with you in my Father's kingdom" (Matt. 26:29), words which would have immediately brought to mind the aforementioned Old Testament images of bountiful wine in the age to come.

Theme #4: Abstinence Is a Good Option, but Not Mandated

A good number of people in the Bible abstain completely from alcohol at various times and for specific purposes, though these examples are never used in a prescriptive or normative sense for all of God's people. Examples of abstinence include Daniel, who in Babylonian exile "resolved not to defile himself with the royal food and wine" (Dan. 1:8) and also abstained during a time of mourning (Dan. 10:3); the Nazirites, who take a vow of separation and "abstain from wine and other fermented drink" (Num. 6:3); Levitical priests instructed to abstain "whenever you go into the tent of meeting" (Lev. 10:8–9); the Rechabites who abstain because their ancestor Jonadab instructed them to (see Jer. 35:14); Samson's mother while she's pregnant (see Judg. 13:4, 7, 14); and John the Baptist (see Luke 1:15). But despite the presence of a biblical tradition of abstinence, "there is nothing that indicates this was either common nor was it seen as the special mark of piety," notes Scot McKnight. "Abstinence is a good and wise option for Christians; it is not the posture of the most advanced Christian or the sign of total dedication."[10]

Theme #5: Moderation

The Latin phrase *abusus non tollit usum* means "the abuse does not invalidate the proper use." Here's one way to think of it:

> Because someone hit another with a hammer isn't an argument against hammers, but an argument for their proper use. The wrong use of sex (or food, or money, etc.) doesn't mean that sex is bad, but that any good thing can be distorted.[11]

This is a biblical principle. When it comes to the use of alcohol, the Bible warns against the *abuse* of it but seems to approve of and even celebrate its proper use. Proverbs reflects this concept when it compares drunkards to gluttons (a comparison also made in Deut. 21:20; Matt. 11:19; and Luke 7:34, among others):

Do not join those who drink too much wine
    or gorge themselves on meat,
for drunkards and gluttons become poor,
    and drowsiness clothes them in rags. (Prov.
    23:20–21)

The pairing of drinking too much and eating too much is significant, because it suggests that the problem resides in overindulgence, not in moderate consumption. Just because Scripture condemns gluttony, and eating food can sometimes lead to gluttony, does not mean it follows that Scripture therefore condemns the eating of food. Likewise with alcohol. Drunkenness is forbidden, but it does not follow that all drinking is thus forbidden. There is a place for proper use.

Time and time again in Scripture, it is the *abuse* of alcohol that is the problem: it's not good to "linger" over wine (Prov. 23:30); whoever is "led astray" by wine or beer is "not wise" (Prov. 20:1). Like food or any other "good thing," too much of it can be a bad thing.

For the New Testament church the issue was the same. Paul instructed church leaders to be those "not given to drunkenness" and "not indulging in much wine" (1 Tim. 3:3, 8), but he never tells them to abstain completely, even advising Timothy to "use a little wine" to help his stomach (1 Tim. 5:23). Paul's position on alcohol should also be understood through the lens of Christian liberty as worked out in passages like Romans 14. The "stronger brother" who can drink moderately should be careful not to cause the "weaker brother" to stumble, but so also should the weaker be careful not to judge the stronger if their faith allows them to eat or drink something. "Do not let anyone judge you by what you eat or drink," says Paul (Col. 2:16). But "whether you eat or drink or whatever you do, do it all for the glory of God" (1 Cor. 10:31).[12]

Much fuller accounts of the biblical treatment of alcohol have been published than this rather brief overview, but I hope for the purposes of what will follow in the next two chapters, this thematic analysis will prove to be a helpful foundation. As we'll see in the next chapter, a variety of cultural/societal/political issues at play have frequently overshadowed Scripture as a determiner of how Christians view alcohol. The biblical era is one thing; the narrative of how Christians have approached alcohol ever since is another story altogether.

* * * * * * * * * *

Interlude

The Summer of the Pub

* * * * * * * * * *

The summer after I graduated from Wheaton College was the summer I discovered beer. I had managed to avoid it completely up until that point (age twenty-two). My evangelical upbringing forbade it, save a tour of the Coors factory in Denver when I was about six (free sample of mediocre beer!). I also stayed "dry" during college, as Wheaton—like most evangelical colleges—requires undergraduates to abstain. But once I graduated from Wheaton and its teetotaling "pledge" was a thing of the past, I began to explore the world of fermented beverages.

I spent that summer with my best friend Ryan, as we both interned at the C. S. Lewis Foundation in California, and together we awkwardly fumbled our way through discovering the differences between lagers, ales, and IPAs. It helped that we went to England for a month. There's nothing like spending a few weeks in Oxford, Cambridge, London, Edinburgh, Belfast, and Dublin to learn the ropes of beer. British pub culture is a different creature—a much more charming one—than the American bar scene, so we learned to drink with dignity and an air of Inklings-homage collegiality.

I remember one night at the St. Catherine's College pub in Oxford during the C. S. Lewis Foundation's Oxbridge Conference. The place was flooded with American evangelicals, euphoric over their pilgrimage to the land of the Inklings and gleefully consuming pint after pint of Boddingtons, Stella, and Strongbow. I remember looking around the room and seeing all these Christians joyfully fellowshiping together with their beer, scotch, and (in many cases) pipes and thinking, "Wow. This is not the evangelicalism I grew up in."

I had mixed feelings about it. On one hand it was a pleasant thing to behold. Jolly good fun. Fellowship. Christians talking freely about God, theology, the church—while sipping alcohol. On the other hand, it occasionally got ugly. Too many beers, too much wine led to ungainly tipsiness and wild behavior. There were hangovers.

Still, there were times at that conference—and during my larger travels in the UK with Ryan—when the conversations and fellowship I had around alcohol were nothing short of transcendent. And that was a revelation. Beer and wine were most definitely present during, and perhaps responsible for, some true spiritual epiphanies that summer.

Two things became very real to me that summer: both the greatness and beauty of alcohol and the dangers it poses when consumed recklessly. It's a tension that has stayed with me ever since.

* * * * * * * * * *

10

Christians and Alcohol

Defining the Relationship

* * * * * * * * * * *

Christians have had a decidedly love-hate relationship with alcohol. The infamous "drink" has been regarded by Christians at various times with awe, horror, religious devotion, fear, obsession, prohibition, addiction, and temperance. It has been one of the most divisive issues within modern American evangelicalism, creating rifts within churches, within families, within Christian institutions. As Mark Noll has noted,

> Some evangelicals have made opinions on liquor more important for fellowship and cooperation than attitudes toward the person of Christ or the nature of salvation. This is particularly unfortunate since the Bible speaks clearly about Christ and salvation, but not about the question of total abstinence.[1]

How did alcohol become the subject of such an emotionally charged cultural debate? Have Christians always been so divided about it? (Short answer: no.) Is it significant that followers of Christ were the first people to invent sophisticated wine- and beer-making techniques (in medieval monasteries) but also the people who led the charge to make alcohol illegal in America?

"A Religious Awe of Beer"

Alcohol hasn't always been seen as a "secular" thing. For ancient Sumerians in the Fertile Crescent, it was elevated to religious heights—a miraculous gift from the gods. The Sumerians had a "religious awe of beer" to the point that they only concocted beer in temples and composed beer-themed poems to the gods, such as "The Hymn to Ninkasi," the Sumerian goddess of beer.[2] Later civilizations also associated these mysterious fermented beverages with the gods—Osiris in the Egyptian dynastic period and Bacchus in classical Greece, for example. In Jewish culture wine was viewed as a blessing of God and a sign of his covenantal abundance, as we saw in the last chapter. And in early Christian culture it was approached with a similar reverence.

In his *Pedagogia*—perhaps the earliest Christian ethic of alcohol consumption—St. Clement of Alexandria discusses the Christian's obligation to drink wine as part of the Eucharist while also being careful to avoid drunkenness. Clement urged believers to not drink in a worldly manner, to excess and intoxication, but to model Christ, who drank wine moderately:

> In what manner do you think the Lord drank when He became man for our sakes? As shamelessly as we? Was it not with decorum and propriety? Was it not deliberately? For rest assured, He Himself also partook of wine; for He, too, was man. And He blessed the wine, saying, *Take, drink: this is my blood*—the blood of the vine. . . . And that he who drinks ought to observe moderation, He clearly showed by what He taught at feasts. For He did not teach affected by wine. And

206

that it was wine which was the thing blessed, He showed again, when He said to His disciples, *I will not drink of the fruit of this vine, till I drink it with you in the kingdom of my Father.*[3]

Indeed, for early Christians, drunkenness was the problem, not alcohol itself. Beer and wine were welcomed by early Christians and "taken as a matter of course."[4] They were good things in moderation.

In the medieval period, as Christians spread the gospel throughout pagan lands, beer played a positive role. As St. Patrick introduced the gospel to the wild pagan land of Ireland, he "captured many an Irish tribal chieftain with his tasty beer before he won the man for God."[5] In the Holy Roman Empire, beer lover Charlemagne promoted improvements in brewing at monasteries throughout the empire, gradually making the church the primary wholesaler of beer in society. Monasteries brewed beer in part as a social service, because it was safer than water and contained less alcohol than some other liquors. Beer was so ubiquitous and so relatively clean that some children in the medieval period were baptized not with holy water but with beer.[6]

Alcohol went hand-in-hand with monastic life in the medieval period (and in many cases still does to this day). Because an ample supply of wine was always necessary in monasteries (for daily Eucharist), monks led the way in cultivating wine wherever the climate permitted. Since their primary focus was to remember their Savior, the monks valued *quality* wine and were the first vintners to apply science to winemaking, in efforts to perfect the finished product and make it worthy of its sacred purpose. The Cistercians, led by St. Bernard of Clairvaux in the twelfth century, were the first to experiment with quality in the Burgundy region of France,[7] and the Cistercian monasteries along the Rhine were also the first to discover the ideal conditions for harvesting the Riesling grape.[8] So the

A Timeline of Christians and Alcohol

AD 27–28: Jesus performs his first miracle: turning 120–180 gallons of water into wine at a wedding banquet in Cana (see John 2:1–11).

AD 30–31: Jesus says of wine, "This cup is the new covenant in my blood, which is poured out for you" (Luke 22:20).

Second Century: St. Clement of Alexandria publishes *Pedagogia*, which included the first scholarly treatment of the subject of Christians and alcohol.

Fifth Century: St. Brigid of Ireland reportedly changes her dirty bathwater into beer so that visiting clerics would have something to drink.

Twelfth Century: Benedictine nun Hildegard von Bingen discovers hops in beer.

1620: Ship carrying John Winthrop to Massachusetts Bay Colony also carries more than 10,000 gallons of wine and three times as much beer as water.

1670: Hard cider is a staple at ministerial ordinations in apple-rich New England.

1673: Increase Mather publishes *Wo to Drunkards*, in which he says, "Drink is in itself a good creature of God, and to be received with thankfulness, but the abuse of drink is from Satan; the wine is from God, but the Drunkard is from the Devil."

1736: The ill effects of gin in England lead Anglican clergyman Thomas Wilson to publish *Distilled Spirituous Liquors the Bane of the Nation*.

1759: Arthur Guinness opens his brewery in Dublin; he eventually uses money from its success to fund Christian charities, hospitals, and Sunday school programs.

1770s–80s: Spanish Catholics plant first vineyards in California at missions up and down the coast.

1805: America's first temperance sermon, "The Fatal Effects of Ardent Spirits," is delivered by Rev. Ebenezer Porter in Washington, CT.

1826: Revivalist pastor Lyman Beecher publishes *Six Sermons on the Nature, Occasion, Signs, Evils, and Remedy of Intemperance*, condemning liquor for "the moral ruin it works in the soul."

1840: The Washingtonian Movement, one of America's first anti-alcohol organizations, is formed.

1869: Methodist pastor Thomas Welch invents a method of pasteurizing grape juice so that it isn't fermented. He persuades local churches to adopt this nonalcoholic "wine" for communion services, calling it "Dr. Welch's Unfermented Wine."

1873–74: "Mother" Eliza Thompson—a devout Methodist—leads "crusade" of women protesting American drinking establishments.

1874: The Woman's Christian Temperance Union (WCTU) is formed.

1893: Ohio pastor Howard Hyde Russell establishes the Anti-Saloon League, a nationwide pressure group aimed at ridding the country of alcohol.

1899: Carrie Nation attacks saloons with hatchets and sledgehammers and becomes an icon of the female-led temperance movement.

January 17, 1920: Eighteenth Amendment goes into effect in America; Billy Sunday holds symbolic funeral service for "John Barleycorn."

1933: Twenty-first Amendment ends Prohibition.

1933–1949: "The Inklings" convenes Christian luminaries including C. S. Lewis, J. R. R. Tolkien, and Charles Williams at the Eagle and Child pub in Oxford for beer-aided literary discussions.

1935: Christians "Bill W." and "Dr. Bob" found Alcoholics Anonymous.

1980: Televangelist Jack Van Impe publishes Alcohol: The Beloved Enemy.

2000s: First "bar churches" begin popping up.

2003: Wheaton College changes rules to allow faculty, staff, and graduate students to drink alcohol in private, when not around undergrads.

2009: Bestselling author Stephen Mansfield publishes The Search for God and Guinness: A Biography of the Beer That Changed the World.

August 9, 2011: In a blog post, evangelical pastor/author John MacArthur chastises the "Young, Restless, and Reformed" community for their reckless approach to alcohol.

next time you enjoy a good Burgundy or Riesling, toast to your medieval Christian forebears who pioneered the science of winemaking for the sake of their Lord.

Modern brewing of beer also can trace its origins to the monks. In the areas of Europe where it was difficult to grow grapevines, monasteries brewed beer—focusing, as with wine, on *quality*. Some brews today—such as Weihenstephan (founded in AD 1040) and Leffe (AD 1240)—originated in medieval monasteries. Nuns also joined in the beer-making business. Hildegard von Bingen was a brewer and is sometimes credited with the discovery that hops added preservative qualities to ale.[9]

The brewing techniques perfected by Christian monastics eventually spread to the secular world, and by the fourteenth and fifteenth centuries consumption of alcoholic beverages was ubiquitous throughout western Europe. In England, ale was consumed at every meal—even with breakfast. It was easy to access and safer than water, which "had an evil and wholly justified reputation . . . of being a carrier of diseases."[10] Soon public drinking houses became popular and taverns and alehouses introduced social drinking and the "bar scene" to the world. This drew the ire of some churches, though, which saw the increasing popularity of taverns as competition. English Christians were going to pubs instead of mass and were opting for taverns over the drinking parties the church itself organized.[11] Still, even as preachers spoke out against pubs and drunkenness, "they did not dare attack drinking per se, which . . . was an essential part of life in medieval England."[12]

The Reformation and the New World

Though today's Protestant evangelical teetotalers owe much of their theology to the heroes of the Reformation, they would likely disagree with the Reformers' views on alcohol. Martin Luther, for example, was an unabashed fan of drinking, particularly good German beer. His hometown of Wittenberg was a brewing center, and he spent much time in the taverns there, studying, mentoring students, even teaching classes. His wife, Catherine, was a skilled brewer.

"We ought to give thanks to God for providing us with food and drink," said Luther, who celebrated moderate drinking even while advising against drunkenness. "You should be moderate and sober; this means that we should not be drunken, though we may be exhilarated. . . . The mind will tolerate a certain degree of elevation, but this must be moderate, not indecent."[13]

Luther viewed drink as a gift from God—something with the potential to be misused, but also something that could be used to honor the Creator. He once said, "Do not suppose that abuses are eliminated by destroying the object which is abused. Men can go wrong with wine and women. Shall we then prohibit and abolish women?"[14]

John Calvin felt similarly about alcohol, writing in his *Institutes*, "We are nowhere forbidden to laugh, or to be satisfied with food . . . or to be delighted with music, or to drink wine."[15] Calvin also noted, "It is lawful to use wine not only in cases of necessity, but also thereby to make us merry,"[16] and insisted in other writings that God created things like alcohol for our benefit and not for our harm.

Luther and Calvin's belief that alcohol was a gift from God to be celebrated in moderation reflect the larger Reformed view that all aspects of creation are redeemable and can speak to the glory of God (think Abraham Kuyper's "every square inch" idea). These ideas filtered down through subsequent generations. Post-Reformation Christians such as George Whitfield and Jonathan Edwards, for example, were known to enjoy rum and hard cider, respectively.[17]

The Puritan Pilgrims in the New World were also largely friendly to alcohol. The *Mayflower* and other ships to the Massachusetts Bay Colony were stocked with ample wine and beer. In 1630, the *Arabella* brought Puritans to New England with at least 10,000 gallons of beer in tow.[18] It was for enjoyment but also for health. Beer was safer to drink than water and thought to have medicinal value essential for survival in the New World. Beer was such a necessary staple for the Pilgrims that a brewery was actually the first permanent building constructed in Plymouth.

Among colonial Christians, "no one felt any tension between Christianity and the moderate use of alcohol," notes Mark Noll. Rather, most believers in America before 1800 "regarded the moderate use of alcoholic beverages, particularly beer and wine, as a privileged blessing from a gracious God."[19] But that attitude shifted dramatically in the centuries that followed.

Temperance and Prohibition

Temperance movements first gained momentum in America in the wake of the Second Great Awakening, when pastors started tying alcohol abstinence to personal holiness and began preaching against even the moderate use of liquor. Revivalist pastor Lyman Beecher, for example, published *Six Sermons on the Nature, Occasions, Signs, Evils, and Remedy of Intemperance*, noting that "there is no prudent use of ardent spirits, but when it is used as a medicine."[20]

By the 1840s, temperance groups such as the Washingtonian Temperance Society debuted, followed later by the Women's Christian Temperance Union (WCTU) and the Anti-Saloon League (ASL). These organizations aimed to rid the nation of "the devastator" (as Abraham Lincoln called liquor) that had ravaged families in both cities and small frontier towns, where saloons and roadside taverns became increasingly popular leisure-time destinations.

Christians led the fight for temperance—particularly Protestant women such as "Mother" Eliza Thompson, who organized a female-led "crusade" against saloons from Ohio to New England in 1874; Mary Hanchett Hunt, who successfully campaigned to get compulsory "scientific" temperance education in the nation's public schools; and perhaps most famously Carrie Nation, who adopted her own "personal doctrine of direct action against alcohol" by violently attacking saloons: smashing kegs of whiskey with a sledgehammer and setting them on fire, shattering bottles and decanters with an iron bar, and battering bar counters with a brass spittoon. Nation was a self-described "bulldog running along at the feet of Jesus, barking at what he doesn't like," and indeed, she had a bite to match her bark.[21]

These passionate women were backed in their efforts by evangelical luminaries such as "Fundamentalist Pope" William Jennings Bryan and ballplayer-turned-preacher Billy Sunday, perhaps the nation's most colorful anti-alcohol expositor. Giving as many as 250 speeches a year in the late 1910s, Sunday spoke to huge crowds about the righteous cause of passing an amendment to outlaw alcohol. Daniel Okrent writes:

> To Sunday, liquor was "God's worst enemy" and "hell's best friend," and he considered those who profited from the alcohol trade earthly Satans. "I will fight them till hell freezes over," he told a rally at the University of Michigan, where he persuaded a thousand students to join the campaign for a statewide Prohibition law. "Then I'll buy a pair of skates and fight 'em on the ice."[22]

On January 17, 1920, Sunday and the broad coalition of anti-alcohol crusaders got their decades-long wish: the

The John MacArthur Controversy

In August 2011, John MacArthur ignited a bit of a firestorm on-line—particularly in the "Young, Restless, and Reformed" (YRR) corner of the blogosphere—when he wrote a blog post entitled "Beer, Bohemianism, and True Christian Liberty," which criticized the somewhat libertine drinking habits of the YRR community. Mac-Arthur didn't mince words, slapping the wrists of YRR Christians for making their passion for drinking "a prominent badge of identity" and admonishing pastors for the "puerile and irresponsible" action of encouraging the recreational use of intoxicants. "It is wrong-headed, carnal, and immature to imagine that bad-boy behavior makes good missional strategy," wrote MacArthur. "The image of beer-drinking Bohemianism does nothing to advance the cause of Christ's kingdom."[23]

Predictably, MacArthur's missive was met with an avalanche of rebuttals, such as a lengthy blog post by Joel McDurmon—author of *What Would Jesus Drink?*—who describes MacArthur as a "wailing imam of the dry jihad" and, in contrast to the YRR, part of the Old, Glum, and Stubborn ("Ogs") contingent of incredulous prohibitionists "trying to give their stump speech without a stump." McDurmon responds to MacArthur by agreeing that the issue is about self-control and maturity but arguing that maturity "is the ability to use the gifts God has given us and even prescribes in places *without* abusing them." He continues,

> Anyone who runs from this standard is not interested in maturity at all. They are interested in keeping Christians childish under the guise of safety. Prohibitionists have always forbidden maturity under the guise of purity. It is legalism, and thus, idolatry.[24]

Somewhat more nuanced responses prevailed on the *Christ and Pop Culture* blog, where Alan Noble took issue with MacArthur's post for downplaying community in the conversation of Christian liberty (see Rom. 14) and attempting "to find a *universal* standard where there can only be *situational* standards," while Canadian pastor Brad Williams defended MacArthur's post as a valuable corrective and "challenge for us to grow up and quit acting silly about alcohol."[25]

prohibition of alcohol went into effect, following the ratification of the Eighteenth Amendment the year prior. To celebrate the occasion, Sunday held a revival meeting in Norfolk, Virginia, in which he announced the death of liquor and the beginning of a new age:

> "The reign of tears is over," Sunday proclaimed. "The slums will soon be only a memory. We will turn our prisons into factories and our jails into storehouses and corncribs. Men will walk upright now, women will smile, and the children will laugh. Hell will be forever for rent."[26]

Of course, things didn't quite turn out that way. Prohibition—in effect for fourteen years before being repealed by the Twenty-first Amendment—had a slew of unintended consequences. It proved a boon to organized crime, for example, launching the era of the Capone-style bootlegger/gangster. It made partying edgier, secret, and thereby more "cool" (think speakeasies and Gatsby), glamorizing vice in the age of jazz and flappers. It "encouraged criminality and institutionalized hypocrisy" and "fostered a culture of bribery, blackmail, and official corruption."[27] Hardly the golden age Billy Sunday envisioned in 1920.

Christians and Alcohol Today

Following Prohibition, most evangelicals still opposed the drinking of alcohol but eased up on their attempts to combat it via prohibitory legislation. In the latter half of the twentieth century, American evangelicals still decried alcohol, particularly in efforts to protect the youth. They supported causes like Drug Abuse Resistance Education (D.A.R.E.) and Mothers Against Drunk Driving (MADD) and took on the media for romanticizing alcohol in movies, pop music, television,

and commercials. Evangelical colleges still remained reso-
lutely "dry" (most do to this day), and many denominations
still required pastors and elders to completely abstain from
alcohol. In the "culture wars" of the 1980s and 1990s, however, alcohol became overshadowed by issues like abortion
and homosexuality. It wasn't the rallying cry for fundamentalist ethics that it once was.

Fast-forward to the 2010s. Alcohol is not nearly the scourge
it once was among many evangelicals. Many churches now
hold services in bars or sponsor outings to go wine or beer tasting. "Theology on Tap"-style gatherings and "bar churches"
aren't hard to find. Graduates of evangelical colleges are making an impact in the craft brewing world: my friend Tyler (a
Biola University graduate) works in sales at LA's Golden Road
Brewery; another friend, Scott (a Calvin College graduate),
started the up-and-coming Greenbush Brewing Co. in Sawyer,
MI. A group of friends who graduated from Taylor University launched ThePerfectlyHappyMan.com, where they offer
reviews of craft beer. I could name at least a dozen Christian
friends of mine who have taken up home brewing.

More and more Christians, particularly of a younger age,
are exhibiting not just a taste for alcohol but a deep love for
it as a gift from God. The pendulum has decidedly swung
away from legalism on the question of alcohol, but is it going
too far? Have younger believers become too reckless and
libertine in their approach to alcohol? Certainly some older
Christians think so (see sidebar "The John MacArthur Controversy"), and I myself have cringed at times when witnessing
the carelessness some of my peers have adopted in this area.
I've been to parties where everyone present is a Christian,
but you wouldn't know it: people doing shots, playing beer
pong, chugging beer, getting drunk, vomiting, smoking, and
so on. Is this appropriate Christian behavior? Certainly not,
as any perusal of Scripture will affirm.

7 Churches That Have Met in Bars

Church	Bar	Location
Kyrie	Mambo's	Fort Worth, TX
Celebration Church	Drunk Monkey Tavern	Tulsa, OK
The Pub Church	The Dugout	Boston, MA
North Brooklyn Vineyard	Trash Bar	Brooklyn, NY
Revolution NYC	Pete's Candy Star	Brooklyn, NY
Country Rock Church	Pub Lounge	Sidney, OH
Evergreen Community	Lucky Lab Brew	Portland, OR

Alcohol is a potentially dangerous thing, not to be approached lightly—especially by Christians who are called to "behave decently, as in the daytime, not in carousing and drunkenness" (Rom. 13:13). Certainly there are ways to enjoy alcohol as Christians in an edifying, God-honoring way (we'll explore that in the next chapter), but there are also ample ways we can go wrong in our consumption of it. Alcohol has been viewed as anathema for many Christians for very good reasons, and part of learning to approach it maturely is recognizing and respecting these concerns.

Common Christian Critiques of Alcohol

Some opponents of alcohol believe the Bible forbids Christians from consuming it in all circumstances. In *Alcohol: The Beloved Enemy*, for example, Jack Van Impe claims that "the Bible forbids the use of wine as we know it today. All wine? Every drop."[28]

But many other Christians, recognizing the "real and

genuine problem in proving that abstinence is a biblical principle,"[29] base their critiques of alcohol on other things—namely, the personal and societal ills caused by intoxicating beverages. The following is a brief overview of some of the frequently voiced, and certainly valid, arguments Christians make against drinking.

Drinking Damages Our Witness

A common reasoning for why Christians should avoid alcohol is that it can tarnish our witness. It's a worldly activity—unwholesome bars and taverns, sloshy tipsiness, vices of all kinds—that Christians should not associate with. Drinking even in moderation can lead us down a path of humiliation and recklessness, compromising our attempts to be salt and light. St. Clement puts it colorfully in his *Pedagogia*:

> But the miserable wretches who expel temperance from conviviality, think excess in drinking to be the happiest life; and their life is nothing but revel, debauchery, baths, excess, urinals, idleness, drink. You may see some of them, half-drunk, staggering . . . vomiting drink on one another in the name of good fellowship; and others, full of the effects of their debauch, dirty, pale in the face, livid, and still above yesterday's bout pouring another bout to last till next morning. It is well, my friends, it is well to make our acquaintance with this picture at the greatest possible distance from it, and to frame ourselves to what is better, dreading lest we also become a like spectacle and laughing-stock to others.[30]

It may not always be as ugly as what Clement depicts here, but the point is well taken: associating ourselves with the excesses of alcohol can be a bad thing for our witness.

Drinking Destroys Families

Anyone who has ever had a friend or family member who's an alcoholic knows this truth all too well. Drinking can wreak havoc on families: drunken and abusive fathers; mothers who can't give up the drink, even in pregnancy; the "drunk uncle" who makes everyone uncomfortable at Christmas dinner; and so on. For many people, destruction is what alcohol breeds. Brokenness. How many families and relationships have suffered throughout history because of alcohol abuse? The women who led the charge against liquor in the days of Prohibition were motivated in part by the deleterious effects it had on their husbands. And who can blame them? Alcohol has the potential to be a ruiner of families, and to flippantly ignore or downplay this fact is unwise.

Drinking Kills

It's hard to argue with the statistics. Worldwide, 2.5 million people die every year because of alcohol-related causes, accounting for nearly 4 percent of total deaths worldwide—more than AIDS, tuberculosis, or violence.[31] Though light to moderate drinking can have beneficial health impacts (e.g., reduced risk of heart disease), heavy drinking can cause all sorts of deadly problems, including cirrhosis of the liver, high blood pressure, epilepsy, liver and breast cancer, poisonings, traffic accidents, and violence. It must be remembered that the chemical at the center of alcohol is ethanol, which is a powerful depressant that affects the central nervous system. In small doses it can simply generate a sense of euphoria or diminish inhibitions, but in large doses it can slow brain activity, impair motor function, and cause slurred speech, drowsiness, and alcohol poisoning. And it's addictive. For many Christians, all of this is enough to say, "We shouldn't even flirt with something proven to be so dangerous."

219

Drinking Impairs Judgment

Because the ethanol in alcoholic beverages affects the brain, it can often lead us to do or say things our inhibitions would normally prevent. We make poor choices "under the influence." Drunk texting. Forgetting important obligations. Violence. Saying things that we'll regret later. Letting one's libido take over instead of using one's brain. The ramifications of reduced inhibitions can be disastrous. Even in the second century, Clement knew how ugly it could get:

> By an immoderate quantity of wine the tongue is impeded; the lips are relaxed; the eyes roll wildly, the sight, as it were, swimming through the quantity of moisture; and compelled to deceive, they think that everything is revolving round them.[32]

As much fun as alcohol can be as a social lubricant, it can swiftly turn into a cringeworthy catalyst for all manner of awkward behavior. For some Christians, the way that alcohol causes one to "lose control" is enough to cause them to avoid it altogether. In a sermon titled "Why I Don't Drink," one pastor, Daniel Walker, said he avoided drinking in part because he wants to be in control of himself. "For myself it is hard enough to lead the good life, without deliberately doing something that makes it harder," he notes.[33] The point is well taken.

Even Moderate Drinking Perpetuates the Problem

But all of those critiques apply only to heavy or intemperate drinking, one might argue. Isn't moderate drinking okay? Some Christians would say no; moderate drinking only supports the alcohol industry. It can make life difficult for those struggling with alcoholism, and it can create the illusion that one is "in control" even while steadily becoming a heavier drinker. "Moderation is only a device for the success of evil affiliated with drinking," Everett Palmer argues. "The only scientific and certain method for preventing the incidence of alcoholism, traffic casualties related to drinking, and other related evils is the practice of abstinence."[34] Some Christians abstain because they want to be a part of the answer, not the problem, and in their view any drip of alcohol they consume only perpetuates the problem.

To Drink or Not to Drink?

Certainly there are plenty of good reasons why abstinence from alcohol is a sensible option, even if "because the Bible says so" isn't one of them. Like the other areas of culture we've explored in this book, alcohol is one of those "gray areas" we are given liberty to assess in our own minds, with the help of the Holy Spirit. One person may decide abstinence is the best option for them while another opts to enjoy alcohol in moderation. Each side needs to bear with the other in patient love and understanding. "To drink or not to drink?" is not a question for which there is a universal answer. It's a question we must each examine and wrestle with individually and in our community contexts.

For those who do opt to partake, one thing is certain: they must do so carefully. For the Christian, there is much to lose if alcohol is consumed recklessly but much to gain if it is consumed properly. What does that look like—"proper" Christian drinking? We'll take on that question in the next chapter.

* * * * * * * * * * *

Interlude

Drinking as Communion

* * * * * * * * * * *

For thousands of years, alcohol has been present in the liturgical practice of drinking the "fruit of the vine" (wine) as part of communion. But there is another sense in which alcohol can create communion, connecting humans and facilitating fellowship in a manner that almost seems sacred.

In his 2011 Grantland.com piece "On Whiskey and Grease,"[1] Wright Thompson beautifully captures the way that alcohol—in this case, bourbon—can create an ineffable aura of connection between humans, as something that can accompany and symbolize what Stephen Mansfield calls "the liturgies of men in concourse with one another."[2]

Thompson narrates an evening of front porch drinking in Alabama, in which a group of men pass around a bottle of Jim Beam that belonged to one of the men's grandfathers, a former church deacon named Herschel Joe York. Herschel's grandson Joe discovered the hidden bottle of his grandfather's bourbon one day when cleaning his grandmother's house following her death.

"Joe took it home and, every year or so, passes it around. It's a communion," writes Thompson. "When he does it tonight, everyone gets quiet. We are laying flowers in our minds."

Thompson goes on to describe the way that as the bottle is passed around the old wooden porch, each of the half dozen men is reminded of some unique memory of their own. "What a wonderful gift, this bottle. It takes everyone to a different place."

As each man holds the bottle and takes a drink, he raises a toast to something meaningful, celebrating the blessing and communion offered by this "heirloom" bottle connecting grandson to grandfather and friend to friend. Thompson's story concludes with a description of the scene after the bottle is empty:

> The stories continue, and the music plays on, until, finally, the porch is empty. The air is cool and the streets of the town are empty now. We all go back to our homes, but we don't leave empty. We take Herschel Joe York with us, a deacon who hid a bottle of Jim Beam in his closet, a man who raised a son who raised a son.[3]

* * * * * * * * * *

11

The Godly Enjoyment of Alcohol

* * * * * * * * * * *

One of the points frequently raised by "drinking is okay" Christians in America is the fact that in many other parts of the world (Europe, for example), drinking alcohol is in no way a faux pas within the church. American evangelicalism is unique in its fear and avoidance of alcohol, they say. And there is some truth in this.

But let's be real here. Whether they like it or not, American Christians live within a culture in which alcohol *is* viewed in a particular way and where certain habits of consumption prevail. Ours is a culture of college binge drinking, keggers, underage drinking as rebellion, and Bud Light commercials. As we saw in the last chapter, it's a culture with a specific historical relationship with alcohol, in which drinking has been seen more often as a scourge than as an art. Things may be shifting (the "artisan" cocktail and craft beer booms are changing the way Americans look at alcohol, to be sure), but we cannot ignore our historical baggage. As we'll see in this chapter, alcohol is culturally and sociologically complex;

225

the consuming of it must be considered in a context much broader than just one's individual opinions.

Throughout recorded history, alcohol has never existed without the accompanying problem of drunkenness. For many people, the ever-present threat that alcohol poses— to become an addiction, a stumbling block, an escape—is enough to warrant complete abstinence. And that's okay. But for others, these threats simply underscore that consuming alcohol is something that must be done with great care.

For Christians who choose to drink, this is especially true. As representatives of Christ we must be mindful that *how we live* matters for mission, that as Christopher Wright notes, "there is an unavoidable ethical dimension to the mission of God's people."[1]

How do our drinking habits fit into the kingdom ethics to which we are called? Are we drinking in a manner that brings glory to Christ, or one that defames his name? Is our drinking a selfish thing—primarily about what it does for us—or is it about the way it helps us connect with and minister to others? These and other considerations are, I believe, crucial in our understanding of what it means to "drink Christianly." In this chapter I'll highlight five principles to elaborate on the notion that, yes, even consuming alcohol can be done to the glory of God.

Don't Drink Alone

For each of the activities of cultural consumption discussed in this book, the case could be made that consuming it in community is better than consuming it alone. For alcohol, it's *especially* true. Drinking alcohol alone, though okay in small doses, can lead to problems: it can become an "escape" in the same way that chowing down on a tub of ice cream alone in one's apartment can be; it can become a private addiction or unhealthy method of de-stressing.

On the contrary, drinking alcohol in community can be incredibly edifying. In the same way that food facilitates fellowship and the table binds people together like little else in life, so too can alcohol be a powerful blessing in the bonding rituals of humanity. From Old Testament Israel and the disciples in the Upper Room to holiday dinners, wedding receptions, and celebratory toasts in today's world, alcohol has long served as a centerpiece in the glad gatherings of mankind.

In my life, some of the most profound moments of connection and deepest occasions of feeling *known* have occurred over fermented beverages: discussing the mysteries of God's grace over pints under the stars in Oxford; gathering at a pub with friends to laugh and share stories together long into the night; toasting to my best friend on the night before his wedding; sipping wine at an oceanside restaurant with the girl I love. These moments can be transcendent.

As Stephen Mansfield describes in *The Search for God and Guinness*, alcohol can help reveal the deeper layers and complexity of a person to us—even our own fathers:

> There was something about those moments alone with his newspaper and beer that seemed to me a liturgy, a mystery of manhood my father had mastered and that I hoped I would one day understand. . . . Somehow I knew early on that the presence of beer changes human interaction, that it gentles the soul and brings about a less guarded state. My father was a different man when he drank a beer and not because he consumed very much of it—he never did—but rather because the beer seemed to give him permission to relax, to stand down and find a human connection to those nearby.[2]

To approach alcohol properly as Christians, we must place a high premium on community—knowing that in gathering together to celebrate and relax with a drink or two, we are participating in a long and biblical tradition of reveling in the blessings of God.

Good wine and beer can be a wonderful way to bring people together. Reformation Brewery in Canton, Georgia, a Christian beer-brewing enterprise affiliated with Isaac's Keep church, celebrates the tradition of Martin Luther, who invited students "to have conversations about theology, life, and culture while sharing a pint of his wife Katy's home-brewed ale." Reformation Brewery fosters conversation and community in downtown Canton around "good beer," in hopes of creating an atmosphere "where you can sit at a table with a businessman, a laborer, artist, or even a politician or preacher to have a conversation and enjoy each other's company."[3] The brewery operates under the conviction that "if there is anything in our culture that could use the redeeming influence of the gospel, it is beer."[4]

For Scott Sullivan, a Calvin College graduate who owns the Greenbush Brewing Company in Sawyer, Michigan, the goal of brewing is less ministry minded but no less community oriented. At the Greenbush taproom, Sullivan's pastors are regulars and thousands of people stop in every week to socialize while enjoying beers like the Traktor ("a kitschy kream ale") or Red Bud ("copper wheat ale with a mind of its own"). "I don't know how you can get a much bigger platform than I have," notes Sullivan.

> We are the community gathering place, in the sense that a public house is the place to gather in England or Ireland, so conversations and debates go on all day and people trade ideas and we have a daily opportunity to show what it is to be a Christian in the world. I'll often have a pastor sitting next to an atheist talking about all sorts of things, which isn't

something that can happen in a conventional church setting. How can you beat that?[5]

Consider the Community You're In

Community should also be considered in the context of Christian liberty: our decision to drink or not to drink may depend on those who are around us. As discussed in earlier chapters, Christian liberty is a biblical principle set forth in passages such as Romans 14 and 1 Corinthians 8 and 10:14–33. Christians are not all at the same level of spiritual maturity, and the "weaker" and "stronger" brethren must bear with one another in Christian love.

In the context of drinking, for example, a believer who has no problem consuming alcohol temperately should nevertheless avoid becoming a stumbling block to the weaker believer who might struggle with intemperance (see Rom. 14:13–21). As Paul says, "It is better not to eat meat or drink wine or to do anything else that will cause your brother or sister to fall" (v. 21).

Some Christian drinkers don't take this verse as seriously as they ought. As Kevin DeYoung notes, "Christians that recognize the good gift of wine or beer need to grow up at times. . . . They should not talk about beer like it's the coolest thing since Sufjan Stevens. Christian liberty is no reason for social life and conversation to revolve around the conspicuous consumption of alcohol."[6]

For pastor Alan Frow, a South African expatriate now serving as pastor of Southlands Church in Brea, California, the question of alcohol consumption for the Christian is contingent on their community. For him, it's less a question of individual conscience as much as the question, "Does it help or hurt the gospel?"

When Frow pastored a church in Johannesburg, for example, he abstained from drinking and required all of his leadership team to as well. Why? Because that particular church contained a large number of people who struggled with alcoholism—a large number of "weaker brothers" who "didn't generally drink socially," but drank "to fall down, to numb the pain."

But since coming to pastor Southlands, Frow no longer makes teetotalism a requirement of his staff because the issue is not a stumbling block for the congregation. If anything, Frow thinks *not drinking* can sometimes be a bigger impediment to reaching the community he's been called to minister to at Southlands.

Frow tells the story of a time when he and his wife invited the parents of one of their daughter's schoolmates to come to church on Easter, with dinner following. The man coming to dinner happened to be French and was a sommelier at an upscale restaurant in Los Angeles. Frow and his wife weren't drinking at the time but knew the man would likely bring over wine—probably very good, expensive wine—for the dinner. Anticipating that, Frow and his wife decided they would drink, because to refuse their guest's wine would be to show no interest in his chief passion in life. It would be a disaster for their Christian witness. Sure enough, the man brought a $300 bottle of wine to dinner.

"We've done a lot of ministry in France, and honestly, not drinking wine is bad for the gospel in that country," said Frow, who has led Alpha outreach courses from homes in which wine is present. "It makes a difference. It's like common currency," he says. "I think it's become a key part of our gospel witness."[7]

Still, Frow is careful to be sensitive to anyone who might be struggling with alcohol, and he makes a point to communicate that people in his congregation have the freedom *not to drink* as well.

Tom Smillie, a Christian beermaker and review writer for The PerfectlyHappyMan.com, also believes that the context of one's community is crucial. When he was in college at Taylor University, Smillie honored the community pledge not to drink because, he says, "I had signed a covenant before God, my school, and my fellow peers." After college he developed a passionate interest in beer and began brewing it himself, which became a source of tension when some of his Christian co-workers openly expressed their belief that alcohol was inappropriate for believers.

The Godly Enjoyment of Tobacco?

Another gray area of cultural consumption is tobacco. Can Christians feel okay about smoking? As with alcohol, opinions about this are all over the map. Some of my evangelical Christian friends wouldn't and haven't ever smoked anything. Others are chain smokers. As with drinking, some of them smoke for the wrong reasons—as a "Look at me! I'm defying your tidy categories for 'Christian' behavior!" form of self-conscious rebellion. Others smoke cigars on special occasions or pipes when in the company of a certain group of friends (especially literary-minded friends or seminary students).

Is smoking in all cases a bad thing? Certainly not. As with alcohol, it can be fine in moderation, in community, and when done with a palate of discriminating appreciation rather than with a need to get a nicotine fix. But as with alcohol, tobacco can also be hazardous to one's health and addictive; it shouldn't be trifled with. Nor should Christians smoke mostly because they want to project a certain image (rebel, cool, fashionable, Don Draper). Tobacco, like alcohol, becomes a damaging thing to our Christian witness when consumed cavalierly, primarily as status marker, or to unhealthy excess.

"I don't want to broadcast my drinking (as controlled and educational as it may be) for fear of being judged or hindering a fellow Christian's walk," notes Smillie. "But at the same time I want to be real, honest, and open with people."

When it comes to our Christian witness and the perceptions of nonbelievers, Smillie thinks it's important that they see examples of Christians drinking responsibly and respecting others, rather than only the "no" Christians who abstain. For Smillie, his love of good beer has allowed him to build relationships and speak into the lives of nonbelievers. "I've had the opportunity to brew alongside the brewmaster, get to know the servers and ask how they are doing, pray for customers, give a Bible to an employee that was leaving the restaurant, and I've been invited to parties," he says. "Beer is communal and appeals to the common man. Interestingly, the gospel message is too."[8]

Drink in Moderation

This one goes without saying, though we all know that "moderation" is much easier said than done. As Christians, however, it's something we must strive toward in our consumption. Just as excessive eating (gluttony) is an unseemly vice forbidden for Christians in the Bible, so too is excessive drinking (drunkenness).

What's the solution? Total abstinence? Maybe, though that wouldn't work with food. Eating is an activity that is potentially hazardous to our health, but we *must* eat for survival. And many people do eat in moderation, so clearly it's possible to consume something potentially addictive in this manner. Likewise with alcohol: it can become addictive and dangerous in excess, but many people throughout history have consumed it in moderation. It's possible.

One of the fruits of the Holy Spirit mentioned in Galatians 5 is self-control (v. 23). The "acts of the flesh" include drunkenness (v. 21), but when we have the Spirit of God within us we have an Advocate who helps us resist those fleshly desires. If you "walk by the Spirit," you "will not gratify the desires of the flesh" (v. 16). This is an encouragement that moderate consumption *is* possible, especially with the help of the Holy Spirit. We are given the gift of self-control from God, so why not use it to properly, moderately enjoy the bounty of his creation?

Drinking in moderation is hard, but it can be a great witness to the world—a manifestation of the work of the Spirit in our lives. If we can consistently enjoy alcohol without drinking it to excess, we also communicate something about the way we view alcohol: that its goodness lies not in its ability to get us drunk but rather in the pleasure of savoring it moderately.

When asked in a video interview if he agreed with Christians who say that "drinking is okay because Jesus drank wine," John Piper responded, "Drinking *can* be okay," but he cautioned that there are also times when drinking is not okay: drinking to drunkenness or drinking with people struggling with addiction, for example.

"People that are cavalier about this thing called alcohol," notes Piper, "make no sense to me. . . . Of course you can't defend, in any absolute way, teetotalism from the Bible. It's clear that wine is a blessing in the Bible."

Even so, Piper has chosen to be a teetotaler, not because he thinks alcohol is evil or forbidden but for other reasons: "It's a context in which I live. It's my children and my grandchildren. It's my addictive personality."[9]

For many people, teetotalism from alcohol does make the most sense. But for those who can handle it, drinking in moderation can be a good thing.

Don't Use Alcohol, Enjoy It

Whenever one *uses* alcohol, things can get messy: using it to make oneself feel better, using it to drown away one's sorrows, using it to mischievously reduce one's inhibitions or the inhibitions of others. When we use it this way we diminish it to nothing more than a tool in service of disordered desires. We lose sight of the fact that alcohol can be as complex and aesthetically rich as a painting or ballet. Just because it's been enjoyed by the masses—in taverns, at ballparks, at keggers—as a decidedly "low" form of culture does not mean this is how it must always be consumed.

"Beer is an art like anything else," remarks Scott Sullivan, whose path to opening Greenbush Brewing Company in 2010 began with his interest in craft beer "as an antidote to the mass market beer world." Sullivan came to brewing by way of making his own bread, sausage, and cheese, which taught him how to work with yeast and formulate recipes. For him, beermaking is as much an art as is making music. It's his medium.

If we think of alcohol as an art, then, we should not approach it in this "user" mindset. To repeat the quote of C. S. Lewis from the introduction, when we *use* a piece of art (or alcohol) rather than *receive* it, it "merely facilitates, brightens, relieves, or palliates our life" but "does not add to it."[10]

A better way to approach alcohol, I would suggest, is to *receive* it as a blessing from God. Think about it less in terms of what it *does* for you and more in terms of how your enjoyment of it brings glory to God. As Mansfield notes,

> Beer is not simply a means of drunkenness nor is it merely a lubricant to grease the skids to sin. Beer, well respected and rightly consumed, can be a gift of God. It is one of his mysteries, which it was his delight to conceal and the glory of kings to search out. And men enjoy it to mark their days

9 Tips for Developing a Discerning Palate

How can we improve our *taste* experience of alcohol and better savor the delights of God's created world? Here are a few brief suggestions:

- Expand your horizons. Don't stick to the drink you *know* you'll like.
- Find a craft brewery that offers a large array of styles and start sampling them.
- Learn to slow down and savor a good drink. A glass of scotch can (and should) last you a good hour if you sip it slowly (preferably while discussing theology or philosophy).
- Read about alcohol on the internet. Do research. Read beer and wine reviews. Become educated.
- Try everything, but don't *love* everything. Find your favorites and don't feel obligated to like the cool or trendy drinks.
- Learn to describe the taste of a drink and why you do or don't like it. This may make you sound pretentious at times, but it will enhance your experience! Maybe even take notes.
- Build your palate sensibly. With beer, for example, don't start with IPAs (intense and bitter). Begin, perhaps, with a quality lager (smooth and easy). Your appreciation for a range of flavors will be a gradual thing.
- Host your own "tastings" in which you share a variety of personally curated types of drinks: wine, beer, bourbon, scotch, and so on. Plan dinners for friends with wine or beer pairings. "Grade" drinks together and compare notes.
- Drink local and support the little guys!

and celebrate their moments and stand with their brothers in the face of what life brings.[11]

Love It More for the Taste Than for the Buzz

As a corollary to the "receive, don't use" approach to alcohol is this advice: love it for how it tastes more than for how it makes you feel. This isn't to say that the "buzz" of alcohol is always a bad thing—it is surely one of its manifold blessings, and we shouldn't pretend otherwise. But when the buzz is the main reason we drink alcohol, it becomes far easier to abuse it. Plus, it turns the activity of drinking into a me-centered activity of "what this drink does to me" rather than "how this drink communicates beauty." This is why people who drink primarily for the buzz—college kids, partiers, "bros," soccer hooligans, and so on—don't mind drinking swill like Coors, Bud Light, Heineken, and Shock Top. It's not about the taste for them. If it's a cold beverage and gives them a buzz, it's enough.

This isn't how alcohol ought to be consumed. And Christians, of all people, should recognize how this "Who cares how it tastes?" approach misses out on a richer appreciation of a well-made beverage.

Over the years I've learned to approach alcohol in a more taste-oriented manner, in the same nuanced way I might approach a piece of art in a gallery. A few of my experiences in the last year might illustrate what I mean:

- At Beachwood BBQ's Sourfest (Seal Beach, CA), I joined a community of beer lovers to taste rare sour ales and hear from the brewers themselves. I particularly enjoyed the "Duck Duck Guava," a tart beer with pineapple and guava, brewed only once (30 gallons total). The preciousness of such a small batch only heightens the experience of truly "craft" beers such as this.

- At a Kindling's Hearth retreat at a Swiss chalet in the Cascades near Seattle, I joined a group of Christians in a blind tasting of wines from the cellar of the host. Hearing the host describe the wines, which were all award-winning reds, and seeing his joy in pouring each of our glasses and then asking us to describe the taste ("nutty," "sweet," "hints of blackberry") was a joyous experience of how the beauty of wine can bring people together.

• Outside of Altea, Spain—a tiny city on the Mediterranean coast—I went wine tasting with some dear friends at Enrique Mendoza winery. For no charge, we were poured about seven generous tastings each. Pepe Mendoza, the second-generation winemaker who runs the place, spoke of each wine with the passion and detail of an artist describing his work. "We are artisans; not industry," he said in broken English as he described a wine called Estrecho, which comes from a local grape called monastrell and tastes faintly of rosemary and pine.

• At Bluestem restaurant in Kansas City, my wife, Kira, and I splurged on a five-course wine-pairing dinner, in which a very nice (and knowledgeable) sommelier handpicked wines for each food either of us ate. The way that each wine was perfectly paired to complement the flavors of the food blew our minds. We both had smiles on our faces the entire meal. It was exquisite.

In each of these cases, the beauty of the experience of drinking was not only that it brought upon me a pleasant, relaxing buzz (which, to be sure, it did). It was also the quality of the drink itself, the nuances of flavor, the details of the grape's local origin, the passion that went into the brewing process. So much wonder can be discovered and enjoyed in the very *tasting* of alcohol: the slow, considered *sipping* of it. It's a shame so many people gulp down their drinks without taking the time to truly appreciate them. When it comes to alcohol, many people are "far too easily pleased," as Lewis might say.

That was the case for Taylor Birkey, a graduate of Taylor University who worked in construction after college and regularly had Buds and other mass market beers with his co-workers at the end of the day. He didn't especially love the taste of beer then—it was just the thing to do. But one day that all changed. On January 1, 2010, he opened a bottle of Three Floyds Dreadnaught IPA.

"All my preconceptions went right out the window," he said. "I was so amazed that a beer could be crafted to smell so much like grapefruit and taste refreshingly bright and bitter and subtly sweet, all in one sip."[12]

Indeed, the fact that beer can be *crafted* to smell and taste in such a way should be a revelation for Christians. Praise be to God that he created things like hops, barley, grapes, grapefruit, and the process of fermentation; and that he created humans with the creative capacity to figure out brewing, distillation, vinification, and all the complexities therein; and finally, that he created us—the drinkers—with taste buds to enjoy it all and faculties to be relaxed by its smooth pleasures.

Conclusion: Drinking as an Act of Worship?

For much of the history of the church, alcohol has literally been consumed as a part of Christian worship in the form of communion wine. But can drinking alcohol socially, for enjoyment, also be worshipful? I think so. Luther and Calvin would say so. Jonathan Edwards too. And of course Jesus himself seemed to value the added layers of joy good wine brought to a wedding banquet.

Let's be very clear: alcohol is not something to be worshiped. It must never be an end unto itself, but rather a blessed glimpse—a sign pointing back to the Creator God who created all things and pronounced them "very good" (Gen. 1:31). It shouldn't be about us as much as it is about God and what he invites us to experience in, through, and on account of his grace.

238

This goes for all of our consumption. Our world sees "consuming" as an individual-oriented, pleasure-gratifying activity of hedonism. I'd like to suggest that Christians should think counterculturally about what it means to be a consumer: that it's not primarily about what I get but about what God gives; that it's not a solitary transaction as much as an activity of communion both with our fellow creatures and with our Divine Creator. It's a way for us to dignify the goodness of a creation God created to bring glory to himself.

If we're willing to do the work, to truly engage the difficult questions of the "gray areas," we can rehabilitate the meaning of "consumer." This has been the project of this book, and in the following concluding chapter I hope to provide a summarizing plan for how this "rehabilitation" can proceed and why it matters for our mission in this world.

* * * * * * * * * *

Interlude

To My Generation:
Let's Stop the Pendulum

* * * * * * * * * *

I don't presume to speak for my generation, but I most certainly speak *to* my generation. And there's one thing I want to say, specifically to those under-forties who might be reading this.

Let's be the generation that stops the pendulum. Christians have for too long been motivated by *reactions* to the errors and excesses of the generations before. For my generation, this means we've reacted against legalism and moralism by drifting away from holiness and engaging in anything and everything under the banner of "freedom in Christ." This is a tragedy. It not only makes a mockery of the generations who raised us; it also makes a mockery of Christ. As we've seen in this book, it also turns our engagement with culture into a "statement" in which we're often more interested in communicating what we're not (legalists, prudes) than what we are (Christ-followers seeking to honor and know him through our cultural activities).

Let's grow up. Let's stop compensating for the wrong-headed approaches to culture that our Christian forebears might have had. Getting drunk proves nothing other than the fact that we can lift a glass of alcohol. Smoking and cussing don't prove we are "more accessible" Christians; they prove we can suck in tobacco fumes and use our lips to utter four-letter words. Oh, and they also might prove that we'd rather look like everyone else than be identifiably "set apart," which probably also communicates that following Christ is in fact as superficial as some skeptics assert. Friends, let's stop deluding ourselves into thinking that by shirking holiness we're advancing the cause of Christ by "breaking stereotypes" people might have of Christians. All we're actually doing is demeaning the name of Christ by cheapening the cost of discipleship. We can do better than that.

There is a middle ground. It's not a place of lukewarm compromise. It's a hard but rewarding place to be: settled in a nonreactionary mode of living where's it's simply about being a faithful disciple of Christ. It's a place of being open-minded about culture but also willing to say no to things. It's a place of thoughtfulness and restraint, where what we do and why is more complicated than a list of moralistic rules and more coherent than the "anything goes" alternative.

Conclusion

Gray Matters for Mission

If you have any doubt about the importance of thoughtful, healthy patterns of consumption, I have a recommendation for you: take a trip to Las Vegas.

In that city—a mirage metropolis rising from the desert like a monument to mammon, neon, and vice—you will see the underbelly of consumption. You will see just how perverted a perfectly good thing can become when it is celebrated in reckless excess. You will see how ugly it is when glorious aspects of God's created world become cheapened and demeaned, reduced to disposable commodities in service of a loud, proud hedonism.

Just before I started writing this chapter, my then fiancée Kira and I spent a few hours in Vegas on the drive back to Los Angeles from a vacation in the Southwestern national parks. After spending four days in the quiet, contemplative spaces of nature—Zion National Park, the Grand Canyon, many long stretches of sage and Joshua tree–lined desert highways in between—Vegas stood out in stark contrast as a self-contained island of overconsumption. It's a place where most people don't slow down to enjoy or thoughtfully consume anything; they consume to escape, to forget. It's a blur of eating, drinking, playing, watching, vomiting, and indulging. The mantra "what happens in Vegas stays in Vegas" is a testament to the city's consumptive ethos: "Go for broke in your consumption here, consequences be damned."

During our time in the national parks, Kira and I relished the ability to be present in the moment, enjoying the small, quiet wonders of our surroundings: the colors of the cliffs, the smell of pine and juniper, the vastness of the sky, the horizon. With (most of) our digital distractions removed, we were able to be fully present, "consuming" the beauty of God's creation in the healthiest sense—that is, in the manner of having our senses heightened and being attuned, curious, patient, and thankful.

By contrast, Vegas was sensory overload. There's so much going on that true enjoyment of anything is almost impossible. Kira and I love food, and Vegas boasts dozens of amazing restaurants from the world's best chefs: Gordon Ramsay, Bobby Flay, Charlie Palmer, Wolfgang Puck, Tom Colicchio, Mario Batali, and so on. But in the context of Vegas's excesses, such a prevalence of five-star cuisine simply depressed us. How many people eating at these restaurants truly appreciate how rare and wonderful are the pleasures of what they are consuming?

Vegas cheapens the experience of amazing food, just as it cheapens the enjoyment of good alcohol. Amazing drinks can be enjoyed in this city, but sadly they are consumed by most people as simply one more beverage on the path to a hangover. Sex is also cheapened and perverted in this city. Like everything else in Vegas, it can be bought for a price and forgotten soon after. It satiates a carnal desire but little more. Also cheapened in Vegas are a glut of amazing architectural wonders, gardens, sculptures, paintings, tapestries, and fashion that are often lost in the onslaught of so many other distractions and excesses vying for one's attention.

Vegas is an extreme example, to be sure. But I believe it is simply a supersized iteration of our culture's broader habits of consumption. It's a microcosm of the manner in which many of us have been raised to consume: to fill our bellies, to appease our desires, to rebel or exert our freedom, and to simply amass *more*.

Consumer is a very ugly word when we think of it in the Vegas sense, but there are other ways to think about it. One can consume in a manner that is passionate yet dignified, sensuous yet controlled, thoughtful yet not academic. One can consume in a manner that makes the world a better place, enhances our experience of it, and deepens our awe of its Creator. This is how I hope Christians will consume, because I believe there is a lot at stake.

What Is Our Purpose on Earth Anyway?

Why does the question of how we consume matter? For Christians, the question behind this question is: What are we here for?

Scripture is clear that our chief purpose on earth is *not* our own personal pleasure or the fulfillment of carnal desires. Christians understand that our lives are not really our own, and thus our own pursuit of pleasure (apart from Christ) is not really the point. We belong to Christ, and our purposes are his. Furthermore, to be Christlike is to be humble (see Phil. 2–4; Rom. 12:3) and sacrificial (see Rom. 12:1; John 15:13), always, out of love, putting the interests of others before our own.

How does consumption—such a seemingly self-interested, pleasure-seeking activity—fit into this? It fits because it's a behavior among many behaviors that manifests our character.

And our character as Christians matters because (ideally) it reflects the glory of God to the world. How we consume, just like how we behave in any other regard, should reflect a character transformation within us that anticipates the virtuous landscape of the coming kingdom of God.

Legalism has tainted my generation so much that we don't even want to go near rules or think in terms of "dos and don'ts." In the process we've lost the idea that character and virtue matter. But we shouldn't think about our behavior in terms of rules. It's more helpful to think of it as part of the bigger picture of the divine purpose for the people of God: to "advance the language of God's new world"[1] by spreading the light of Christ outward and being a blessing to the nations.

Our ethical choices matter because they are always linked to the effectiveness of our mission, notes Christopher Wright:

> It is never merely a matter of me and my conscience and God. The moment we fail to walk in the way of the Lord, or fail to live lives of integrity, honesty, and justice, we not only spoil our personal relationship with God, we are actually hindering God in keeping his promise to Abraham. We are no longer the people of blessing to the nations.[2]

Ethical living matters, notes N. T. Wright, because it is part of our "truly human" vocation to extend the Garden of Eden outward, reflecting God into the world and reflecting the world back to him.[3] As God's image-bearing creatures, we have both a royal and a priestly vocation, representing our two primary tasks of mission and worship: "to stand at the interface between God and his creation, bringing God's wise and generous order to the world and giving articulate voice to creation's glad and grateful praise to its maker."[4]

We should think of our life's purpose as that of being an angled mirror, reflecting God to the world (mission) and the world back to God (worship). Likewise, I believe when we think about consuming culture as Christians, we should think about it in terms of both worship and mission. Everything in this book has been intended to shape our consumptive habits toward these ends, which are closely related.

When we consume in a thoughtful, virtuous manner, we honor God and reflect the grandeur of his creation back to him. Our healthy enjoyment of the created good is a way that we demonstrate worship to the Creator.

But this inevitably has an outward, missional component as well. If we strive to consume virtuously in a manner consistent with Christ and his kingdom, the light of Christ will naturally be reflected outward. People will take notice. The glory of Christ will be expanded; the light will penetrate new territories of darkness. And this, ultimately, is why *consuming well* matters. It matters for mission, and the following are a few specific reasons why.

Being a Better Consumer: Four Reasons It Matters for Mission

Here's the "so what?" conclusion to this book—the summarizing takeaways for Christians seeking to be better consumers "in but not of" this world, unafraid of deep engagement with the gray areas of life. These are the reasons it matters, I believe, that we strive to honor Christ through the way we consume culture.

1. Consuming Culture Connects Us to Others

Everyone consumes. It's a shared experience unique to humanity: we create feasts to enjoy together; we plan parties; we go to concerts and movies and discuss them together; we cheer wildly in the sports bar when our team scores.

Thus, on a basic level, Christians should take consumerism seriously because it's a way we can connect with others. It's a method of outreach. And it can take many forms.

Learning how to engage an area of culture more deeply and appreciate it more fully can open doors to develop friendships and launch meaningful conversations. If a Christian becomes an informed, passionate wine connoisseur and strikes up a meaningful conversation with a secular sommelier, it can be a great opportunity to share the love of Christ and break down barriers to the receiving of the gospel. If a Christian attending a secular college becomes a passionate fan of Iranian cinema, it can become an important point of loving connection with others who share that interest. A youth pastor who genuinely loves the music of M83 or Phoenix will have a great opportunity to bond with the students who share those tastes—not to mention a more general opportunity to exhibit patterns of healthy, informed consumption to everyone else in his impressionable community.

For my friend Arianna, who runs a mission to nonbelieving artists in Spain, demonstrating a serious, earnest interest in culture is central to her outreach. "Taking in their culture, eating the food they eat, drinking the things they drink is one of the most vital things I can do," she says. "It's what Jesus did: he ate with us, walked with us, identified with our humanity."

Loving artists, affirming others' passions for culture, and joining them in the enjoyment and discussion of God's good creation can be a powerful way to connect with others and spark conversations about the big questions. Art is a mysterious force: it awakens desire, stirs longings, and—as Makoto Fujimura said at Calvin College's 2009 Festival of Faith and Music—"poses the questions for which faith is the answer."

But Christians won't have a missional impact in the realm of culture if we don't first value it ourselves. Deep conversations and relationships with secular communities will not happen if we haven't first developed a cultural literacy, notes Kevin Vanhoozer. We must learn to read culture well rather than merely consume it passively:

> For I cannot love my neighbor unless I understand him and the cultural world he inhabits. Cultural literacy—the ability to understand patterns and product of everyday life—is thus an integral aspect of obeying the law of love. . . . Christians must read popular culture in order to understand the way in which it affects us, our neighbors, our children, and the church.[5]

It's vital that we see the world of cultural consumption as a fertile field where important conversations and connections can plants seeds of faith. This is not to say that we should neglect *preaching* the gospel outright. Dialoguing about culture is in no way a replacement for evangelism. But if we do the former well, it can certainly be beneficial for outreach. The way we engage culture can testify to the far-reaching ramifications of the gospel, which among other things can invigorate one's appreciation for art and culture and infuse new meaning and interpretation to all manner of beauty.

2. Our Consumer Choices Set Us Apart

What we consume or do not consume and *why* we choose to consume or abstain is another key part of this notion of consumption as mission. As a people charged with the task of being salt and light (see Matt. 5:13–16) and a "royal priesthood" called out of darkness and into light (see 1 Peter 2:9), Christians must consider how our consumer choices contribute or detract from this vocation. What is communicated about our identity and values via our consumer behavior?

20 Questions for Christian Consumers

When you're in that moment of deciding whether or not to take that drink, watch that movie, or engage in that cultural activity, here are some questions that might be helpful for you to consider:

1. Is there anything good, true, or beautiful in what I'm about to consume?
2. Everything is permissible, but is what I'm about to consume *beneficial*?
3. Did the creation of what I'm about to consume harm others or make the world a worse place?
4. Will my consuming of this lead me to sin?
5. Will my consuming of this lead others to sin?
6. If a non-Christian saw me consuming this and knew I was a Christian, how would that affect his or her view of Christianity?
7. Am I consuming this primarily because I'm sad, angry, stressed, lonely, or [insert other emotion here]?
8. Am I consuming this because when I was growing up I was told it was evil?

If we are Christians seen at church one minute but seen throwing money away at casinos or guzzling cheap beer at keggers the next, what does that communicate? If we give no thought to the health of the food we eat and frequently indulge in gluttonous displays of junk food eating, what does that say about our appreciation of God's gifts (including the gift of our own body)?

If Christians are just as prone to overeating, drunkenness, thoughtless movie-watching, and status-driven music consumption as everyone else, something is wrong. We should ask, "Our lifestyle, the music we listen to, the values we endorse in practice, are they different from those of society around us?"[6]

9. Am I consuming this because I don't want to be a legalist and/or don't want to be labeled a prude by non-Christians?
10. Am I consuming this primarily to check it off of a list?
11. What will the consuming of this add to my life?
12. Would Jesus consume this with me if he were here? (Seriously!)
13. Do I have enough background knowledge to know whether or not the experience of this will be edifying and worth my investment?
14. If I am spending money on this, is it a wise use of the resources I've been given?
15. Have I thanked God for this?
16. Would I be embarrassed to thank God for this (e.g., if I'm about to watch *The Jerry Springer Show* or something)?
17. Am I consuming this alone? Would it be better to find someone else to enjoy it along with me?
18. Have I given myself enough time to truly consume this well?
19. Will the consuming of this add joy to my life rather than fleeting pleasure?
20. Would I feel comfortable consuming this in church?

Like it or not, the way we consume is a big part of how many people perceive who we are. Sometimes the only thing people see of us is what we buy or the music, movie, and book "likes" we list on our social media profile pages. So the stakes are high: Are we communicating healthy, thoughtful, temperate patterns of consumption to the observing world? Or do people only see us as giving lip service to Jesus on Sundays and thoughtlessly bowing before Mammon the rest of the week?

As we've previously mentioned in this book, sometimes what we *don't* consume sends the most significant message. Christians must be willing to say no to things, but we should have good reasons for our abstention. If we choose to say no to a particular television show but don't really know anything about it and simply have a knee-jerk, fear-driven reaction to it, we'll simply come across as culture warriors uninterested in deep engagement. But if we can thoughtfully, carefully, and compassionately give good reasons for why our faith identity leads us to abstain from a particular cultural item or genre, it can be a solid witness that might elicit even more respect from observers who might otherwise cast us as prudes.

For Jesus during his ministry on earth, culture wasn't something wholly bad or wholly good. Jesus drew upon "various [cultural] artifacts (coins, clothing, implements, tools), conventions (language, holy days, instructional methods), and institutions (kingdoms, marriage, civil and religious authority structures) as illustrations or vehicles through which to assert his unique callings and pursue the unfolding of the kingdom of God." But other aspects of culture he regarded "as corrupt or corrupting, and he opposed them for the sake of the greater good of the kingdom of God."[7]

For Jesus and for us, culture is inescapable. It's part of the ambience of human existence. But we must recognize that some of it is edifying and life giving and some of it isn't. Some things in culture contribute to our human flourishing; others lead us into sin. As Christians, our discernment in choosing what to consume or not consume (and how, and why) communicates important things about our orientation toward Christ and his kingdom.

3. Healthy Consumption Affirms Creation's Goodness and Brings Glory to God

Madonna isn't exactly a trusted source of wisdom in this world, but she was onto something when she said we are living in a material world. We are. This is a world of materiality: watermelon juice, grass stains on denim jeans, sunburns. We breathe in air, consume food, and drink for sustenance, and, well, we live a very bodily existence. We are fundamentally consuming beings. We take things in, desire and enjoy them, chew on them, dance to them, cry to them, and sometimes get ill because of them.

Our experience as embodied creatures consuming material things is one of the ways that we experience, very viscerally, the dual realities of the goodness of creation and the "not yet" groanings of it. If we consume thoughtfully, gratefully relishing the pleasures of the tangerine, the sunset, the symphony, or the romantic comedy, we receive little foretastes of the new creation to come. Of course, if we eat too many tangerines, we'll know all too well—in the form of a stomachache—the "not yet" part of it.

It's no accident that the central act of Christian worship—the Eucharist—is itself an act of consumption that affirms the material goodness of creation while also pointing to the renewed creation of the eschaton. Through the physical consumption of communion bread and wine, notes James Smith, we are reminded that "we meet God in the material realities of water and wine, that God embraces our embodiment, embraces *us* in our embodiments."[8] As Christians, the notion that creation is good "makes sense for us because we first experience the blessing, sanctification, and riches of the material world in the joy and pleasure of Christian worship," notes Smith. "There is a performative sanctioning of embodiment that is implicit in Christian worship, invoking the ultimate performative sanctioning of the body in the incarnation."[9]

But communion not only affirms our embodiment and the physical realities we inhabit; it also affirms the realm of human culture:

> After all, it's not wheat and grapes that are on the table; it's bread and wine. These are not naturally occurring

phenomena; they are the fruit of *culture*, the products of human making. . . . The affirmation of the goodness of creation includes not just the furniture of "nature" but also the whole panoply of cultural phenomena that humanity, by its cultural labor, teases out of creation.[10]

In the very heart of Christian worship, then, is a liturgical affirmation of materiality and culture that confirms what we are hardwired as humans to suspect: that the Creator of the universe reveals himself to us and touches our hearts through the art, culture, oceans, colors, and heavens that declare his glory (see Ps. 19:1).

Indeed, Christians should consume with a passion and confidence that indeed, "the earth is the LORD's, and everything in it" (Ps. 24:1). We should recognize that becoming more attuned to the diverse beauty of creation—more literate, nuanced consumers—isn't a waste of time in the life of faith. Rather, it serves to help us become more fully human. As Makoto Fujimura has said, "What is good, true, and beautiful rehumanizes all of us."[11]

While in Oxford I once heard the Eastern Orthodox bishop Kallistos Ware define the Christian as "the one who, wherever he looks, sees Christ everywhere." I don't think he meant that the Christian sees Jesus's face on tortillas; rather, I think the bishop was getting at the same thing Lewis was getting at when he famously said, "I believe in Christianity as I believe that the sun has risen, not only because I see it, but because by it I see everything else."[12] It's what Kuyper was getting at when he said, "There is not a square inch in the whole domain of our human existence over which Christ, who is Sovereign over all, does not cry: 'Mine!'"[13] It's the idea that Christ illuminates and animates all things, that our enjoyment of culture is both justified and amplified by his incarnation, and that "sacred" and "secular" are reductive categories that inhibit our ability to behold all the goodness, truth, and beauty that exists by God's grace.

4. Consumer Power Can Be Used for Good

Consuming culture has consequences. It's not just a recreational diversion that can be bracketed off from the things that "matter" in our spiritual development. What happens in Vegas does *not* just stay in Vegas. On the contrary, our consumption of culture often *is precisely what shapes us*, spiritually and in every other way. We should take it seriously.

James Smith articulates this well in *Desiring the Kingdom*, noting that our cultural practices and rituals are actually shaping our desires, forming our identities, instilling in us visions of the good life, and specifying our "ultimate concern." They are thus "liturgies" that "are after nothing less than our hearts."[14]

Smith notes that even secular and seemingly "thin" cultural practices such as shopping at the mall or attending a football game are deeply formative and embedded with a sense of *telos* (purpose) and a vision of what ultimately matters. He writes:

> "Secular" liturgies are fundamentally formative, and implicit in them is a vision of the kingdom that needs to be discerned and evaluated. From the perspective of Christian faith, these secular liturgies will often constitute a *mis*-formation of our desires—aiming our heart away from the Creator to some aspect of the creation as if it were God. Secular liturgies capture our hearts by capturing our imaginations and drawing us into ritual practices that "teach" us to love something very different from the kingdom of God.[15]

Christians should be savvy about the power of these cultural "liturgies." We should develop a toolbox of cultural exegesis that allows us to avoid being mis-formed by the false visions of the good life we receive through the music, movies, television shows, and other cultural items we consume. At the same time, we should recognize that "even the secular is ultimately about love of something ultimate" and that "even these secular liturgies, with their misdirected desires, are a witness to the desire for God."[16]

Smith likens this to Calvin's *sensus divinitatis* (sense of the divine), which he says is "best understood not as a primarily intellectual disposition to form theistic beliefs but as a passionate disposition to worship." Because of the *sensus divinitatis* within every human—this disposition to worship *something*—there is thus something [for Christians] to work with, something to build on, a point of contact for articulating the gospel."[17]

We could perhaps go so far as to say that all culture (both the making and the enjoying of it) is motivated by a desire for God. Now, to be sure, not all of it communicates truth about God, and much of it ends up going in precisely the opposite direction. The point is that as readers of culture and informed consumers of it, we often do not need to stretch that much to find in culture something salvageable for the purposes of knowing and glorifying God. Often it takes just a little reshaping, redirecting, reinterpretation. As consumers, we have that power.

Michel de Certeau's essay "Reading as Poaching" is the classic apologia for the empowered consumer. In it, de Certeau suggests that consumers of culture should not think of themselves as doomed to passivity, beholden to whatever *telos* of meaning (or vision of the good life) the producer intends. Rather, reading culture is an act of power and creativity. "By challenging 'consumption' as it is conceived," he notes, "we may be able to discover creative activity where it has been denied that any exists."[18]

In de Certeau's view, the reader of cultural texts "invents in texts something different from what [the author] 'intended.' . . . He combines their fragments and creates something unknown in the space organized by their capacity for allowing an indefinite plurality of meanings."[19]

Now, for Christian consumers of culture, this does not mean that a Marilyn Manson album can be reinterpreted as a prophetic commentary on the destruction of the temple or that the latest Marvel Comics movie can be read through a Johannine lens. There are limits to "poaching." But where it's appropriate, sensible, and informed by more than just a desire for a convenient sermon illustration, the savvy Christian consumer should consider how a misdirected cultural liturgy might be redirected toward a Christian *telos*.

This is one among many powers that a consumer has: interpretive power. There are others, as we've seen in this book. Consumers also have *economic* power: they choose what organizations, companies, or artists to support through their purchasing power, and if enough people favor a certain type of company (a locally sourced grocer, for example), the market will adjust accordingly. Imagine how transformed the world would be if Christians recognized the consumer power at their fingertips and used it wisely! Imagine how improved would be the reputation of Christianity if Christians became known as the most thoughtful, informed, careful consumers of all.

Be Consumed

In the hubbub of our contemporary consumer world—where our very identities have become intertwined with our media tastes and Amazon preferences, where an app or online amusement is just a click away, and where to be unplugged is to feel

257

frighteningly impotent—it's a wonder any of us has a capacity to slow down and worship an invisible God. It's miraculous that in spite of the glut of amusements and the breakneck pace of our lives, God is still present and active—speaking to us if we are keen to listen. Praise him from whom all blessings flow!

If I can leave you with one thing, it is this fundamental suggestion: Christians cannot be good consumers unless they are first, foremost, and passionately consumed by Christ. He must be at the center of our lives: the Giver of all good things who gave himself up for us so that we would have life and have it *abundantly* (see John 10:10). None of the tips, lists, thoughts, questions, or guidelines offered in this book will matter in the least for Christians unless they are first consumed by Christ.

If we are utterly consumed by him, however, oh how our perspective as consumers should change! We will no longer consume primarily for immediate gratification or to satisfy some desire to "be cool" or communicate superior status, because we'll realize that the pleasures go deeper than that. We will no longer consume on binges or in excess, because we'll see that the short-lived thrills of me-centered consumption pale in comparison to the joys of a more careful consumption, one that is focused on Christ and community. We will start to enjoy things more profoundly as we see them in a context far greater than the iConsume model of a billion little islands of cultural intake.

We will consider the redness and sweetness of the strawberries more fully, recognizing the majestic wonder of something so gloriously gratuitous. We will relish more deeply the way a film rearranges time, the way a book transports us to other worlds, the way certain chords of music make us long for home. We will recognize and give thanks for the manifold blessings of enjoying culture in community: a drink with a long-lost friend, a baseball game between father and son, a group of friends watching the season finale of *Mad Men*.

And we will ultimately worship God more continually, feeling his presence in the daily engagements of our senses and praising him constantly for the gray matters and mysteries of his multitudinous gifts.

For the wonderfully complex world of color, taste, smell, texture, timbre, and tone; for the way God created humanity not only to create but to consume; and for how through all of this we can worship God and reflect his wonders outward like sunlight on a mirror . . .

Thanks be to God!

Acknowledgments

To my dear wife Kira—my editor, reader, encourager, and muse throughout the writing of this book: thank you for joining me on this Psalm 34:8 journey and helping me see beauty in a whole new way.

To Jeff, Rhonda, Russ, Judy, and all of my family: thank you for believing in me and teaching me to believe in the abundance of God's grace.

To the many friends and colleagues who read chapters or offered feedback in the shaping of the book manuscript—Erik Wolgemuth, Roberta Ahmanson, Darian Lockett, Ryan Hamm, Allison Budimlija, Judy Williams, Jason Newell, Albert Rios, Laurel Dailey, Larry Eskridge, Alan Frow, and those I'm probably forgetting: your input was invaluable.

To Robert Hosack, Ruth Anderson, Wendy Wetzel, and all of the Baker Books team: thanks for a great partnership!

And to the chefs, brewers, vintners, musicians, thinkers, filmmakers, creators, and critics whose work I encountered in the writing of this book: thank you for creating, contemplating, and celebrating culture in all of its gray glory.

Notes

Introduction

1. Kevin J. Vanhoozer, Charles A. Anderson, and Michael J. Sleasman, eds., *Everyday Theology: How to Read Cultural Texts and Interpret Trends* (Grand Rapids: Baker Academic, 2007), 33.

2. C. S. Lewis, *An Experiment in Criticism* (Cambridge: Cambridge University Press, 1961), 85, 88.

3. I should note that while I do believe everyone is a consumer of culture and can benefit from the ideas explored in this book, the primary cultural context I will be writing from and to is that of Western, economically comfortable Christian culture. This is not to diminish the importance of these issues for Christians in other parts of the world, nor is it to suggest that only "affluent Western Christians" will understand and appreciate the underlying principles of this book; it's simply to note that the particularities of the culture under discussion in this book—food, music, movies, alcohol—are informed by my specific cultural context (American evangelicalism) and may not be as relatable to a believer in, say, Egypt or Indonesia.

4. C. S. Lewis, "The Weight of Glory," *The Weight of Glory and Other Addresses* (New York: Macmillan, 1949), 38.

5. Vanhoozer, Anderson, and Sleasman, *Everyday Theology*, 34.

Chapter 1 Food and Faith

1. L. Shannon Jung, *Food for Life: The Spirituality and Ethics of Eating* (Minneapolis: Fortress, 2004), 22.

2. Brian MacDonald-Milne, "The Eucharist as Witness to the Kingdom of God and Experience of God's Reign," *International Review of Mission* 69, no. 274 (April 1980): 146.

3. Tim Chester, *A Meal with Jesus* (Wheaton: Crossway, 2011), 12.

4. Eugene LaVerdiere, *The Breaking of Bread* (Chicago: Liturgy Training Publications, 1970), 10–11.

5. Chester, *Meal with Jesus*, 68.

6. Ibid., 13.

7. Robert Farrar Capon, *The Supper of the Lamb: A Culinary Reflection* (New York: Pocket Books, 1970), 86.

8. Jung, *Food for Life*, 48.

9. Chester, *Meal with Jesus*, 66.

10. Ibid., 14.

11. See Robert Busey, "Luke 22:7–23," *Interpretation* 52, no. 1 (January 1998): 73.

12. Peter Leithart, *Blessed Are the Hungry: Meditations on the Lord's Supper* (Moscow, ID: Canon Press, 2000), 11.

13. Tom Wright, *The Meal Jesus Gave Us* (Louisville: Westminster John Knox, 1999), 33.

14. Robert J. Banks, *Paul's Idea of Community* (Peabody, MA: Hendrickson, 1994), 81.

15. Ben Witherington, *Making a Meal of It: Rethinking the Theology of the Lord's Supper* (Waco: Baylor University Press, 2007), 14.

16. Thomas R. Schreiner, *Paul: Apostle of God's Glory in Christ* (Downers Grove, IL: InterVarsity, 2001), 315.

17. Rob Bell, *Velvet Elvis: Repainting the Christian Faith* (Grand Rapids: Zondervan, 2005), 171.

18. Jung, *Food for Life*, 31.

19. Chester, *Meal with Jesus*, 125.

20. Matthew Lee Anderson, *Earthen Vessels* (Minneapolis: Bethany House, 2011), 79.

21. Jung, *Food for Life*, 45.

Chapter 2 Where We Go Wrong (and Right) in Eating

1. Chester, *Meal with Jesus*, 10.

2. Norman Wirzba, *Food and Faith: A Theology of Eating* (New York: Cambridge University Press, 2011), 2.

3. Tom Beaudoin, *Consuming Faith* (Lanham, MD: Sheed & Ward, 2003), 86.

4. L. Shannon Jung, *Sharing Food: Christian Practices for Enjoyment* (Minneapolis: Fortress, 2006), 111.

5. "Learn the Facts," Let's Move!, http://www.letsmove.gov/learn-facts/epidemic-childhood-obesity, accessed January 20, 2013.

6. "Adult Obesity Facts," Centers for Disease Control and Prevention, http://www.cdc.gov/obesity/data/adult.html, updated August 13, 2012.

7. "Learn the Facts," Let's Move!

8. Dennis Okholm, "RX for Gluttony," *Christianity Today*, September 4, 2000, http://www.christianitytoday.com/ct/2000/september4/3.62.html?start=1.

9. Jung, *Food for Life*, 99.

10. "Hunger Stats," World Food Programme, 2013, http://www.wfp.org/hunger/stats, accessed January 21, 2013.

11. Okholm, "RX for Gluttony."

12. Clotaire Rapaille, *The Culture Code* (New York: Broadway Books, 2006), 146–47.

13. Jung, *Sharing Food*, 102.

14. Ibid., 106.

15. Chester, *Meal with Jesus*, 104.

16. Jung, *Sharing Food*, 105.

17. Stephen H. Webb, "Against the Gourmands: In Praise of Fast Food as a Form of Fasting," *The Other Journal* 19 (August 2, 2011), http://theotherjournal.com/2011/08/02/against-the-gourmands-in-praise-of-fast-food-as-a-form-of-fasting/.

18. Frank Bruni, "Unsavory Culinary Elitism," *The New York Times*, August 24, 2011, http://www.nytimes.com/2011/08/25/opinion/bruni-unsavory-culinary-elitism.html.

19. Lisa Graham McMinn and Megan Anna Neff, *Walking Gently on the Earth* (Downers Grove, IL: InterVarsity, 2010), 54.

20. Webb, "Against the Gourmands."

21. McMinn and Neff, *Walking Gently*, 66.

22. Beaudoin, *Consuming Faith*, x.

23. Paraphrased from McMinn and Neff, *Walking Gently*, 68, 73–75, 83–85, 107–8.

24. Elisha Witt, email to the author, September 15, 2011.

25. Jung, *Sharing Food*, 113.

26. T. M. Moore, *Culture Matters: A Call for Consensus on Christian Cultural Engagement* (Grand Rapids: Brazos, 2007), 110.

Interlude: Music Means

1. John Van Sloten, *The Day Metallica Came to Church* (Grand Rapids: Square Inch, 2010), 181–82.

Chapter 3 Christians and "The Devil's Music"

1. Quotes from John R. McMahon, "Unspeakable Jazz Must Go," *Ladies' Home Journal* 38 (July–December 1921): 34.

2. See Steve Lawhead, *Rock of This Age* (Downers Grove, IL: InterVarsity, 1987).

3. David A. Noebel, *Rhythm, Riots and Revolution* (Tulsa: Christian Crusade Publications, 1966), 12. In the foreword, Noebel writes: "The Communist use of music is a two-edged subversive sword, cutting deeply and effectively into the American will to resist a 'Soviet America.' One cutting edge is aimed at removing the barrier between classical music and certain types of popular music by substituting perverted form, e.g., jungle noises (atonality) for standardized classical form. The other edge of the blade is more psychological than cultural and consists of the Communist use of music directed at destroying the mental and emotional stability of America's youth through a scheme capable of producing mass neurosis."

4. Ibid., 81.

5. Ibid.

6. Ibid., 79.

7. Bob Larson, *Rock and the Church* (Carol Stream, IL: Creation House, 1971), 9.

8. Ibid., 62–63.

9. Ibid., 58–59.

10. Ibid., 55.

11. Ibid., 67.

12. Dan Peters, Steve Peters, and Cher Merrill, *What about Christian Rock?* (Minneapolis: Bethany House, 1986), 23–29.

13. Ibid., 66.

14. Steve Lawhead, *Rock of This Age*, 59.

15. Ibid., 36.

16. Ibid., 97.

17. Terry Mattingly, *Pop Goes Religion* (Nashville: Thomas Nelson, 2005), 1–2.

18. Charlie Peacock, *At the Crossroads: An Insider's Look at the Past, Present, and Future of Contemporary Christian Music* (Nashville: Broadman and Holman, 1999), 203.

19. Ibid., 100.

20. Ibid., 125.

21. Ibid., 70.

22. Ibid., 89, 92.

23. Ibid., 64.

24. Ibid., 140.

25. Jay R. Howard and John M. Streck, *Apostles of Rock* (Lexington: The University Press of Kentucky, 1999), 187.

26. Steve Turner, *Hungry for Heaven* (Downers Grove, IL: InterVarsity, 1988), 14, 220.

27. Charles Colson and Nancy Pearcey, *The Christian in Today's Culture* (Wheaton: Tyndale, 2001), 290.

28. Ibid., 290–91.

29. Howard and Streck, *Apostles of Rock*, 18.

30. "The Battle for Our Culture: An Interview with Francis Schaeffer," *New Wine* 14, no. 2 (February 1989): 4–9, available online at http://www.samizdat.qc.ca/arts/FS_cult_e.htm#ref.

Chapter 4 What Are You Listening To?

1. "By the Numbers: Tyler, the Creator's *Goblin*," *Fader*, May 10, 2011, http://www.thefader.com/2011/05/10/by-the-numbers-tyler-the-creators-goblin/.

2. Tom Breihan, "Odd Future Mixtapes," *Pitchfork*, March 4, 2011, http://pitchfork.com/features/articles/7940-odd-future-mixtapes/.

3. Frannie Kelly, "Why You Should Listen to the Rap Group Odd Future, Even Though It's Hard," *The Record* (blog), NPR, February 22, 2011, http://www.npr.org/blogs/therecord/2011/06/21/132283971/why-you-should-listen-to-the-rap-group-odd-future-even-though-its-hard.

4. Nitsuh Abebe, "Odd Future, Energy, Inclusion, and Exclusion," *a grammar* (blog), March 28, 2011, http://agrammar.tumblr.com/post/4166624859/odd-future-energy-inclusion-and-exclusion.

5. David Gross, "The Religious Critique of Culture: Paul Tillich and Hans Urs von Balthasar," *Philosophy Today* 54, no. 4 (December 2010): 398.

6. Jeremy Jernigan, "The Devil Has No Right to All the Good Tunes," *Tomorrow's Reflection* (blog), November 23, 2010, http://tomorrowsreflection.com/the-devil-has-no-right-to-all-the-good-tunes/.

7. James D. Bratt, ed., *Abraham Kuyper: A Centennial Reader* (Grand Rapids: Eerdmans, 1998), 461.

8. Abraham Kuyper, *Lectures on Calvinism* (Grand Rapids: Eerdmans, 1943), 30.

9. John Calvin, *The Institutes of the Christian Religion*, book 2, chapter 2, section 15. Available online at the Christian Classics Ethereal Library, http://www.ccel.org/ccel/calvin/institutes.iv.iii.html.

10. Van Sloten, *The Day Metallica Came to Church*, 87.

11. Philip Ryken, *He Speaks to Me Everywhere* (Phillipsburg, NJ: P&R Publishing, 2004), 15.

12. Rex M. Rogers, *Christian Liberty* (Grand Rapids: Baker, 2003), 97.

13. Ibid., 91.

14. Peacock, *At the Crossroads*, 157.

15. Rogers, *Christian Liberty*, 139.

16. Van Sloten, *The Day Metallica Came*, 216.

17. Vanhoozer, Anderson, and Sleasman, *Everyday Theology*, 40.

18. Ibid., 56–57.

19. Van Sloten, *The Day Metallica Came*, 143.

Chapter 5 A Christian Approach to Music Appreciation

1. C. S. Lewis, *Reflections on the Psalms* (London: Fontana Books, 1958), 81.

2. Miroslav Volf, *Work in the Spirit: Toward a Theology of Work* (Oxford: Oxford University Press, 1991), 136–37.

3. Andrew Braine, interview with the author, June 29, 2010.

4. Marissa Nadler, "Help Marissa Nadler Record Her New Album," Kickstarter project launched October 25, 2010, http://www.kickstarter.com/projects/marissanadler/help-marissa-nadler-record-her-new-album-0.

5. Letter from Linford Detweiler and Karin Bergquist, April 23, 2010, http://www.overtherhine.com/letters/april-23-2010.

6. Hans Rookmaaker, *Art Needs No Justification* (Leicester, UK: Inter-Varsity Press, 1978), 48–49.

7. Frank Burch Brown, *Good Taste, Bad Taste, and Christian Taste* (Oxford: Oxford University Press, 2000), x.

8. Ibid., 11.

9. Ibid., 23.

10. Ibid., 166.

11. Ibid., 12.

12. Tom Beaudoin, *Consuming Faith* (Lanham, MD: Sheed and Ward, 2003), 107.

Chapter 6 A Brief History of Christians and Movies

1. Nancy Bayley, "Review of *Our Movie Made Children*," *The American Journal of Psychology* 46, no. 1 (January 1934): 185.

2. Francis G. Couvares, "Hollywood, Main Street, and the Church: Trying to

Censor the Movies Before the Production Code," *American Quarterly* 44, no. 4 (December 1992): 589.

3. The text of the "Don'ts and Be Carefuls" document appears in Appendix D of Raymond Moley, *The Hays Office* (New York: Bobbs-Merrill, 1945), 240.

4. When Monsignor Amleto Cicognani visited New York from the Vatican in 1934, he "mourned the movies' 'massacre of innocence of youth' and urged Catholics to unite in a campaign 'for the purification of the cinema.'" Marjorie Heins, "The Miracle: Film Censorship and the Entanglement of Church and State," *University of Virginia Forum for Contemporary Thought* (October 28, 2002), available at http://www.fepproject.org/commentaries/themiracle.html.

5. Thomas Doherty, *Pre-Code Hollywood* (New York: Columbia University Press, 1999), 321. An excerpt from the Oath: "I shall do all that I can to arouse public opinion against the portrayal of vice as a normal condition of affairs. . . . I hereby promise to remain away from all motion pictures except those which do not offend decency and Christian morality. I promise further to secure as many members as possible for the Legion of Decency."

6. Ibid., 7.

7. "Movies Improving, Catholics Report," *New York Times*, October 13, 1934, 15.

8. Quoted in Doherty, *Pre-Code Hollywood*, 47–48.

9. Ibid., 320.

10. Mark Noll, *A History of Christianity in the United States and Canada* (Grand Rapids: Eerdmans, 1992), 369, 373.

11. Quoted in Noll, *History of Christianity*, 385.

12. Edward de Grazia and Roger K. Newman, *Banned Films: Movies, Censors, and the First Amendment* (New York: Bowker, 1982), 79.

13. Charles Lyons, *The New Censors: Movies and the Culture Wars* (Philadelphia: Temple University Press, 1997), 156.

14. Ibid., 147.

15. "About Us: What We Do," *Plugged In*, 2013, http://www.pluggedin.com/aboutus.

16. Steven Isaac, review of *American Pie*, directed by Chris Weitz and Paul Weitz, PluggedIn.com, http://www.pluggedin.com/videos/1999/q3/americanpie.aspx.

17. Steven Isaac, review of *About Schmidt*, directed by Alexander Payne, PluggedIn.com, http://www.pluggedin.com/videos/2003/q1/aboutschmidt.aspx.

18. Review of *The Grey*, directed by Joe Carnahan, Movieguide.org, http://www.movieguide.org/reviews/movie/the-grey.html.

19. Ted Baehr and Tom Snyder, "A Hollywood Stimulus Plan: Make More Uplifting Movies," *The Wall Street Journal*, February 13, 2009, http://online.wsj.com/article/SB123449031400180527.html.

20. Ted Baehr and Tom Snyder, "Americans Want Movies with Morals, Christian Values," *The Washington Post*, February 19, 2009, http://newsweek.washingtonpost.com/onfaith/guestvoices/2009/02/americans_want_movies_with_mor.html.

21. "About Dr. Baehr and Movieguide," Movieguide.org, October 30, 2008, http://www.movieguide.org/c/info/about-movieguide.html.

22. "The Most Redeeming Films of 2010," *Christianity Today*, February 4, 2011, http://www.christianitytoday.com/ct/movies/commentaries/2011/10redeemingmovies2010.html.

23. "Arts and Faith Top 100 Films," *Image*, 2011, http://artsandfaith.com/t100/.

24. Steven D. Greydanus, "Reading the Eternities: The 2011 Arts and Faith Top 100 Films," *Image*, February 14, 2011, http://imagejournal.org/page/blog/reading

-the-eternities-the-2011-arts-faith-top-100 -films.

25. Anderson, *Earthen Vessels*, 28–29.

Chapter 7 Where Do We Draw the Line?

1. Paraphrased from Robert K. Johnston, *Reel Spirituality: Theology and Film in Dialogue* (Grand Rapids: Baker Academic, 2000), 41–58.

2. Ibid., 57.

3. K. L. Billingsley, *The Seductive Image* (Westchester, IL: Crossway, 1989), 21.

4. Ibid., 23.

5. Comments on Brett McCracken, review of *Gran Torino*, directed by Clint Eastwood, *Christianity Today*, December 12, 2008, http://www.christianitytoday.com/ct/movies/reviews/2008/grantorino.html.

6. Comments on Brett McCracken, review of *Taking Woodstock*, directed by Ang Lee, *Christianity Today*, August 28, 2009, http://www.christianitytoday.com/ct/movies/reviews/2009/takingwoodstock.html.

7. Justin Chang, interview with the author, March 5, 2012.

8. Rebecca Cusey, "Christians and Movies: Recognizing the Danger Within, Not Without," *Tinsel* (blog), Patheos.com, January 12, 2012, http://www.patheos.com/blogs/tinseltalk/2012/01/christians-and-movies-recognizing-the-danger-within-not-without/.

9. William D. Romanowski, *Eyes Wide Open* (Grand Rapids: Brazos Press, 2001), 15.

10. Justin Chang, interview with the author, March 5, 2012.

11. Cusey, "Christians and Movies."

12. Rebecca Ver Straten-McSparran, email interview with author, April 3, 2012.

13. Rebecca Ver Straten-McSparran, unpublished lecture, "Thirteen Ways of Looking at a Blackbird: The Dark Side of

Beauty," The Princeton Forum on Youth Ministry, Santa Barbara, CA, January 25, 2012.

14. Ibid.

15. Gregory Wolfe, speaking at the 2011 Festival of Faith in Music, Calvin College.

16. Billingsley, *Seductive Image*, 21–22.

17. Miroslav Volf, "Soft Difference: Theological Reflections on the Relation Between Church and Culture in 1 Peter," *Ex Auditu* 10 (1994), http:www.yale.edu/faith/resources/x_volf_difference.html.

18. Darian Lockett, "Strong and Weak Lines: Permeable Boundaries between Church and Culture in the Letter of James," *Review and Expositor* 108, no. 3 (Summer 2011): 402.

19. James K. A. Smith, *Desiring the Kingdom* (Grand Rapids: Baker Academic, 2009), 188.

20. Ibid., 210–11.

Chapter 8 The Art and Pleasure of Moviegoing

1. Rookmaaker, *Art Needs No Justification*, 17.

2. All Eugene Suen quotes are from an email interview with the author, March 26, 2012.

3. Newton N. Minow, "Television and the Public Interest," address to the National Association of Broadcasters, Washington, DC, May 9, 1961.

4. Emily Nussbaum, "When TV Became Art," *New York Magazine*, December 9, 2009, http://nymag.com/arts/all/aughts/62513/.

5. Rookmaaker, *Art Needs No Justification*, 60.

6. Dana Gioia, "An Evening With Dana Gioia," lecture, Biola University, February 7, 2012.

7. Alan Jacobs, *The Pleasures of Reading in an Age of Distraction* (Oxford: Oxford University Press, 2011), 23.

8. Philip Ryken, *Art for God's Sake* (Phillipsburg, NJ: P&R Publishing, 2006), 47.

9. Jacobs, *Pleasures of Reading*, 97.

10. Chuck Klosterman, *Chuck Klosterman IV: A Decade of Curious People and Dangerous Ideas* (New York: Scribner, 2006), 269.

11. Nigel Goodwin, quoted in Ryken, *Art for God's Sake*, 51.

12. Rookmaaker, *Art Needs No Justification*, 51.

13. Ibid., 34.

Chapter 9 A Biblical History of Intoxicating Beverages

1. Stephen Reynolds, *The Biblical Approach to Alcohol* (Princeton: Princeton University Press, 1989), 147.

2. John MacArthur, "Beer, Bohemianism, and True Christian Liberty," *Grace to You* (blog), August 9, 2011, http://www.gty.org/blog/B110809.

3. Scot McKnight, "Response to a Letter about Alcohol Consumption," *Jesus Creed* (blog), September 9, 2011, http://www.patheos.com/blogs/jesuscreed/2011/09/09/response-to-a-letter-about-alcohol-consumption/.

4. Kevin DeYoung, "Sobering Report on College Drinking," *DeYoung, Restless, and Reformed* (blog), The Gospel Coalition, August 25, 2011, http://thegospelcoalition.org/blogs/kevindeyoung/2011/08/25/sobering-report-on-college-drinking/.

5. Reynolds, *Biblical Approach to Alcohol*, 44.

6. Reynolds essentially says this in his *Biblical Approach to Alcohol*, noting that "favorable references to *oinos*" in the New Testament "mean the unfermented kind, and unfavorable ones the fermented." See ibid., 43.

7. Kenneth Gentry, *God Gave Wine: What the Bible Says about Alcohol* (Lincoln, CA: Oakdown, 2001), 47.

8. Ibid., 32.

9. Ibid., 51.

10. McKnight, "Response to a Letter."

11. Anderson, *Earthen Vessels*, 194.

12. I'm very indebted in this chapter to the thorough, detailed listings of biblical passages related to alcohol chronicled in the blog post by John Anthony Dunne, "Alcohol in the Bible: Part Two (The New Testament)," *Two Cities*, August 23, 2011, http://www.thetwocities.com/biblical-studies/alcohol-in-the-bible-part-two-the-new-testament.

Chapter 10 Christians and Alcohol

1. Mark Noll, "America's Battle with the Bottle," *Christianity Today*, April 1, 2000, Web-only, http://www.christianitytoday.com/ct/2000/aprilweb-only/53.0.html.

2. Stephen Mansfield, *The Search for God and Guinness* (Nashville: Thomas Nelson, 2009), 14–15.

3. Clement of Alexandria, *Pedagogia*, book 2, chapter 2. Online at http://www.newadvent.org/fathers/02092.htm.

4. Mansfield, *Search for God and Guinness*, 20.

5. Ibid., 21.

6. Ibid., 23.

7. Iain Gately, *Drink: A Cultural History of Alcohol* (New York: Gotham Books, 2009), 78.

8. Ibid., 93.

9. Ibid., 79.

10. Ibid., 81.

11. Ibid., 86.

12. Ibid., 90.

13. Martin Luther, "Sermon on Soberness and Moderation against Gluttony and Drunkenness" (May 18, 1539), http://www.prca.org/standard_bearer/volume79/2002oct15.html#meditation.

14. Quoted in Mansfield, *Search for God and Guinness*, 29.

15. Calvin, *Institutes of the Christian Religion*, III, XIX, 9.

16. John Calvin, Commentary on Psalm 104:15. Online at http://calvin.biblecommenter.com/psalms/104.htm.

17. Mansfield, *Search for God and Guinness*, 32.

18. Ibid., 7.

19. Noll, "America's Battle."

20. Lyman Beecher, *Six Sermons on the Nature, Occasions, Signs, Evils, and Remedy of Intemperance* (New York: American Tract Society, 1827), 38.

21. Gately, *Drink*, 350, 352.

22. Daniel Okrent, *Last Call: The Rise and Fall of Prohibition* (New York: Scribner, 2010), 97.

23. MacArthur, "Beer, Bohemianism, and True Christian Liberty."

24. Joel McDurmon, "John MacArthur Drops the Booze Bomb," Zionica.com, August 16, 2011, http://zionica.com/2011/08/16/john-macarthur-drops-the-booze-bomb/.

25. Alan Noble and Brad Williams, "Alcohol, John MacArthur, and the Growing Pains of Christian Liberty," *Christ and Pop Culture*, August 23, 2011, http://www.christandpopculture.com/featured/alcohol-john-macarthur-and-the-growing-pains-of-christian-liberty/.

26. Quoted in Okrent, *Last Call*, 2.

27. Ibid., 373.

28. Jack Van Impe, *Alcohol: The Beloved Enemy* (Nashville: Thomas Nelson, 1980), 140.

29. Gordon L. Addington, *The Christian and Social Drinking* (Minneapolis: Free Church Publications, 1984), 9.

30. Clement, *Pedagogia*.

31. Reuters, "Alcohol-Related Deaths Kill More Than AIDS, TB Or Violence, WHO Reports," *The Huffington Post*, February 11, 2011, http://www.huffingtonpost.com/2011/02/11/alcohol-related-deaths-_n_821900.html.

32. Clement, *Pedagogia*.

33. Daniel D. Walker, "Why I Don't Drink," in Everett Palmer and Glenn Peters, eds., *The Christian Case for Abstinence* (New York: Association Press, 1955), 45.

34. Everett W. Palmer, "Lift Up a Standard," in Palmer and Peters, eds., *The Christian Case for Abstinence*, 7.

Interlude: Drinking as Communion

1. Wright Thompson, "On Whiskey and Grease," Grantland.com, July 14, 2011, http://www.grantland.com/story/_/id/6769890/on-whiskey-grease.

2. Mansfield, *Search for God and Guinness*, xxvi.

3. Thompson, "On Whiskey and Grease."

Chapter 11 The Godly Enjoyment of Alcohol

1. Christopher J. H. Wright, *The Mission of God's People* (Grand Rapids: Zondervan, 2010), 95.

2. Stephen Mansfield, *Search for God and Guinness*, xxiii.

3. Reformation Brewery, "Our Story," April 9, 2012, http://www.launch.reformationbrewery.com/?p=65.

4. Isaac's Keep, "Reformation Brewery," September 22, 2009, http://www.isaacskeep.com/reformation-brewery/, accessed May 26, 2012.

5. Quotes from Scott Sullivan, email interview with the author, May 13, 2012.

6. DeYoung, "Sobering Report on College Drinking."

7. Quotes from Alan Frow, personal interview with the author, May 24, 2012.

8. Quotes from Tom Smillie, email interview with the author, May 24, 2012.

9. John Piper, "Is It Okay to Drink Alcohol?" Desiring God, May 8, 2010, http://www.desiringgod.org/resource-library/ask-pastor-john/is-it-okay-to-drink-alcohol.

10. Lewis, *An Experiment in Criticism*, 88.

11. Mansfield, *Search for God and Guinness*, xxv.
12. Taylor Birkey, email interview with the author, April 24, 2012.

Conclusion

1. N. T. Wright, *After You Believe* (New York: HarperOne, 2010), 69.
2. Wright, *The Mission of God's People*, 95.
3. Wright, *After You Believe*, 74–75.
4. Ibid., 81.
5. Vanhoozer, Anderson, and Sleasman, *Everyday Theology*, 19, 28.
6. Rookmaaker, *Art Needs No Justification*, 25.

7. Moore, *Culture Matters*, 20.
8. Smith, *Desiring the Kingdom*, 140.
9. Ibid.
10. Ibid., 200.
11. Makoto Fujimura, presentation at Encounter 2011 conference, New York, NY, March 3, 2011.
12. Lewis, *The Weight of Glory*, 140.
13. Bratt, *Abraham Kuyper*, 461.
14. Smith, *Desiring the Kingdom*, 87.
15. Ibid., 88.
16. Ibid., 122.
17. Ibid., 123.
18. Michel de Certeau, *The Practice of Everyday Life* (Berkeley: University of California Press, 1984), 167.
19. Ibid., 169.

Brett McCracken is a graduate of Wheaton College and UCLA. He works as managing editor for Biola University's *Biola* magazine and regularly writes movie reviews and features for *Christianity Today*. He is a contributing writer for MereOrthodoxy.com and maintains a personal blog, *The Search*, at http://stillsearching.wordpress.com. He lives in Southern California.

Connect with

BRETT
McCracken

• • •

READ MORE AT BRETT'S BLOG:
stillsearching.wordpress.com

OR CONNECT WITH HIM ON:

 brett.mccracken

 @brettmccracken

 @bwmccracken

What Happens When
Church and *Cool* Collide?

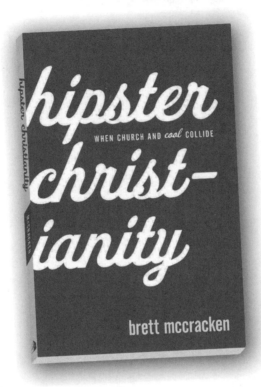

Brett McCracken examines an emerging category he calls "Christian hipsters"—an unlikely fusion of the American obsession with being "cool" and the realities of a faith that is often seen as anything but. His insightful analysis explores what they're about, why they exist, and what it all means for Christianity and the church's relevancy in our youth-oriented culture.

BakerBooks

Relevant. Intelligent. Engaging.

Available wherever books and ebooks are sold.
 ReadBakerBooks • @ReadBakerBooks